For Fi

Without her unapologetic love of God,
Her spirit-fueled, stoic nature,
And always pointing others to Jesus,
none of this would exist.

- Outlining Alpha as a key tool for change
- Understanding the key appeal of Alpha for these generations, as a dynamic environment and an inclusive space where meaningful connections are formed
- Practical insights into the reasons why Alpha works

Chapter 5: Empowering Youth Leadership: 152

- Recognising the leadership potential within the youth and empowering them to take active roles
- Establishing mentorship programs to support and guide young leaders
- Encouraging intergenerational collaboration and learning within the Church community

Chapter 6: Embracing Technology and Innovation: 229

- Exploring the role of technology in connecting with and engaging the youth
- Leveraging social media platforms and digital tools for effective outreach
- Embracing innovative approaches to deliver messages and create meaningful experiences

Chapter 7: Investing in Education and Discipleship: 277

- Prioritising the educational and spiritual development of the youth
- Implementing comprehensive discipleship programs that meet the needs of different age groups
- Equipping youth with relevant skills and knowledge to navigate the challenges of the modern world

Chapter 8: Nurturing Relationships and Community: 377

- Fostering a sense of belonging and community among the youth

- Promoting healthy relationships and friendships within the Church
- Creating opportunities for intergenerational bonding and support

- Summarising the key strategies for making the Church more relevant to today's youth
- Encouraging the adoption of a long-term mindset and commitment to ongoing adaptation
- Inspiring hope for a vibrant future Church built on the engagement and enthusiasm of today's youth

NOW OR NEVER

As a bit of a long-in-the-tooth youth worker, I tend to steer clear of anything that suggests Christians should engage in youth work to vouchsafe the future of the church. Ministering to young people *is* an end in itself. Our congregations and Christian communities are all the poorer, *right now,* without the dynamism of young people's gifts, faith, risk-taking and leadership.

But the church in the West is in decline. Serious, rapid decline. And the focal point of this decline? Younger people. A recent report says that in the past ten years there's been a 40% drop in the number of young people in the UK identifying as Christian, and very few consider themselves to be part of a church. The number of young people who don't identify with any religion has risen by almost 60%. Even if they're not aware of the stats, most churches in the UK and wider Europe know the truth of this. If you have two under 16's in your Sunday services, it would appear you're doing better than 50% of churches within mainstream denominations. Many churches are at risk of closing in the next ten to twenty years, because they've not passed on faith to younger generations.

There are exceptions of course - churches that are reaching, raising and releasing young people - and those exceptions are incredible. You may be part of such an exception. Whatever you're doing, keep doing it. Keep resourcing it, getting out of the way for it, praying for it, backing it, being bold with it. But these exceptions are few and, sadly, more likely to be in areas that have more resources. We know that the vast majority of churches who do have more than two young people *only* engage with young people who are *already within the church.*

So what do we do?

The answer isn't for the church to 'be cool'. We don't need to make the Gospel relevant; the Gospel has always been and will always be the most relevant news for the whole of creation. But we do need to radically rethink how we're sharing the Gospel with young people. If the medium is the message, what message are young people getting from us about the best news they will ever hear? What's happening that means they're not hearing or, worse still, not trusting us? What sort of messenger does the church need to be to be relevant to younger generations? Questions of cultural relevance aren't just for the missionaries who head to other countries and cultures: they're for the church who is seeking to meaningfully connect with younger generations in their community. Churches that are making bold moves into this new territory will need guides to help them navigate this landscape.

Dez is one such guide. His years of youth ministry and church leadership have given him a deep appreciation of where the church is reaching, and failing to reach, young people. Where our methodology, power dynamics and communication styles are negating the message of the Gospel to young people. Spend any time with Dez and you can't help but catch his fire for the power of the Gospel to transform lives, churches and communities.

Over the years I've seen this passion take Dez to speak to all sorts of people across the rich diversity of church tradition and culture, from the faithful few in a village chapel in the Highlands, to thousands at Christian conferences across Europe. His ability to create community and stir people to action is an extraordinary gift to the church right now. I thank God for leaders like Dez who love equipping the body of Christ to pass on the unchanging life changing news of all God has done in Christ.

So I'm delighted that Dez has written *Now or Never*. Challenging, practical and rooted in Scripture, it's the invitation we, the church, need to hear and respond to - because the consequences of the church in the UK *not* being relevant in the lives of young people are serious.

But imagine what could happen if the church takes up the challenge to listen deeply, demonstrate humility, release power and be relevant to emerging generations? Imagine if they hear, grasp and share the Gospel with their peers because we, the people of God, are good and trustworthy messengers of the greatest news ever? The consequences are infinite.

So what will you do with what you read? And who's hands (or device) will you drop this into?

For the sake of those yet to hear the Good News, and for the glory of King Jesus, who is unstoppable in building his church.

"For I am not ashamed of the Good News of Christ, because it is the power of God for salvation for everyone who believes, for the Jew first, and also for the Greek. For in it is revealed God's righteousness from faith to faith. As it is written, "'But the righteous shall live by faith.'" Romans 1:16-17 (WEB)

Rachel Gardner 2024

Introduction:

In the vast tapestry of time, certain moments emerge as pivotal crossroads, demanding our attention and deliberate action. This is one such moment for the Christian Church—a juncture where the echoes of the past meet the vibrant pulse of the present, and the future of our sacred institution hangs in the balance. *Now or Never* is not just a title; it encapsulates the urgency that permeates these pages, as we navigate the intricate terrain of contemporary theology and grapple with the imperative of connecting with Generations Z and Alpha.

Generation Z, born into the kaleidoscope of the late 20th century, and Generation Alpha, emerging as digital natives in the early 21st century, bring with them a unique set of characteristics that challenge and inspire. Their world-view is shaped by unprecedented access to information, a global interconnectedness that defies borders, and a relentless pursuit of authenticity in an age of constant flux. In *Now or Never*, we embark on an exploration of what makes these generations distinctive and, more importantly, how the Christian Church can not only understand but actively engage with their aspirations, doubts, and yearnings.

I bring to these pages not only a commitment to theological discourse but also a wealth of practical experience garnered over fifteen years. My intention is clear: to bridge the gap between theory and practice, offering a response to the future that is rooted in both biblical wisdom and the lived realities of contemporary Church life.

This book unfolds as a journey, weaving together biblical evidence and practical theology to provide a comprehensive roadmap for the Church. Each chapter is a step toward understanding the nuanced dynamics of faith in the context of Generations Z and Alpha, and each page is a call to action for the Church to adapt without compromising its core principles.

The urgent question before us is, "How do we connect with younger generations to keep the Church alive?" This isn't a theoretical inquiry; it's a rallying cry for a Church that not only survives but thrives in the years to come. Through biblical insights, real-world examples, and practical strategies, *Now or Never* invites clergy, congregants, and leaders to embark on a transformative journey toward a Church that is both timeless in its essence and timely in its engagement. The time is now, the choice is ours, and the future of the Church hangs in the balance.

Chapter 1: Understanding the Challenges

In this chapter, we will take a trip to better understand the issues that the Church faces in engaging youth ministry in today's ever-changing cultural landscape. In his letter to the Romans, the Apostle Paul warns against conforming to worldly patterns: "Don't be conformed to this world, but be transformed by the renewing of your mind, so that you may prove what is the good, well-pleasing, and perfect will of God" Romans 12:2 (World English Bible [WEB]). These remarks serve as a reminder that as the cultural landscape changes, the Church must remain watchful in modifying its strategy to reach the younger generation.

Culture's shapes never stay the same; they change, grow, and remake themselves over time. When we look at the first part of this investigation, we look at the modern cultural landscape and its great effects on young people's involvement in religious issues. We will examine the things that shape the spiritual stories of the younger generation, from how technology affects their daily lives to how morals are changing. Through this lively interaction, we are trying to figure out how changes in culture help or hurt the spiritual journey of young people in the Church.

Beyond the cultural currents that cause change, there are barriers—obstacles that sometimes make it hard for young people to fit in with the Church's fabric. The second part of this chapter talks about these issues. We want to find and understand the different types of problems that often make it hard for young people to get involved in their faith groups. Whether these problems are caused by differences between generations, social pressures, or the way institutions work, they need to be carefully looked into in order to be removed and replaced with strategies that make youth participation not only accepted but also celebrated.

Neglecting the active participation of youth in the Church has effects that go beyond the present moment; they affect the spiritual landscape of future generations and the fabric of religious groups. If we don't listen to or value the opinions, ideas, and contributions of young people, we might face problems in the future (as discussed in the third subsection). We want to show how ignoring the spiritual needs of younger people can have a big effect on the health and longevity of religious communities by using both ancient wisdom from the Bible and new ideas from today.

As we start this theological trip, the chapters that follow will break these down in a way that will make you think, talk, and act. We want to add to the story of a faith that supports and empowers its young people by navigating the currents of cultural change, breaking down barriers, and learning about the effects of neglect. This story will resonate with the timeless truth that faith, when nurtured in an open way, becomes a source of hope for future generations.

The Impact of the Shifting Cultural Landscape on Youth Involvement in Generations Z and Alpha

As the cultural landscape shifts, it is critical for the Christian Church to identify and solve the specific difficulties that affect the involvement of Generation Z (born between 1997 and 2012) and Generation Alpha (born after 2012) in Church life. These generations are growing up in a world that is fast changing, affected by various philosophies and technical breakthroughs. Let us study biblical advice for managing these issues in light of their unique situation.

1. **Generations Z and Alpha are real digital natives,** having grown up immersed in technology and social media. This constant connectivity brings with it both advantages and disadvantages. Young people have access to a great wealth of information, quick connection, and limitless entertainment, thanks to the digital world at their fingertips. However, with these advantages comes the requirement for guidance and discernment.

In an age when "likes" and follower counts can quickly become measurements of self-esteem, it is critical to remind our young people of the significance of their hearts and souls. "Keep your heart with all diligence, for out of it is the wellspring of life," Proverbs 4:23 says (WEB). This ancient wisdom tells us that our ideas, feelings, and behaviours all come from the condition of our hearts. It exhorts us to guard our hearts against bad influences and to cultivate a spirit that is in line with holy values.

It is critical to help young people to use judgement in their online interactions in the digital realm. Remind them to be conscious of the content they consume and to make sure it is consistent with their values and beliefs. Teach young people to think critically, to challenge the veracity of information, and to avoid becoming engrossed in internet trends that may jeopardise their integrity.

It is critical for our youth's spiritual well-being to equip them with biblical principles for navigating the digital world. Teach young people the value of kindness, integrity, and compassion in both online and offline settings. Encourage active engagement in online networks that promote happiness, encourage others, and provide a forum for people to share their beliefs.

We should emphasise the importance of striking a good balance between virtual and real-world experiences. Encourage them to do things that will nourish their minds, bodies, and souls, away from screen-only alternatives. Encourage face-to-face conversations, outdoor activities, and meaningful time with family and friends.

We equip our young digital natives to navigate the digital world ethically by mentoring them with biblical wisdom. We are assisting them in understanding that their value and impact extend well beyond the virtual domain. Let us work together to ensure that they develop into resilient persons who use technology to effect positive change and continue to guard their hearts, as everything they do flows from them.

2. **Relativism and pluralism** are the two dominant secular world-views in our current society; they have influenced how young people see truth and morality. In an era of information overload and a wide range of opposing viewpoints, today's youth must navigate a complicated landscape of ideas and beliefs. In this context, Ephesians 4:14 (WEB) serves as a timely reminder to believers, encouraging them not to remain "children, tossed back and forth and carried about with every wind of doctrine, by the trickery of men, in craftiness, after the wiles of error."

It is critical for the Church to actively engage young people in intelligent, Scripture-based discourse. By doing so, the Church may lay a solid foundation for young people based on the unchanging truth of God's Word. This foundation is more than just a spiritual anchor; it is also a source of insight and discernment, enabling young people to distinguish between the numerous world-views and ethical systems they meet. Furthermore, it gives individuals the ability to make educated, principled decisions in an increasingly complex world.

The Church can assist young believers to create a solid world-view that can survive the challenges of relativism and pluralism by creating an atmosphere in which they can investigate, question, and improve their understanding of their faith. In creating this space, we are helping them to build a solid foundation against the shifting sands of modern culture. This foundation will enable young people to evolve into mature, grounded individuals capable of confronting the moral quandaries and philosophical questions that they face in a world filled with varied ideas.

In essence, the Church plays a critical role in overcoming the modern age's intellectual and moral turpitude by giving the youth a solid, biblically-based foundation. The Church ensures that young people may successfully navigate the intricacies of their secular surroundings while remaining true to their religion and God's unchanging truth, as their spiritual growth and intellectual development are supported.

3. **Individualism and Isolation**: Individualism, a cultural phenomenon that promotes personal liberty and self-expression, has seen a major increase in the modern period. At the same time, conventional communal structures that previously provided a sense of belonging and support have disintegrated, leaving many young people feeling profoundly isolated. In the face of these challenges, Hebrews 10:24-25 (WEB) serves as a poignant reminder of the value of communal connection, advising us not to be "forsaking our

own assembling together." This biblical wisdom highlights the critical role that the Church can play in addressing the pervasive issue of youth isolation.

As a faith community, the Church occupies a unique position in this terrain. By emphasising genuine relationships and promoting a sense of belonging, it can provide a loving and inviting environment that counteracts the consequences of isolation. The Church develops spaces for community and support where young people can form meaningful connections with fellow believers, and hopefully non-believers too, through frequent gatherings, worship services, and numerous community programmes.

The Church provides a spiritual as well as a social home by fostering the practise of gathering. Young people might find a sense of purpose and unity in these events, which can help them battle the loneliness that is all too common in the secular world. They can share their joys, sorrows, and spiritual journeys with people who care about their development and well-being.

The role of the Church in combatting isolation goes beyond simple social connection. It can also provide emotional and spiritual assistance. In times of crisis or personal difficulty, young people might seek help, encouragement, and empathy from their Church community. The Church at its best show provides a haven for them to find peace and strength, increasing their resilience in the face of life's adversities.

Furthermore, the Church's teachings on love, compassion, and service urge young people to apply these ideals to the larger community, bridging the gap between individualism and a feeling of civic responsibility. As a result, the Church becomes more than just a place of sanctuary; it also serves as a catalyst for positive change in both the lives of the young and society as a whole.

To summarise, in today's environment, the increase of individuality and the resulting isolation among youngsters is a major issue. Hebrews 10:24-25 emphasises the critical need of community, and the Church is uniquely positioned to meet this need. The Church can effectively counteract isolation among young people by building genuine relationships, creating spaces for fellowship and support, and promoting a culture of compassion and care. This provides them with a sense of belonging and purpose that is frequently lacking in the greater secular community.

4. **Scepticism and a Desire for Authenticity**: Our society's youngest cohorts, Generations Z and Alpha, have earned a reputation for their inherent scepticism and a strong desire for authenticity in numerous parts of life, including their faith. They are looking for faith experiences that truly match with their beliefs and go beyond the surface. "Even so faith, if it has no works, is dead in itself" (James 2:17 [WEB]). This verse emphasises the significance of faith accompanied by action, speaking directly to the need for authenticity and depth in their spirituality.

The Church has a critical role to play in responding to this appeal for authenticity. To engage and inspire these younger generations, the Church must invite them to participate actively in service projects, missions, and attempts to address critical social issues. Young people can observe faith in action and experience firsthand the reality of a Christ-centred existence through these relevant and hands-on activities.

Young people can put their religion into action by participating in service programmes and missions. It gives them a real means to live out Christ's teachings by exhibiting love, compassion, and selflessness in service to others. They not only contribute to the betterment of their communities, but they also cement their own sense of what it is to be a Christian. These encounters give their faith new vitality and make it relevant and applicable in their daily lives.

It also serves as an introduction to wider social issues, creating a space for young people to struggle with complicated and important moral challenges. They are able to apply their beliefs to real-world challenges, which generates a strong sense of sincerity and purpose. When they are confronted with concerns such as poverty, injustice, and inequality, people can see how their faith can be a beneficial force for change, fostering a rich and meaningful spirituality.

Participating in service and mission work also helps people to connect with others who share their beliefs and dedication to making a difference. These connections provide a powerful support network, validating the genuineness of their faith experience. The fraternity and camaraderie of their fellow believers encourages them, creating a sense of belonging and shared purpose.

Finally, Generation Z's and Generation Alpha's scepticism and quest for authenticity are strongly entrenched in their desire for authentic religious experiences that accord with their beliefs. The focus in James 2:17 on faith in action is a significant direction for the Church to solve this need.

By actively integrating youth in service, missions, and social issues, the Church not only allows them to see faith in action, but it also provides them with a road to a genuine and Christ-centred life. These encounters change faith from an abstract belief to a dynamic, practical, and purposeful way of life.

5. **Mentorship and Discipleship**: In the ever-changing environment of youth difficulties, mentorship and discipleship play a vital role. Young individuals benefit significantly from the nurturing influence of solid mentorship as they seek direction and knowledge. Titus 2:7-8 (WEB) emphasises the importance of mentorship by encouraging older believers to serve as guides and examples: "In all things show yourself an example of good works...show integrity, seriousness, incorruptibility, and soundness of speech."

The Church is well-positioned to cultivate these intergenerational ties by providing a welcoming environment that promotes mentorship and discipleship. The Church can promote the transmission of wisdom, faith, and life lessons from one generation to the next by partnering seasoned believers with youth in need of guidance and support. This deliberate pairing weaves a rich tapestry of spiritual mentorship, providing young people with trustworthy partners on their spiritual journey.

Mentorship and discipleship go well beyond knowledge transfer; they involve character development, value development, and faith strengthening. Youth can learn about faith in action through these partnerships. They learn not only from words but also from the behaviours, attitudes, and choices of their mentors, who serve as living examples of the Christian life.

Young people can find a secure environment in these connections to express questions, seek guidance, and discuss their concerns. They get the support and accountability they need to negotiate life's difficulties, make sensible decisions, and stay strong in their faith. As they face the hardships of adolescence and young adulthood, their mentors' advice and expertise serve as a source of inspiration and security.

Unique intergenerational connections formed via mentoring and discipleship add to the Church's overall unity and strength. They break down generational barriers and foster a sense of belonging and mutual respect among people of various ages. These connections bridge the gap between experience's wisdom and youth's excitement, resulting in a more dynamic and resilient Church community.

Finally, mentorship and discipleship, guided by Titus 2:7-8 principles, are strong instruments that the Church can utilise to encourage and nurture its young members. By encouraging older believers to actively participate in the spiritual formation of the youth and promoting intergenerational ties, the Church not only provides young people with the guidance they require, but it also enriches the entire faith community. Faith is not only taught but also lived, experienced, and handed on in these transforming connections, improving the lives of both mentors and mentees and bolstering the Church's future.

The Church can respond with biblical wisdom by acknowledging the cultural landscape and its impact on the involvement of Generations Z and Alpha. Understanding their issues and strategically engaging with them through relevant lessons and focused discipleship, developing authentic relationships, and establishing venues for worship, service, and community are all part of this. The Church may effectively reach the youthful generations with the unchanging message of hope found in Christ through these activities.

Identifying the Hurdles that Restrict Youth from Participating in Church Activities:

To effectively engage with youth, it is critical to recognise and comprehend the barriers that limit their active participation in the Church. In the Parable of the Prodigal Son (Luke 15:11-32), Jesus gives us a vital lesson about the difficulties that certain young people may endure on their religious journey. It makes us think about the value of empathy, compassion, and creating a safe space for young people to share their doubts, fears, and wants.

The Apostle Peter widens this call for Christians to "Sanctify the Lord God in your hearts. Always be ready to give an answer to everyone who asks you a reason concerning the hope that is in you" (1 Peter 3:15 [WEB]). This verse reminds us that providing thoughtful responses to the youth's concerns and objections is critical in removing obstacles and developing meaningful discussion that supports their active participation in the Church.

Here are several potential impediments to Generations Z and Alpha Church participation, along with biblical and supporting references:

1. **Lack of Authenticity**: Many young people today are concerned about a lack of authenticity, particularly in matters of faith. They appreciate authenticity, genuineness, and integrity, and they might be acutely aware of any deceit or insincerity inside religious institutions. Several scriptural texts, such as Matthew 6:2 and Matthew 23:28, emphasise the necessity of real faith and the negative consequences of hypocrisy in this context.

• Matthew 6:2-3 (WEB), " Therefore, when you do merciful deeds, don't sound a trumpet before yourself, as the hypocrites do in the synagogues and in the streets, that they may get glory from men. Most certainly I tell you, they have received their reward."

This Sermon on the Mount statement is a strong warning against hypocritical shows of righteousness. It emphasises that acts of charity and kindness should be undertaken out of a genuine desire to help others, rather than for public praise. As seen above, hypocrisy can tarnish one's behaviour and motivations.

• Matthew 23:28 (WEB) says, "Even so you also outwardly appear righteous to men, but inwardly you are full of hypocrisy and iniquity."

In this text, Jesus criticises the religious leaders of his day for their outer shows of piety that concealed inner deceit and moral corruption. He emphasises that true faith and righteousness must be genuine, coming from the heart and not only for show.

To address the issue of lack of authenticity and to connect with young people, the Church's actions and teachings must prioritise transparency, integrity, and honesty. Here's how the Church can do it:

A. Transparent Leadership: Church leaders should set an example of transparency by admitting their own flaws and challenges. They should be candid about their personal religious journeys, indicating that faith development is a lifelong process for everyone.

B. Create a culture inside the Church that supports open and honest discussions about doubts, concerns, and problems. Young people should feel free to communicate their concerns without fear of judgement or censure.

C. Consistency: The Church should guarantee that its teachings and deeds are in sync. When the Church teaches love, acceptance, and compassion, it must exemplify these traits in its dealings with the congregation and the community.

D. Admitting Mistakes: When the Church or its leaders make a mistake, they should admit it and make repairs. This not only indicates humility but also the Church's commitment to correcting its mistakes.

E. Focusing on Heart Transformation: Encourage true, heart-based faith rather than rote rituals and traditions. Stress the importance of having a personal relationship with God.

F. Servant Leadership: Church leaders should demonstrate servant leadership by being willing to serve and help others rather than seeking positions of power and influence.

By emphasising these authentic values, the Church may create an environment that resonates with young people and helps strengthen their trust. As a result, there may be a deeper feeling of community and a more real and passionate expression of religion inside the Church, harmonising with the values and aspirations of the younger generation.

2. Irrelevance: The issue of irrelevance is one that the Church must face, especially when it comes to communicating with young people. Young people are navigating a fast-changing environment that presents them with new difficulties and dilemmas. If the Church does not engage with this generation's problems or fails to give meaningful connections to their life, the youth may feel distant and disengaged. In passages such as 1 Corinthians 9:22-23, the Bible explains the significance of cultural relevance and modifying the message of faith to communicate with varied audiences.

1 Corinthians 9:22-23 (WEB) says, "To the weak I became as weak, that I might gain the weak. I have become all things to all men, that I may by all means save some. Now I do this for the sake of the Good News, that I may be a joint partaker of it."

The Apostle Paul emphasises the notion of cultural relevance and flexibility in this text. He recognised the significance of meeting people where they were and engaging on a personal and cultural level. Paul's method, characterised by adaptability and flexibility, embodies the belief that the Church should actively interact with the issues and questions of its contemporary audience.

The Church should examine the following measures to solve the challenge of irrelevance and engage with young people:

A. Listening and Understanding: The Church must first actively listen to young people's issues, challenges, and questions. The Church can better personalising its message and approach by recognising their individual experiences and opinions.

B. Giving Meaningful Answers: Young people frequently struggle with complex themes such as identity, relationships, ethics, and social justice. The Church should be prepared to provide relevant, biblically-informed responses to these issues, demonstrating the relevance of faith in solving current challenges.

C. Bridging the Gap: The Church can act as a link between the timeless truths of the Gospel and the ever-changing realities of modern life. This entails translating and applying biblical concepts to current circumstances, making faith relevant and actionable.

D. Engaging in Open Discourse: Creating a space inside the Church for open and respectful discourse allows young people to share their concerns and questions. It creates an atmosphere in which they feel heard and respected.

E. Embracing Innovation: Use new techniques of worship, communication, and community-building that are appealing to today's youth. This could include the use of technology, modern worship styles, and interactive learning opportunities.

F. Promoting Social Justice: Given young people's increased knowledge of social justice issues, the Church should take an active role in addressing these concerns, advocating for justice, and participating in activities that promote good change.

G. Authenticity and Relationship Building: Connecting with young people requires developing authentic relationships with them, exhibiting care, love, and acceptance. Such interactions create a setting for young people to explore their faith and discover their position in the Church community.

By implementing these actions, the Church may avoid becoming irrelevant, while also demonstrating its commitment to interacting with the younger generation. It can demonstrate that faith is a living, dynamic force that tackles contemporary challenges and provides significant advice. This strategy demonstrates to young people that their faith is both relevant and responsive to the complexities of their lives, establishing a sense of belonging and connection within the Church community.

3. Judgmental Attitudes: Judgmental attitudes within a Church community can have a substantial impact on young people's religious participation. The concepts contained in biblical texts like Luke 6:37 and Romans 14:10 emphasise the significance of not having a judgmental mentality. When young people consider the Church to be judgmental or condemning, it creates a barrier that prevents them from fully participating in the religious community.

The Church must prioritise modelling a culture of acceptance, love, and grace in order to promote a vibrant and inclusive atmosphere. This entails creating a safe atmosphere in which young people feel not only accepted but also encouraged in their own faith journeys. Rather than focusing on judgement, the emphasis should be on understanding, empathy, and compassion, in accordance with Jesus' instructions to us, "Don't judge, and you won't be judged" (Luke 6:37 [WEB]).

The Church may encourage young people to communicate their opinions, questions, and concerns without fear of condemnation, by fostering an accepting environment. This open discourse allows for a more in-depth investigation of faith, boosting spiritual growth and strengthening the bond between youth and the Church community.

The principle of grace takes precedence in removing judgmental attitudes. Understanding that everyone is on their own spiritual journey, and that they may face difficulties along the way, provides for a more compassionate attitude. The Church may play an important role in expressing this grace by recognising its members' flaws while guiding them towards a path of atonement and personal improvement.

The goal is to create a Church atmosphere in which young people not only take consolation in their faith but also actively participate in various aspects of the community. A nonjudgmental culture is consistent with Christ's teachings, fostering a sense of togetherness, understanding, and mutual support among the Church family. As the Church attempts to embrace these ideals, it can become a light of love and inclusion, bringing young people closer to faith's transformational power.

4. Demanding Schedules and Priorities: The demanding nature of modern life, particularly for young people, makes regular Church attendance difficult. Finding time for religious activities can become a lower priority with academic commitments, a plethora of extracurricular activities, and the pursuit of personal objectives (Matthew 6:33). Recognising this fact is critical for the Church to properly engage with and support the younger generations as they journey through life.

Understanding the complex web of commitments that young people must traverse, the Church should take a compassionate and adaptable approach. This entails appreciating the various demands on their time and energy, including academic expectations that might be particularly high at times. The Church not only exhibits empathy in this way, but it also promotes itself as a relevant and understanding institution in the lives of young people.

To accommodate the youth's hectic schedules, offer flexible service hours, different formats, or even virtual options for those who are unable to attend in person. Embracing technology, such as livestreams or online communities, can extend the reach of the Church beyond its physical boundaries, making it more accessible to individuals who are time- or place-constrained. This adaption enables young people to incorporate their faith into their active lifestyles.

Perhaps the Church might attempt to create meaningful participation opportunities that correspond with the tastes and interests of the younger generation on a proactive basis. This may entail organising events, conversations, or study groups that cater not only to spiritual progress but also to their current circumstances. The Church can bridge the gap between conventional religious practises and the everyday life of young people by providing relevant and approachable content.

It is critical to create a space where the Church actively supports and fosters the personal ambitions of its youth. This may entail incorporating mentorship, instruction, and encouragement, in accordance with the biblical idea of seeking God's Kingdom first (Matthew 6:33). The Church plays an important role in assisting young people in reconciling their spiritual interests with other elements of life, by guiding them in navigating the difficulties of their busy schedules.

In essence, by adapting to the realities of hectic schedules and fluctuating priorities, the Church not only shows understanding but also becomes a dynamic and important part of the lives of young people. The Church may provide a solid foundation for the spiritual growth of youth via flexibility, empathy, and meaningful interaction, building a connection that transcends beyond the limitations of traditional worship places.

5. Cultural and Technological Disparities: The widening gaps between established Church practises and the fast-evolving, technology-driven world of Generations Z and Alpha present religious institutions with a unique challenge

(Matthew 9:17). As these younger generations navigate a world defined by continual connectedness and rapid information interchange, the Church must modify its techniques while remaining committed to biblical values. Accepting innovation becomes not just a must but also an opportunity to transcend cultural and technological divides that may impede effective interaction.

The first step is to understand the cultural and technological intricacies of Generations Z and Alpha. These generations have grown up in a digital world characterised by quick access to information, social media interactions, and immersive technologies. Recognising this, the Church might look at methods to incorporate technology into its practises while remaining true to its essential principles. This could include using social media channels for outreach, providing live-streaming services, or creating engaging and user-friendly apps that promote spiritual growth.

The Church might reinvent its old methods of communication and outreach in the spirit of Matthew 9:17, which talks of new wineskins for fresh wine. This adaptation does not require a departure from biblical concepts, but rather their imaginative use in a modern environment. For example, storytelling, a popular practise in the Bible, can be revitalised through multimedia presentations, podcasts, or visual storytelling techniques that appeal to a younger audience.

In order to cultivate genuine connections in the digital era, the Church must look beyond its physical limits. Virtual communities, online forums, and interactive digital platforms facilitate discourse and the sharing of experiences. The Church can use these tools to build a sense of belonging and community among today's youth, who frequently connect through digital platforms.

Education and assistance on how to navigate the internet realm from a biblical standpoint are also essential. As young people meet various ideas and influences online, the Church may serve as a moral compass, assisting them in determining the ethical consequences of their online interactions and decisions.

In essence, the Church must be deliberate in its embrace of modern innovations while remaining committed to its fundamental ideals. This entails not only adapting to a changing cultural and technical landscape but also actively creating it, in order to transmit the eternal message of faith. The Church can effectively bridge the gap between tradition and innovation by embracing creative approaches, judiciously utilising technology, and building genuine connections, ensuring its relevance and impact in the lives of Generations Z and Alpha.

6. A Lack of Sympathetic and empowering Mentors: A lack of compassionate and empowering mentors within the Church can be a substantial impediment to young people's meaningful engagement in their religious journeys (1 Timothy 4:12). Recognising the importance of mentorship in spiritual growth and personal development, the Church must take purposeful steps to close this gap by investing in intentional mentorship programmes.

1 Timothy 4:12 emphasises the need of young people having positive role models in the Christian community. To carry out this biblical duty, the Church can launch structured mentorship programmes that link seasoned and mature

Christians with others who are just starting out on their spiritual journeys. These mentorship connections serve as a foundation for discipleship, providing direction, support, and a wealth of insight gained through years of faith and life experiences.

Creating a mentoring atmosphere entails fostering genuine ties between older and younger Christians. Community-building efforts, workshops, and events aimed at fostering interpersonal relationships can help achieve this. The Church creates a forum for the interchange of information, faith, and life lessons by building a culture that encourages intergenerational connections.

Mentorship should not be a one-size-fits-all strategy, but rather a customised experience that addresses the specific needs and obstacles that young people confront. The Church can help by identifying mentors who have the abilities and attributes that match the mentees' objectives and problems. This deliberate matching approach fosters confidence and guarantees that the mentoring relationship is relevant and impactful.

The mentorship path is travelling alongside young people, listening to their concerns, and providing practical advice based on biblical principles. Mentors act as sounding boards for young people's questions, worries, and doubts, creating an environment in which they feel secure to explore and deepen their religion.

Group mentorship settings, in addition to individual mentorship, can be effective. Small group conversations, Bible studies, and mentoring circles foster a collaborative and supportive learning atmosphere. This group dynamic not only provides a variety of perspectives, but it also fosters a sense of community among the mentees, emphasising the idea that they are not alone on their spiritual path.

Investing in purposeful mentorship programmes demonstrates a dedication to the biblical concept of discipleship, in which older Christians actively guide and nurture the next generation. The Church becomes a place where young people not only learn about faith but also see it lived out in the lives of those who have gone before them, by providing opportunites for meaningful interactions and personalised mentorship experiences. In doing so, the Church creates the groundwork for a thriving and integrated community that will last for generations.

The Church may effectively break down the hurdles that inhibit Generations Z and Alpha from fully engaging, by understanding and addressing these barriers in a biblically grounded manner. This entails building a culture of authenticity, relevance, inclusion, and support, as well as adjusting to their specific needs and welcoming possibilities for discipleship and mentorship.

Investigating the Repercussions of Ignoring Youth Participation:

Neglecting youth active engagement in the Church can have far-reaching implications. According to Proverbs 29:18 (WEB), "Where there is no revelation, the people cast off restraint." When young people are not included, mentored, and given opportunities to offer their unique perspectives and talents, a vision for the Church's future may be lost. Their absence can lead to a decrease in Church community passion, energy, and innovation.

The Apostle Paul emphasises the importance of unity among the body of believers. He compares the Church to a Body in 1 Corinthians 12:12-14, emphasising the interdependence of its members. Neglecting youth engagement can break this balance, making it difficult for the Church to fully embrace its many skills and abilities. By failing to nurture and involve the youth, the Body of Christ remains incomplete.

Here are several possible outcomes, along with biblical references and supporting remarks:

1. Spiritual Growth: By ignoring youth engagement, the Church risks missing out on the spiritual growth and development of the next generation (Proverbs 22:6). Investing in their involvement and discipleship allows individuals to grow spiritually while also contributing to the overall vitality of the Church.

Neglecting young people's involvement in the Church might lead to a loss of spiritual growth. Proverbs 22:6 recommends teaching young people in the way they should go, implying that investing in their engagement and discipleship is critical for their spiritual development. When the Church fails to prioritise young people's inclusion and active engagement, the young people miss out on opportunities to foster their faith and future contributions. By empowering the younger generation, the Church not only nurtures their spiritual growth but also ensures the Church community's overall vitality and relevance.

2. Diminished Relevance: If the Church fails to engage Generations Z and Alpha successfully, it risks becoming irrelevant to modern culture and unable to properly transmit the timeless truth of the Gospel (1 Corinthians 9:22). Accepting their opinions, addressing their issues, and applying biblical principles to their lives helps the Church remain relevant and impactful in their faith journey.

Failure to interact effectively with Generations Z and Alpha risks reducing the Church's relevance. The Church must adapt and engage with the ever-changing contemporary culture in order to successfully transmit the timeless message of the Gospel. In order to successfully proclaim the Gospel, 1 Corinthians 9:22 emphasises the significance of relating to various categories of people.

Engaging with Generations Z and Alpha entails not just knowing their distinct points of view but also actively addressing their issues and challenges. The Church may demonstrate its relevance and the usefulness of biblical ideas in their lives by acknowledging and addressing the challenges that they encounter. This reveals that the Gospel is more than an intellectual concept; it is a transformative force in their daily lives.

To stay relevant, you must be willing to listen to and learn from the next generation. Their life experiences, cultural context, and technology fluency can provide unique ideas and perspectives that can assist the Church in connecting with them more effectively. By embracing and incorporating their ideas into the life and ministry of the Church, the Church may successfully communicate the timeless truth of the Gospel in a language that Generations Z and Alpha understand.

In this way, the Church can stay vital and active in the lives of young people, ensuring that the transformational force of the Gospel remains relevant and influential in their spiritual journey. The Church can bridge the gap between the timeless truths of the Gospel and modern culture by connecting with Generations Z and Alpha, ensuring that the message of hope and salvation remains accessible and meaningful to future generations.

3. Church Attendance Drop: Neglecting young people's participation can lead to a drop in Church attendance and activity (Psalm 145:4). Failure to provide genuine connections, address spiritual needs, and provide spaces for their contributions may lead to disengagement from the Church community.

Neglecting young people's participation can have a negative impact on Church attendance and involvement. Psalm 145:4 emphasises the necessity of passing on one's faith to the next generation, implying that engaging and involving young people is critical to the Church's general growth and sustainability.

If the Church fails to establish meaningful connections for young people, the youth may become disengaged. It is critical to create environments in which youth may form relationships with peers and mentors who can help them on their spiritual journey. Without these ties, young people may feel alone and separated from the Church community, which may lead to a decrease in attendance and involvement.

Addressing young people's spiritual needs is critical to keeping them interested. They have specific questions, doubts, and struggles that must be addressed in order for them to develop a strong and real faith. The Church can ensure that young people find spiritual nutrition and growth within its community by providing relevant and meaningful lectures, mentoring opportunities, and open dialogue places.

It is critical to provide chances for young people to contribute to and actively participate in the life of the Church. They experience a feeling of ownership and involvement in the Church community when their voices, talents, and ideas are valued and supported. Failure to provide spaces for their contributions, on the other hand, might make young people feel marginalised and irrelevant, leading to disengagement and, ultimately, a drop in Church attendance.

In conclusion, ignoring the participation of young people can lead to a decrease in Church attendance and activity. To avoid this, the Church must prioritise making real connections, meeting their spiritual needs, and giving chances for them to contribute. By doing so, the Church can assure young people's active participation and establish a healthy and thriving community that continues to grow and affect lives.

4. Loss of Future Leaders: According to 1 Timothy 4:12, Generations Z and Alpha are the Church's future leaders. If they do not participate actively, they will miss out on opportunities to develop their leadership abilities, use their gifts and talents for the benefit of the Church, and prepare for future ministry responsibilities. This could result in a leadership void in the Church in the future.

Neglecting Generations Z and Alpha's active involvement in the Church can result in the loss of future leaders. 1 Timothy 4:12 emphasises the significance of not dismissing young people and encourages them to be role models in their faith.

Recognising this potential and developing their leadership qualities is critical for the Church's future.

When we fail to engage young people as active participants in the Church, they miss out on opportunities to develop their leadership skills. Leadership is about enabling and empowering individuals to use their strengths and talents to serve others, not just about age or experience. When young people have the opportunity to lead, they can improve their abilities, build confidence, and develop a sense of purpose within the Church community.

It is critical to allow young people to actively contribute and use their strengths and talents inside the Church. When students are given meaningful opportunities to serve, youth not only learn new skills but also gain the satisfaction and fulfilment that comes from making a difference. This involvement fosters a strong commitment to the Church's mission and vision by instilling a sense of ownership and investment in it.

Failing to involve young people in leadership roles can result in a leadership void in the Church later on. It is critical to recognise that they are the Church's future leaders and to purposefully prepare and coach them for future ministry roles. The Church promotes a smooth succession of leadership, maintains vitality, and retains its mission for future generations by investing in their growth.

In conclusion, failing to actively engage Generations Z and Alpha in the Church can result in the loss of future leaders. The Church preserves leadership continuity and the vitality of its purpose by allowing people to develop their leadership abilities, use their gifts and talents, and prepare for future roles in ministry. Accepting and empowering young people as leaders benefits them personally, as well as having a positive effect on the general growth of the Church community.

5. Disconnection from Biblical Truth: If young people are not intentionally engaged, they may seek solutions and guidance from sources that do not fit with biblical truth (Colossians 2:8). If they do not participate, they will miss out on experiencing the transformative power of God's Word and understanding its relevance in their lives.

Neglecting Generation Z's and Generation Alpha's active participation in the Church might lead to a detachment from biblical truth. Colossians 2:8 warns against being led astray by false ideologies and human traditions that are not based on the truth of God's Word. Without purposeful interaction, young people may seek answers and guidance from sources that are not always consistent with biblical truth. By ignoring their participation, the Church denies them the opportunity to experience the transformative power of God's Word and comprehend its relevance to their lives.

Engaging young people in Bible study and application is critical for their spiritual development and formation. They can learn about God's character, His plan of redemption, and how to live according to His principles by studying the Scriptures. Young people can build a firm foundation of biblical knowledge and a profound awareness of God's truth by participating in the Church's teaching and discipleship programmes.

Neglecting their participation disconnects young people from the transformational power of the Word. The Bible has the power to bring deep spiritual growth, insight, and direction into their lives. Young people can experience personal transformation and build a firm biblical world-view that informs their decisions and actions, by actively engaging in the study of Scripture and being allowed to engage with its realities.

Ignoring their participation can lead to young people seeking answers and guidance from places that may not be biblically accurate. They are exposed to a wide range of ideas and beliefs through social media, popular culture, and their immediate surrounds in a quickly changing and linked world. Young people are better equipped to manage these influences and identify what aligns with the reality of God's Word when they are actively involved in biblical teachings and discussions within the Church.

Young people discover the significance and application of God's Word for their lives by engaging with biblical truth. They realise that the Bible's ageless ideas and teachings can help them navigate the intricacies and problems of their relationships, personal development, and decision-making. They can experience a deeper relationship with God and a more fulfilling and purposeful existence by pursuing God's truth and applying it in their lives.

In conclusion, neglecting the active participation of Generations Z and Alpha in the Church poses a serious risk of detachment from biblical truth, as warned in Colossians 2:8. The potential consequences include seeking guidance from sources that may not align with the timeless principles of God's Word. By deliberately engaging young people in Bible study and application, the Church provides them with the opportunity to build a solid foundation of biblical knowledge and experience the transformative power of God's Word.

Participation in the Church's teaching and discipleship programs is crucial for the spiritual development and formation of the younger generation. It enables them to understand God's character, His redemptive plan, and how to align their lives with His principles. Active engagement in the study of Scripture equips young individuals to navigate the complexities of the modern world with a biblical world-view, ensuring they are not led astray by false ideologies prevalent in society.

By embracing their participation, the Church empowers young people to discern truth from falsehood in a rapidly changing and interconnected world. This active involvement allows them to identify and counteract the influences of popular culture, social media, and surrounding ideologies that may not align with the truth of God's Word. Through intentional engagement with biblical teachings, young people develop the skills and understanding needed to live in accordance with God's timeless truths.

Ultimately, the Church plays a pivotal role in helping young individuals discover the relevance and application of God's Word in their lives. This active engagement fosters a deeper relationship with God, equipping them to face the challenges of relationships, personal development, and decision-making with the guidance of biblical wisdom. Ignoring their participation denies them the transformative power of the Word, while intentional engagement opens the door to a more fulfilling and purposeful existence grounded in the eternal truths of Scripture.

6. Missed Evangelistic Opportunities: Within their peer groups and spheres of influence, Generations Z and Alpha form a distinct mission field (Matthew 28:19-20). By ignoring their participation, the Church limits its ability to reach and touch their generation with the message of Christ, so passing up evangelistic possibilities.

Neglecting the active participation of Generations Z and Alpha in the Church has ramifications for not only future leaders and Church growth but also for wasted evangelistic chances. Matthew 28:19-20, sometimes known as the Great Commission, emphasises the significance of spreading the Gospel of Christ and making disciples of all nations. This entails reaching out to and influencing the next generation.

Within their respective peer groups and spheres of influence, Generations Z and Alpha represent a distinct mission field. They have unique values, experiences, and issues that necessitate a specialised strategy in order to effectively convey the Gospel of Christ to them. By ignoring their participation, the Church diminishes its potential to engage with and influence their generation.

Young people have considerable power inside their own social circles, which include friends, classmates, and online groups. They become ambassadors of the faith when they actively participate in the life of the Church, sharing the Word of Christ to their peers and broadening the reach of the Church's evangelistic efforts. Their presence and testimonies can be a powerful witness, resulting in life transformation and Kingdom expansion.

Neglecting young people's involvement limits them the opportunity to use their strengths, talents, and enthusiasm for evangelisation. The Church actively involves them, not just to equip and encourage young people to confidently express their faith, but also to profit from their unique viewpoints and approaches to reaching their generation. They understand the cultural intricacies and trends that impact their peers' lives, making them great evangelistic preachers in their own right.

By ignoring Generations Z and Alpha, the Church misses out on great evangelistic chances. These young people have the potential to reach out to their classmates and bring them into the family of believers. By welcoming and involving them, the Church broadens its evangelistic influence, presenting Christ's transformative message to a wider audience and fulfilling the Great Commission mandate.

In conclusion, failing to actively engage Generations Z and Alpha in the Church results in missed evangelistic possibilities. By involving people, the Church may tap into their specific sphere of influence, empower them to share their religion, and eventually broaden its reach and impact. Accepting young people as mission partners strengthens the Church's evangelistic efforts and allows Christ's revolutionary message to reach their generation in a personal and relevant way.

In this chapter, we looked at the problems of altering cultural landscapes, highlighted impediments to young involvement, and discussed the repercussions of ignoring their role in the Church. Let us continue to think on these biblical realities, seeking direction and discernment in order to successfully engage and empower the youth, creating a healthy and inclusive Church that embraces future generations.

Chapter 2: Rediscovering the Church's Purpose

Revisiting the Underlying Values and Teachings that Determine the Mission of the Church:

The Church is at a crossroads in the dynamic and rapidly changing world of the twenty-first century, with a once-in-a-lifetime chance to reconnect with the younger generations, particularly Generation Z and Generation Alpha. To rediscover and recreate its mission for these generations, the Church must go on an introspective and reaffirmative journey, beginning with a deep dive into the fundamental principles and teachings that have served as the foundation of its mission for centuries.

Drawing inspiration from biblical links becomes crucial in this path of rediscovering. A key verse that captures the essence of these virtues is Matthew 22:37-39 (WEB): "'You shall love the Lord your God with all your heart, with all your soul, and with all your mind.' This is the first and great commandment. A second likewise is this, 'You shall love your neighbor as yourself.'" These verses serve as a perpetual beacon, illuminating the path for the Church and inspiring it to continue spreading love, building unity, and inspiring positive change.

To "Love the Lord" resonates as an invitation to a profound, intimate relationship with the Divine, highlighting the importance of a sincere and authentic relationship with God. This love is not superficial; it requires the participation of the entire being—heart, soul, and mind. It signifies an all-encompassing dedication to living out Christ's teachings in all elements of one's life, both individually and collectively as a community.

The second commandment, "Love your neighbour as yourself," extends this love beyond the individual, requesting that the Church build a compassionate and inclusive culture. This concept serves as a counterweight to the widespread individualism in today's culture, reminding the Church that its mission is not insular but outward-facing. It highlights the communal aspect of faith, encouraging Christians to extend the same love and grace that they have received from God to others.

By revisiting these fundamental beliefs and teachings, the Church not only rediscovers its identity but also re-establishes its relevance for future generations. Love, compassion, and community are eternal concepts that are unaffected by time or societal shifts. By embracing these essential truths, the Church positions itself as a living, breathing entity capable of meeting the spiritual needs of a new era, rather than a relic of the past.

On this path of rediscovery, the Church serves as a bridge between the ancient wisdom of Scripture and the present difficulties confronting Generation Z and Generation Alpha. It reinterprets and revitalises tradition, ensuring that the fundamental ideas that have defined the Church for centuries become a vibrant and meaningful guide for the present and future.

In essence, rediscovering the fundamental values and teachings that characterise the Church's mission is a deliberate and forward-thinking effort, not a sentimental glance back. It acknowledges that the substance of the Church's vocation transcends generations, and that when anchored in timeless principles of love and community, it has the capacity to speak to the hearts of our society's youngest members, offering them a path of meaning, purpose, and transformational grace.

In order to engage the young and revitalise the Church, we must return to the underlying principles and teachings that define our purpose. As we investigate these timeless truths revealed in the Bible, we rediscover the Church's mission and calling.

In a message to His followers, Jesus revealed the essence of His mission: "For the Son of Man also came not to be served, but to serve, and to give his life as a ransom for many" Mark 10:45 (WEB). This insightful statement reminds us that the Church exists to serve people selflessly, offering a haven of hope and compassion in a society that frequently nurtures division and despair.

Fostering the spiritual growth of kids is a critical responsibility for any society or organisation, but especially for the Church. Psalm 119:9 (WEB) serves as a strong reminder of the significance of this undertaking. In this passage, the psalmist asks, "How can a young man keep his way pure? By living according to your word." This question highlights the need of leading and nurturing the next generation with the lessons and wisdom found in God's Word.

This verse underlines above all the fact that young people are especially vulnerable to the plethora of influences and temptations that surround them in today's environment. It is vital to provide adolescents with a solid foundation based on God's Word during a time when they are developing values, beliefs, and ideals. We can help them navigate the intricacies and barriers they face, allowing them to make decisions that are compatible with their faith's beliefs and teachings.

The verse also emphasises that the responsibility for leading and protecting young people's paths lies not only with the youth but also with the community, particularly the elder generations. This notion highlights the importance of mentors, parents, and Church leaders in passing on Bible wisdom and information to the next generation. The community can help young people stay on track by providing a safe and supportive environment in which they can learn and grow spiritually.

In Romans 12:2 (WEB), the Apostle Paul highlights the concepts of transformation and regeneration, which apply not only to adult Christians but also to the younger generation. "Be transformed by the renewing of your mind" encourages a lifelong process of spiritual growth and personal development by increasing understanding of God's truth and intimacy with Him.

This shift can occur for the youth through a variety of techniques inside the Church or spiritual community. Providing opportunities for young people to encounter God through Church, prayer, and community involvement can be transforming. Studying God's Word is also important because it allows young people to research and comprehend the Bible's teachings, helping them to internalise and apply its principles in their lives.

Experiencing God's presence through meaningful events, retreats, and spiritual gatherings can also inspire youth to pursue spiritual growth. These encounters allow people to experience the reality of their religion and improve their relationship with God, inspiring them to pursue a more meaningful and sincere relationship with Him.

Finally, as emphasised by Psalm 119:9 and the teachings of the Apostle Paul, a vital goal for every faith-based community is to prioritise the spiritual well-being of the youth. The Church may play an important role in supporting spiritual growth in the younger generation, preparing them to face life's challenges while remaining rooted in their faith. This is achieved by guarding their path according to God's Word, offering guidance, and providing transformative experiences.

Emphasising the Potential Benefits of Youth Involvement in the Church Community:

Young people's involvement in the Church community has huge potential for positive consequences that spread across the congregation and beyond. In 1 Timothy 4:12, Paul offers a meaningful message to the youth, asking them not to underestimate their importance because of their age, but to instead set an example in speech, conduct, love, faith, and purity. This biblical insight reminds us that young Church members are not only the future but also an important part of the present, capable of making significant contributions.

When adolescents actively participate and share their unique gifts, they contribute boundless energy, unwavering passion, and fresh perspectives to the Church community. Their fervour instills a renewed sense of vitality, and their vibrant vision inspires a spirit of zeal and ingenuity in people of all ages. Young people find a sense of purpose and belonging by actively engaging in Church events and taking on leadership roles. They also give their energy as a precious resource, invigorating the entire congregation.

1. The Biblical Basis: Youth as Faith Models

The counsel Paul delivers to Timothy in 1 Timothy 4:12 is a basic assumption for appreciating the value of young Church membership. The Scripture warns young believers not to underestimate their impact because of their youth but rather to set an example via their speech, conduct, love, faith, and purity. This biblical insight calls into question the widely held assumption that adolescents are passive recipients of knowledge, highlighting their power to actively influence the spiritual environment of the community.

A. The Articulation Effect in Public Speaking

When young people are given the freedom to express their ideas and opinions, they add to the rich tapestry of voices inside the Church. Their new perspectives, unburdened by years of history, may stimulate debate and foster an atmosphere of open communication. "The heart of the righteous weighs answers," Proverbs 15:28 (WEB) says, "but the mouth of the wicked gushes out evil." Through their words, the youth have the ability to communicate wisdom, challenge misconceptions, and reinvigorate the Church's communicative fabric.

B. Inspiring Behaviour: Setting a Good Example

Paul's exhortation includes a call for adolescents to be role models of virtue. This extends beyond observing moral principles to putting Christ's teachings into practise in daily life. Galatians 5:22-23 (WEB) highlights the transformational power of such behaviour: "But the fruit of the Spirit is love, joy, peace, patience, kindness, goodness, faith, gentleness, and self-control." By embracing these fruits, the children become live examples of religion's transformative power, inspiring others to follow in their footsteps.

C. Spiritual Influence Pillars: Love, Faith, and Purity

The instruction to show love, faith, and purity highlights the varied nature of the youth's influence. 1 Corinthians 16:14 (WEB) highlights love as a guiding force: "Let all that you do be done in love." The teenagers establish a Church community where compassion and acceptance flourish by displaying genuine love. Faith, as expressed in Hebrews 11:1 (WEB), becomes a driving force: "Now faith is assurance of things hoped for, proof of things not seen." Through their unwavering faith, the children energise the spiritual atmosphere. Purity becomes a standard as a result of Philippians 4:8 (WEB): "Finally, brothers, whatever things are true, whatever things are honorable, whatever things are just, whatever things are pure, whatever things are lovely, whatever things are of good report: if there is any virtue and if there is any praise, think about these things." The youth's commitment to purity sets a standard that challenges the mainstream culture.

2. Energising the Congregation: The Vitality of Youthful Involvement

A. Renewal Catalysts with Endless Energy and Unrelenting Passion

The children are a source of energy and passion for the Church community, working as a catalyst for regeneration.

Their enthusiasm pervades the audience, invigorating it and instilling a renewed feeling of purpose. "Rejoice, young man, in your childhood, and let your heart be pleasant in the days of your young manhood," Ecclesiastes 11:9-10 (Amplified Bible [AMP]) states. "And walk in the ways of your heart and in the desires of your eyes, but know that God will bring you into judgment for all these things. Therefore, remove sorrow and anger from your heart and put away pain from your body, for childhood and the prime of life are fleeting." By channelling this energy into meaningful activities, the Church not only benefits from the vitality of youth, but it also gives a platform for young people to express their joy and creativity in service to God.

B. New Viewpoints and Perspectives: Innovation Catalysts

Unburdened by the weight of tradition, the youth offer new perspectives that serve as catalysts for change within the Church community. Proverbs 20:29 (WEB) emphasises the value of both youth and wisdom: "The glory of young men is their strength. The splendor of old men is their gray hair." This appreciation underlines how the mix of youth and wisdom results in a comprehensive understanding of the spiritual journey. By actively including youth in decision-making processes and leadership roles, the Church taps into a wellspring of innovation, ensuring that its practises remain relevant and accessible to a changing world.

C. Leadership Responsibilities: Instilling a Sense of Purpose and Belonging

When young people take on leadership roles, they receive a sense of purpose and belonging while also becoming valuable members of the Church community. Proverbs 3:5-6 (WEB) reads in this regard, "Trust in Yahweh with all your heart, and don't lean on your own understanding. In all your ways acknowledge him, and he will make your paths straight." By entrusting leadership roles to the youth, the Church demonstrates its trust in God's guidance while also establishing an atmosphere in which young leaders can grow and thrive.

3. Beyond the Congregation: The Expansion of Youthful Participation

A. Community Outreach: Making a Difference Outside of the Church

Through good community outreach projects, youth involvement has a positive impact that extends beyond the Church community and into the larger society. "Even so, let your light shine before men, that they may see your good works and glorify your Father who is in heaven," according to Matthew 5:16 (WEB). Motivated by their faith and zeal, the youth become positive change ambassadors, taking part in initiatives that address social issues and reflect Christ's loving teachings.

B. Social Justice and Activism: Catalysts for Positive Change

Youth who are motivated by a feeling of justice and driven by a desire for positive change can become community catalysts for social justice and action. "He has shown you, O man, what is good," Micah 6:8 (WEB) states. What does the Lord anticipate from you? "Act justly, to love mercy, and to walk humbly with your God." By accepting these ideas, the youth contribute to the creation of a more egalitarian and compassionate society as they align their actions with the teachings of the Bible.

C. Mentoring for Future Leaders: Investing in the Next Generation

Youth involvement in leadership positions creates a mentorship dynamic that continues to the next generation, ensuring that favourable effect continues. Titus 2:7-8 (WEB) highlights the need of mentorship: "In all things show yourself an example of good works. In your teaching, show integrity, seriousness, incorruptibility, and soundness of speech that can't be condemned, that he who opposes you may be ashamed, having no evil thing to say about us." By actively mentoring younger people, we enable the youngsters to contribute to the development of future leaders who are rooted in religion, wisdom, and a desire to effect positive change.

Conclusion:

Finally, the potential benefits of young people becoming involved in the Church community are wide and significant, encompassing spiritual, communal, and societal dimensions. The scriptural foundation, as demonstrated in 1 Timothy 4:12, offers the groundwork for a thorough grasp of the youth's role as faith models. By embracing their unique gifts, unrelenting passion, and new perspectives, the Church community not only revitalises its internal dynamics but also broadens its positive influence far beyond its walls. As the youth actively participate, take on leadership roles, and engage in community outreach, they help to construct a future in which faith's transformative power is recognised in all aspects of life. Recognising and developing the potential of its young people ensures that the Church remains a dynamic and relevant force in an ever-changing world.

The idea of Christ's body in 1 Corinthians 12:12-27 is a powerful metaphor that highlights the importance of every member of the Church community. The Church thrives when it embraces and absorbs its youth's different abilities, talents, and perspectives, just as a physical body needs all of its parts to function well. Each member, young and old, possesses a distinct set of abilities and characteristics that, when correctly combined, convert the Church into a vibrant and holistic organisation.

Involvement of youth serves the Church community in a variety of ways. Their innovative thoughts shake up routines and encourage creative problem-solving, which can lead to the creation of new programmes and approaches. Their commitment to social justice and community service can inspire the entire congregation to act with compassion and charity.

The Church fosters a stronger sense of unity and diversity by actively involving the youth. It bridges generational divides and encourages intergenerational mentorship and collaboration, where the knowledge of the elders and the zeal of the youth complement each other. This combination of experience and vitality results in a more peaceful, diversified, and inclusive community that mimics the Body of Christ, with its various parts working together towards a common purpose.

The involvement of young people in the Church community has the potential to be a powerful force for positive transformation. When adolescents participate actively, they not only provide new energy to the congregation, but they also reflect the spirit of 1 Timothy 4:12 and 1 Corinthians 12:12-27, enriching the Church with their unique gifts, perspectives, and passions. Accepting and strengthening youth in the Church community shows not only faith strength but also a commitment to a more cohesive, diverse, and purpose-driven body of believers.

Revisiting the Underlying Values and Teachings that Determine the Mission of the Church:

In this section, we addressed the major beliefs and teachings that constitute the Church's mission, highlighting the need of nurturing spiritual growth in youth and emphasising the potential positive impact of their involvement in the Church community. By grounding ourselves in these biblical principles, we rekindle our enthusiasm for the Church's purpose and become agents of change, both in the lives of the youth and in the greater Church body.

1. The Great Commandment: Love God and Your Neighbour

Anchoring ourselves in Matthew 22:38-39 revitalises our mission. We are not only called to follow rules but also to love passionately. This commandment establishes the tone for our contacts with the youth, emphasising the necessity of developing a deep, personal relationship with God and establishing a community in which love is the driving force.

For our young people, delving into the profound wisdom of Matthew 22:38-39 and embracing the spirit of The Great Commandment becomes a transforming experience. It is not simply a collection of rules to follow; it is an invitation to immerse ourselves in a radical, all-encompassing love. This commandment is the cornerstone of our mission, giving it life and moulding the culture of our relationships with adolescents.

To begin with, we recognise that this commandment is a call to transcend beyond the surface and ritualistic parts of faith. It invites us to go on an in-depth and personal examination of our connection with God. This is more than just memorising passages or attending services for the youth; it is an invitation to engage in a dynamic, living connection with the Divine. It inspires individuals to seek God with all of their hearts, souls, and minds, cultivating spiritual depth that extends beyond the surface.

We emphasise the transformational power of love in our relationships with youth. It is an active force that motivates us to serve, comprehend, and empathise, not a passive sentiment. This love propels all areas of our ministry, shaping our programmes, discussions, and outreach initiatives. The goal is to establish a community in which love is a tangible and lived experience rather than an ideal.

The Great Commandment establishes the tone for how we approach unity in our young group. It provides the foundation for relationships—relationships characterised by genuine caring, support, and a shared commitment to spiritual progress. We emphasise the value of a community in which each member is appreciated not for their achievements or compliance but for the love they bring to the collective journey.

This entails infusing love-centred practises into our youth ministry. We encourage acts of kindness, service projects, and focused conversations that foster a culture of love and acceptance. The emphasis is on providing a space where every youngster feels seen, heard, and, most importantly, loved, whether in small group talks or big gatherings.

Anchoring ourselves in the Great Commandment, in essence, revitalises our mission by shifting our focus from external compliance to personal reform. It moves the focus from a list of religious obligations to a passionate pursuit of a God who is personally involved in every part of our lives. As youth workers, we are not just mentors but also facilitators of a journey in which the transformative power of love is not only recognized but also experienced, resulting in a lively and spiritually rich community in which the young can thrive.

2. The Great Commission: Proclaiming the Gospel

Matthew 28:19-20, also known as the Great Commission, serves as a compass for our youth ministry, directing our efforts towards a transformative purpose. This biblical mandate moves us beyond the boundaries of our immediate community, challenging us to embrace a global and eternal mission.

In light of the Great Commission, the youth ministry takes on a dynamic role as a training ground for discipleship and Gospel proclamation. We recognise that this commission is more than a suggestion; it is a divine mandate to go and make disciples of all nations. As a result, our emphasis switches from just supporting the spiritual growth of youth within the Church to training them as Christ's ambassadors, actively engaged in sharing the Gospel with the world.

A major aspect of our youth ministry is instilling a sense of responsibility for Gospel preaching. We recognise that the youth are not only the Church's future but also active players in the unfolding story of God's redemptive plan. We equip youth to articulate their faith, express the transformative power of Christ's message, and courageously share the good news with others around them via deliberate instruction, mentorship, and immersive experiences.

This empowerment is not a one-size-fits-all approach in youth ministry. We value each individual's unique gifts, passions, and situations. Some people are exceptional speakers, while others specialise in interpersonal connections or artistic expression. The purpose is to develop a wide range of skills and ways that contribute to the overarching mission of Gospel proclamation.

We emphasise that their purpose extends well beyond the boundaries of the Church. Youth are encouraged to regard their communities, schools, jobs, and even social media platforms as fertile ground for sowing Gospel seeds. We encourage young people to see every interaction as an opportunity to exemplify Christ's love and truth, knowing that their influence has the power to reach every part of the globe.

To provide hands-on chances for Gospel proclamation, practical initiatives such as outreach programmes, mission trips, and community service projects are interwoven into the youth ministry. This not only reinforces theoretical understanding but also allows the youth to see the real-world impact of their role as Christ's ambassadors.

The Great Commission, in essence, transforms our youth ministry into a hub of discipleship and mission. It drives us to equip and empower students to be active agents of change in a world hungry for Christ's redeeming message, rather than passive recipients of spiritual enlightenment. As youth workers, we find satisfaction in seeing the youth embrace their calling, realising that their goal is a worldwide movement that resonates with the heartbeat of God's compassion for all humanity.

3. Spiritual Growth and Discipleship

2 Timothy 2:1-2 and Colossians 1:18-19 outline our approach to spiritual progress. We value not only personal spiritual maturation but also preparing youth to become mentors and teachers themselves. It's a chain reaction that turns discipleship into a never-ending cycle of growth and mentorship.

These two passages serve as essential pillars in our journey as youth workers, guiding our approach to spiritual development and discipleship within the youth ministry. These verses invite us to a profound knowledge not only of personal spiritual progress but also of the transformational power of passing on this wisdom to future generations.

2 Timothy 2:1-2 (WEB) becomes our guidepost, with its call to "be strengthened in the grace that is in Christ Jesus" and to "commit the same things to faithful men." This letter emphasises the importance of personal resilience in the face of life's hardships, gaining strength from Christ's grace. As youth workers, we instill in the young the notion that spiritual development is a lifelong path of drawing from the source of grace.

Colossians 1:18-19 adds to this viewpoint by emphasising Christ as the head of the Body, the Church. The text encourages us to preach and teach wisely, with the goal of presenting everyone fully developed in Christ. This becomes the overarching purpose of our discipleship efforts: to facilitate an encounter with the transformational presence of Christ, leading to complete faith maturity.

Our method goes beyond simply instilling biblical information in the brains of the kids. We try to establish a strong and authentic relationship with God in our surroundings. Spiritual disciplines such as prayer, meditation, and Scripture study are considered as opportunities to encounter the living Christ, rather than as obligations. We guide the youth in establishing a lively and personal religion that transcends the surface via focused teaching and experiential activities.

Equally crucial is the realisation that spiritual development is not a solitary endeavour. It's a group effort, and 2 Timothy 2:2 encourages us to transmit what we've learned to trustworthy individuals who will then teach others. As a result, the kids are not only recipients of wisdom but also active participants in the mentoring cycle. We encourage them to take on leadership responsibilities, such as conducting small group discussions and even leading portions of our worship sessions.

In our youth ministry, discipleship is considered as a continuous cycle of growth and mentorship, rather than a linear procedure. As the youth spiritually mature, they are urged to invest in the spiritual development of their peers. This fosters a culture in which discipleship becomes a dynamic and intergenerational interchange of insight, experience, and faith.

In practise, this entails mentorship programmes in which older youth guide and support younger members on their spiritual path. It includes opportunities for youth to share their testimonies, allowing personal tales to inspire and encourage others. The goal is to build a community in which each member is both a disciple and a disciple-maker.

In essence, our approach to spiritual development and discipleship is about facilitating encounters with Christ's transformative power rather than giving knowledge. We hope to build a community where spiritual growth is a continuous and enjoyable journey through this intentional and relational approach.

4. Unification and Community

Ephesians 4:11-16 reminds us of the interconnectivity of Christ's body. We emphasise the idea that each kid has a distinct role to play in the overall growth and maturity of the Church. Unity is more than a goal; it is a requirement for a functioning Church community.

The message in Ephesians is a lighthouse that guides our youth ministry in establishing a sense of community and harmony. This profound verse not only emphasises the importance of unity within the Body of Christ, but it also gives a vivid picture of how each individual's unique abilities and contributions play an important role in the Church's collective growth and maturity.

As youth workers, we recognise the intrinsic value of community, realising that spiritual growth is not a solo quest. Ephesians 4:11-16 challenges us to see the youth ministry as a microcosm of the broader Body of Christ, in which each member, who has a unique ability and calling, is an indispensable element of the whole. This viewpoint serves as the cornerstone for our strategy to create a thriving and linked youth community.

This passage's emphasis on oneness is not a call to conformity, but rather a celebration of difference. We teach young people to recognise and value the various qualities, gifts, and views that each person provides to the community. Every member is seen as a meaningful contributor to the depth of the collective journey, regardless of spiritual skills, talents, or personal experiences.

In practise, we create an environment in which the young actively engage with one another. Small group talks, collaborative projects, and interactive activities provide outlets for developing relationships and finding the community's unique abilities. We provide spaces for the youngsters to share their stories on purpose, knowing that each narrative contributes a unique thread to the fabric of the group's collective experience.

Ephesians 4:11-16 serves as a model for leadership development in youth ministry. We encourage youth to identify and cultivate their spiritual abilities, understanding that these skills are supposed to be shared for the benefit of the entire community rather than only for personal edification. We build a culture of shared accountability and collective ownership by empowering youth to take on leadership positions in worship, service projects, and outreach efforts.

The verse also emphasises the significance of spiritual development in attaining unity. As youth workers, we help the youth develop in a holistic way, nourishing not just their spiritual understanding but also their emotional and relational intelligence. This comprehensive development benefits the community's overall health and vitality.

In essence, Ephesians 4:11-16 becomes more than a verse in our youth ministry; it becomes a living reality. It shapes our community's culture, providing a sense of belonging and purpose. The youth are not just spectators; they are active participants in a vibrant and flourishing community of believers. This method not only prepares children for a lifelong journey within the greater Body of Christ, but it also cultivates a community in which each member's collective growth and maturity is honoured as a testimonial to our Lord's grace and wisdom.

5. Social Participation and Justice

Micah 6:8 and James 1:27 emphasise the significance of social responsibility. We teach young people to be just, merciful, and involved in their communities. Addressing societal challenges, caring for the marginalised, and actively participating in efforts to bring about constructive change are all part of this.

Our approach to youth ministry is based on the profound truths found in Micah 6:8 and James 1:27. These verses serve as a moral compass for the kids, directing them towards a holistic view of faith that extends beyond personal salvation to active engagement with the world's issues.

Micah 6:8 (WEB) is an impassioned exhortation to action. "He has shown you, O man, what is good. What does Yahweh require of you, but to act justly, to love mercy, and to walk humbly with your God?" It becomes the ethical framework within which we manage our roles as individuals and as a community.

We unpack Micah 6:8 in our youth ministry to emphasise the practical implications of acting justly. This entails making a commitment to solving systemic challenges of inequality and injustice on a local and global scale. We involve the kids in social justice discussions, urging them to be champions for the marginalised and downtrodden. Volunteering at local shelters, participating in community outreach programmes, or campaigning for legislation reforms that promote justice could all be examples of this principle.

The commandment to love mercy encourages youth to develop a compassionate heart. We investigate mercy as more than a passive emotion, but as an active force seeking to alleviate suffering and extend forgiveness. We guide the young in building a compassionate mindset that extends grace and mercy to people who may have been marginalised or disregarded; we do this through hands-on service initiatives and thoughtful talks.

Walking humbly with God becomes our spiritual anchor. This humility is not self-deprecating, but rather recognises our dependency on God's guidance and grace. It promotes a mindset of continuous learning and receptivity to other people's opinions and experiences. As youth workers, we demonstrate this humility by encouraging youth to address societal challenges with an open mind and open ears.

James 1:27 underscores the commitment to social justice by characterising a pure and flawless religion as caring for orphans and widows in need while being unstained by the world. This verse becomes a call to action on behalf of those who are vulnerable and marginalized, to actively participate in their well-being. This manifests itself in our youth ministry through establishment of programmes centred on community service, collaboration with organisations that assist orphans and widows, and participation in conversations about the ethical dilemmas that the world presents.

In practise, youth are encouraged to participate in community outreach programmes that address the needs of the most vulnerable members of society. Initiatives to support orphanages, mentorship programmes for at-risk adolescents, and collaborations with organisations working on topics such as poverty alleviation and refugee relief are examples of this.

Justice and social participation in our youth ministry are not optional extras, but rather essential components of a dynamic and authentic faith. Micah 6:8 and James 1:27 challenge the students to turn their spiritual convictions into concrete deeds that reflect the heart of a God who is passionately concerned with justice, mercy, and the well-being of all people. We hope that by sharing these teachings, we might inspire a new generation to actively contribute to the creation of a more equitable and compassionate world.

6. International Outreach & Missions

Acts 1:28 pushes us to think outside the box. Youth are urged to respond to the call to be witnesses, not only locally but also nationally and internationally. This broadens their horizons, cultivating a worldwide understanding of God's mission and their role in it.

The call to missions and international outreach inspired by Acts 1:28 crosses geographical boundaries in our youth ministry. This verse becomes a driving force, pulling the kids beyond the familiar landscapes of their local communities and encouraging them to embrace a greater perspective of their participation in God's redemptive purpose on a national and international scale.

Acts 1:28 sets the tone for our approach, reminding the youth that they are called to be witnesses, not only in their immediate surroundings but also to the ends of the globe. This biblical foundation serves as a catalyst for widening their viewpoints and establishing a feeling of global awareness in them. We hope to instill in the kids a fundamental knowledge that God's work knows no boundaries, and that their duty as witnesses includes a commitment to engage with humanity's variegated tapestry.

In practise, this entails cultivating a culture of openness and curiosity about the world. We encourage young people to learn about different cultures, appreciate different customs, and comprehend the unique issues that communities around the world confront. This could involve organising cross-cultural activities, inviting international speakers, or incorporating global themes into the curriculum.

Furthermore, we actively encourage participation in national and international missions. This could include collaborating with existing missionary organisations, going on short-term mission trips, or working on projects that address global issues including poverty, healthcare disparities, and educational inequality. These experiences expose the youth to the breadth of God's Kingdom and their vital part in its expansion.

International outreach becomes a transformative trip for the youth, allowing them to see directly the global influence of their faith. It pushes them out of their comfort zones, encourages adaptability, and fosters empathy for the different realities that communities around the world confront. These encounters shape their perceptions and enhance their resolve to be ambassadors of Christ's love outside their current surroundings.

Furthermore, technology is critical in linking youngsters to the worldwide mission field. Virtual collaborations, online forums, and partnerships with foreign youth organisations allow the youth to interact with peers from all cultures, share experiences, and together explore how their faith can be a unifying factor in a diverse society.

Ultimately, Acts 1:28 becomes a commission for the youth to regard themselves as active partners in God's goal to reconcile all nations to Himself. It converts the youth ministry into a dynamic hub where the limits of location are transcended, and a generation is empowered to affect the world with the transformative message of Christ's love. Through missions and international outreach, the youth find that their duty as witnesses goes far beyond the familiar, encouraging them to contribute to a global narrative of redemption and restoration.

7. Contemplative Spirituality

Exploring contemplative spirituality, especially pulling from Celtic and monastic traditions, gives richness to our spiritual growth approach. We present activities that inspire reflection, stillness, and a deeper connection with God. This meditative part strengthens the youth's spiritual journey, creating a profound and intimate contact with God.

In our youth ministry, the infusion of contemplative spirituality, with a particular emphasis on drawing from Celtic and monastic traditions, serves as a transforming dimension to our spiritual development strategy. This purposeful inclusion goes beyond the surface of typical religious traditions, encouraging the youth into a deeper and more intimate connection with God. Contemplative spirituality becomes a hallowed space where the cacophony of the world diminishes, and the youth can encounter the Divine in profound and meaningful ways.

Celtic and monastic traditions offer a rich tapestry of meditative practices that have lasted the test of time. Drawing inspiration from these historic wells, we introduce the youth to practices that transcend beyond the busy noise of ordinary life. We guide children to explore the beauty of silence, promoting periods of thought, meditation, and prayer that give a counterweight to the fast-paced and noisy world they occupy.

One of the hallmarks of contemplative spirituality is the cultivation of inner calm. Through practices such as centering prayer, Lectio Divina, or mindfulness, the youth learn to quiet the commotion of their minds and create a sacred place for connection with God. These activities not only provide a relief from the hustle of life but also serve as a pathway to deeper self-awareness and a more profound relationship with the Divine.

The contemplative aspect is not confined to traditional rituals alone; it extends to interaction with the natural environment. Inspired by Celtic spirituality's great love for creation, we encourage the youth to connect with God via nature. This could involve contemplative hikes, outdoor meditation, or simply finding a peaceful location in nature for prayer. By infusing the beauty of the created world into their spiritual practices, the young discover new aspects of God's presence and creativity.

We introduce the youth to the rhythm of liturgical seasons by incorporating components from monastic traditions. This cyclical view of time leads individuals to adopt a contemplative posture, recognising the sacred in the mundane and discovering God in the midst of routine. Advent, Lent, and other seasons provide opportunities for focused reflection, assisting youth in developing a sense of spiritual discipline and mindfulness.

In practise, we build contemplative places within our youth ministry. This could involve setting aside time for silent thought during gatherings, adding contemplative components into spiritual retreats, or giving tools for personal contemplative practises that the young can apply in their daily lives.

The purpose of adopting contemplative spirituality is to connect with reality more truthfully rather than to retreat from it. As youth workers, we help the kids understand that contemplative practises are not just for the elite, but are available to anybody seeking a deeper connection with God. This part of spiritual development becomes a journey of self-discovery, cultivating a profound and intimate relationship with God that improves their overall spiritual journey and helps them to negotiate life's complexity with a grounded and centred spirit.

In essence, by incorporating these biblical principles into the fabric of our youth ministry, we not only rekindle our enthusiasm for the Church's mission, but we also serve as catalysts for dramatic change in the lives of the young and the greater Church body.

These biblical verses reflect the principles and beliefs that direct the activities of the Church. By practising these ideals, the Church strives to fulfil God's purposes by bringing people into a loving relationship with Him, nurturing their faith, fostering unity, promoting justice, and spreading the good news of salvation through Jesus Christ to all corners of the world.

Highlighting the Positive Impact of Encouraging Spiritual Growth in Youth across the Church Community:

From a broader perspective, encouraging spiritual growth in youth within a Church community can have various possible positive effects. Here are some important factors to consider:

1. Continuation and Future Leadership: Investing in the spiritual development of youngsters supports the Church community's continuation. Young individuals who have a strong faith foundation are more likely to become active and dedicated members of the Church. This can also help the Church's future leadership, since these people may take on roles in ministry, administration, and other areas.

Continuity and future leadership within a Church community are critical factors that rely heavily on investments in the spiritual development of its youth. Here's an extension of that thought:

A. Laying the Groundwork for Lifelong Faith:

Encouraging spiritual growth in youth entails providing them with a solid foundation in their faith's beliefs and teachings. As young people have a better knowledge of their religious beliefs, they are more likely to carry them into adulthood. This continuity ensures that the Church's essential values survive from generation to generation.

B. Membership that is Active and Committed:

Youth who grow spiritually are more likely to become active and dedicated members of their Church community. Actively engaged youth not only add to the energy of contemporary Church life but also serve as the congregation's backbone in the years to come. Regular attendance, participation in events, and a willingness to donate their time and talents to various Church initiatives can all demonstrate their involvement.

C. Transitional Leadership Positions

A religious community that prioritises its youth's spiritual growth is more likely to see young persons assume leadership roles as they enter adulthood. Spiritually grounded youth can serve as a bridge between elder generations and younger generations, whether in formal positions such as ministry or administration duties, or in informal roles such as mentors and community influencers.

D. Regeneration and Adaptation:

Youth frequently provide new insights and an eagerness to adjust to changing circumstances. Investing in their spiritual development can infuse the Church with new ideas, enthusiasm, and service ways. These individuals, as future leaders, may play a critical role in guiding the Church through periods of transition, assisting it in remaining relevant and responsive to the changing needs of its members and the larger society.

E. Transmitting Traditions and Values:

Spiritual development entails not just personal faith development but also an awareness of the Church's traditions and principles. The Church ensures the true transmission of its rich traditions and basic principles by investing in the spiritual training of youngsters. This constancy leads to a sense of group identification and belonging.

F. Developing Mentoring Relationships:

Churches that prioritise spiritual growth frequently offer mentorship programmes in which older, more experienced members guide and support younger members on their faith journeys. These intergenerational interactions promote a sense of connection and offer vital counsel to adolescents as they manage life's difficulties, adding to their overall development and preparation for leadership roles.

G. Addressing Modern-Day Challenges:
The Church faces a variety of obstacles in a fast-changing world, including shifting cultural norms, technological breakthroughs, and evolving societal expectations. Youth who experience real spiritual growth are better prepared to face these problems while remaining committed to their faith. Their future leadership can help the Church to manage contemporary difficulties with wisdom and grace.

Investing in the spiritual growth of adolescents is an investment in a Church community's long-term health and resilience. It not only maintains the continuation of fundamental values, but it also raises a generation of leaders who are dedicated, adaptive, and capable of leading the Church into the future with a strong sense of purpose and conviction.

2. Community Building: Fostering spiritual growth in youth can help to strengthen the Church's feeling of community. Young people build friendships with each other and with elder members of the Church when they participate in spiritual activities together. This intergenerational link helps to make the community more alive and supportive.

Fostering spiritual growth in youth is critical to improving a Church's sense of community. This dedication to fostering young people's spiritual development has a rippling effect on the congregation's overall cohesion and liveliness. Here's an explanation of how this technique helps to establish community:

A. Spiritual Experiences Shared:

Encouragement of youth participation in spiritual activities fosters shared experiences that serve as the foundation for community building. These shared spiritual endeavours establish a common basis for interaction among the adolescents, whether through worship services, study groups, retreats, or community service projects. These common experiences serve as touchstones, binding them together and contributing to a sense of unity.

B. Deep Friendship Formation:

Personal introspection, vulnerability, and a search for meaning are all common components of spiritual growth. When young people travel together on this adventure, they frequently create strong and meaningful connections. These connections extend beyond the boundaries of formal Church events, forming a supporting network that fosters emotional, spiritual, and practical assistance within the youth community.

C. Bonds between Generations:

Fostering spiritual growth in youth naturally leads to intergenerational Church connections. Young people interact with elder members of the congregation who serve as mentors, advisors, and role models while they participate in spiritual activities. This intergenerational exchange of wisdom, experiences, and perspectives generates a feeling of continuity and shared history within the community, resulting in a tapestry of relationships spanning many age groups.

D. Acceptance and Inclusion:
The emphasis on spiritual growth fosters an accepting and inclusive environment among the Church community. Youth are encouraged to explore their beliefs in an atmosphere of openness and tolerance. This acceptance culture extends beyond religious beliefs to incorporate varied backgrounds, experiences, and opinions, resulting in a friendly society in which everyone feels appreciated and included.

E. Service and Outreach in Collaboration:
Involving youth in spiritual development frequently includes a call to service and outreach. As young people collaborate on community-benefiting projects, they acquire a shared sense of purpose and responsibility. Collaborative service activities create a strong bonding experience, reinforcing the notion that the Church is more than just a venue for personal growth, but also a community actively involved in making a positive difference in the world.

F. Challenge Support Systems:
The obstacles that young people experience during their early years are broad and complex. Fostering spiritual growth offers a friendly environment in which people can seek direction, encouragement, and understanding from one another. This support structure is especially important at times of personal difficulty or crisis, reinforcing the idea that the Church

community is a place where people are cared for and supported on their spiritual journey.

G. Diversity Celebration:

Spiritual development invites investigation of the Church community's rich tapestry of religious and cultural variety. Youth gain an awareness of other opinions and backgrounds as they mature spiritually. This celebration of diversity adds to the richness of the community by encouraging members to learn from one another and grow together in a spirit of togetherness despite their differences.

H. Rituals and Traditions of the Community:

Spiritual development frequently includes involvement in rituals and customs that are central to the community's religious identity. Youth participation in these rituals not only connects them to the Church's tradition but also reinforces a sense of belonging. These common practises become a unifying factor, strengthening communal relationships throughout generations.

Supporting spiritual growth in youth extends beyond individual development; it serves as a catalyst for the formation of a close-knit and supportive Church community. Youth contribute greatly to the vibrancy and resilience of the overall Church community through shared experiences, deep friendships, intergenerational relationships, inclusivity, collaborative service, support networks, diversity celebration, and common rituals.

3. Service and Outreach: Spiritually grounded young people are more likely to participate in acts of service and outreach.

Encouragement to live out their faith by acts of kindness, social justice, and community service benefits not only individuals in need but also the Church's good impact on the larger community.

Intergenerational ties formed by supporting spiritual growth in youth are the foundation of a flourishing and integrated Church community. This deliberate effort in bringing people of diverse ages together generates a dynamic tapestry of relationships that adds significantly to the congregation's overall strength and vitality. Here's an extension of the idea of intergenerational ties in the context of spiritual development:

A. Guidance and Mentorship:
As youth participate in spiritual activities, they inevitably encounter older, more experienced members of the congregation who serve as mentors and leaders. These seasoned folks share their personal faith journeys to provide insights, wisdom, and practical assistance. Mentorship becomes a two-way street, with senior members providing direction while also learning from the youth's fresh insights and energy.

B. Spiritual Practises in Common:
Sharing spiritual practises is a common way for intergenerational ties to form. Participating in religious ceremonies, prayer groups, or study sessions becomes a community activity that brings people of different ages together. This shared commitment to spiritual growth fosters a sense of unity within the Church, bridging generational gaps.

C. Tradition and Values Transmission:

Through their interactions with the youth, older members of the congregation play an important role in transferring the Church's traditions and essential beliefs. This intergenerational exchange ensures that the faith's tradition is authentically passed forward. It develops into a living tradition in which stories, practises, and beliefs are passed down, preserving a sense of continuity and identity within the community.

D. Creating a Community History Awareness:

The intergenerational exchange of experiences helps to shape a shared community history. A collective narrative emerges through conversations, storytelling, and collaborative activities that encompasses the diverse journeys of individuals of various ages. This shared history becomes a source of strength and resilience for future generations to build on.

E. How to Develop Empathy and Understanding:

Interacting with people from various generations fosters empathy and understanding. Young people learn about the challenges, triumphs, and life experiences of their elders, and vice versa. This mutual understanding dispels stereotypes and generational misunderstandings, resulting in a more inclusive and harmonious Church community where everyone feels valued and appreciated.

F. Strengthening the Church's Fabric:

Intergenerational connections formed through spiritual growth activities contribute to the Church's overall strength and cohesiveness. When people of various ages work together, worship together, and learn from one another, they form a strong and resilient fabric that can withstand the ravages of time and external challenges. This interconnectedness strengthens the community's sense of belonging and shared responsibility.

G. Promote Collaborative Leadership:
Intergenerational relationships are necessary for the development of collaborative leadership within the Church. As youth progress in their spiritual journeys, the relationships they form with older members can develop into leadership partnerships. This collaborative approach ensures a range of perspectives and skills, enriching leadership dynamics and promoting a more comprehensive and inclusive decision-making process.

H. Coming Together to Celebrate Milestones:
The intergenerational community provides a welcoming environment for commemorating life's significant events. Whether it's baptisms, confirmations, weddings, or funerals, these shared moments bring people of all ages together to offer support, love, and a sense of collective joy or mourning.

Encouraging spiritual growth in youth creates a dynamic and resilient Church community by fostering intergenerational bonds. The exchange of wisdom, shared practises, tradition transmission, cultivating empathy, strengthening the fabric of the Church, encouraging collaborative leadership, and celebrating milestones together all contribute to a community that is not only spiritually rich but also deeply connected across generations.

4. Informed and Critical Thinking: Spiritual growth requires education and reflection. This procedure can help to develop critical thinking skills as well as a better understanding of religious beliefs and practises. As young people grow in their faith, they are better able to engage with current issues, contribute to discussions, and make informed decisions in their personal and professional lives.

Encouragement of informed and critical thinking as part of the spiritual development process represents an investment in the intellectual and spiritual development of youth within a Church community. This approach goes beyond rote learning and aims to equip individuals with the skills and knowledge needed to navigate complex issues, both within the context of faith and in their daily lives. Here's how providing opportunities for spiritual growth can help with informed and critical thinking:

A. Foundations of Education:
Spiritual development frequently involves structured education, such as study groups, Sunday school, or educational programmes. These contexts provide a solid foundation for understanding religious texts, historical context, and theological principles. This educational component gives youth the knowledge they need to have thoughtful and informed conversations about their faith.

B. Encouraging Inquiry and Exploration:
Spiritual growth involves not only accepting information but also questioning and exploring one's beliefs. Providing a safe space for youth to ask questions, express doubts, and explore different

points of view fosters a critical thinking environment. It encourages people to dig deeper into their faith rather than relying on dogma.

C. Religious Text Analysis:
In-depth study of religious texts is an essential component of spiritual development. This process entails not only reading the Scriptures but also critically analysing and interpreting them. It encourages young people to investigate historical and cultural contexts, consider alternative interpretations, and cultivate the skills necessary to discern the core messages and values embedded in the texts.

D. Interacting with Theological Ideas:
Spiritual development frequently entails grappling with difficult theological concepts. Engaging with these concepts, whether it's understanding the nature of God, theodicy, or theological doctrines, necessitates critical thinking. Youth are encouraged to investigate the nuances, challenge assumptions, and form their own opinions on these important issues.

E. Application of Faith to Current Issues:
In spiritual growth, an emphasis on critical thinking extends to the application of faith to contemporary issues. Youth are encouraged to consider how their religious beliefs intersect with modern-day social, ethical, and moral challenges. This process prepares them to connect their faith to real-world issues, fostering a sense of relevance and applicability.

F. Taking Part in Thoughtful Discussions:

Spiritual development entails not only personal reflection but also discussions with peers, mentors, and the larger community. These discussions allow youth to express their beliefs, listen to others, and participate in a dialogue that promotes critical thinking. The exchange of ideas fosters intellectual development and broadens perspectives.

G. How to Navigate Ethical Dilemmas:
The development of critical thinking skills allows young people to navigate ethical quandaries within the context of their faith. They learn to analyse situations, consider the ethical implications of their choices, and make decisions using their moral compass. This skill set extends beyond religious contexts, contributing to the development of responsible and ethical individuals.

H. Interfaith Dialogue Preparation:
A strong spiritual growth process prepares youth for interfaith dialogue. Critical thinking skills enable them to understand and respect various religious perspectives, fostering a climate of mutual understanding and cooperation. This ability to engage with people of different faiths thoughtfully contributes to the larger goals of religious tolerance and harmony.

I. Improving Personal and Professional Decisions:
As young people grow in their faith through critical thinking, the skills they learn transfer to their personal and professional lives. The ability to analyse information, weigh options, and make sound decisions is a valuable skill. This combination of critical thinking and faith builds a solid foundation for

navigating life's challenges with wisdom and discernment.

Providing opportunities for spiritual growth that emphasise education and critical thinking equips youth with the intellectual tools they need to approach their faith and the world around them thoughtfully and informedly. This approach not only increases their engagement with religious beliefs and practises, but it also prepares them to be thoughtful, informed, and ethical people in all aspects of their lives.

5. Adaptability and Innovation: Young people frequently bring new perspectives and innovative ideas. Encouraging spiritual growth in a dynamic and inclusive manner within the Church can foster a culture of adaptability and innovation. This can result in the creation of new approaches to worship, outreach, and community engagement that are appealing to a diverse and changing population.

Embracing youth's adaptability and innovative potential within a Church community is an investment in the faith community's dynamic evolution and relevance. Churches can foster a culture that not only adapts to change but also actively seeks innovative ways to connect with the ever-changing needs of its members and the broader society, by encouraging spiritual growth in a way that recognises and values the unique perspectives of youth. Here's more on how this approach contributes to Church adaptability and innovation:

A. Receptivity to New Ideas:
Because of their stage of life, youth frequently bring new perspectives and ideas. Encouraging spiritual

growth in a way that values these distinct points of view fosters an open environment. This willingness to listen to and learn from the youth fosters a culture in which new ideas are welcomed rather than resisted, contributing to the Church's adaptability.

B. Creative Worship Methods:

Spiritual growth can inspire innovative approaches to worship that are in tune with the congregation's changing needs. Youth may bring new elements to traditional worship services, such as multimedia, interactive components, or creative expressions such as art and music. This injection of creativity has the potential to make worship more engaging and relevant to a wide range of people.

C. Experiment with Different Outreach Strategies:

Youth-led spiritual development promotes experimentation with outreach strategies. This could include using social media, organising community events, or employing new communication methods. The Church can reach new audiences and connect with individuals who may not be engaged through traditional means, by supporting and empowering youth in these endeavours.

D. How to Adjust to Changing Community Dynamics:

Communities change over time, as do their members' needs. Youth, who are frequently deeply involved in current issues, can provide valuable insights into these shifting dynamics. Encouragement of spiritual growth that recognises and responds to these changes enables the Church to adapt its ministries, programmes, and services to meet the changing needs of its members.

E. Using Technology to Enhance Spiritual Practises:

The digital age opens up new avenues for spiritual engagement. Because they are digital natives, youth may have novel ideas for incorporating technology into spiritual practises. This could include virtual prayer groups, online study sessions, or interactive apps to help with the spiritual journey. By embracing these technological innovations, the Church can remain accessible and engaging.

F. Initiatives for Community Engagement:

Young people frequently have a strong sense of social responsibility. Encouragement of spiritual growth that emphasises community engagement can lead to the development of innovative social initiatives. The Church becomes a hub for positive change in the community, whether it is organising service projects, partnering with local organisations, or advocating for social justice.

G. Flexible and Inclusive Programming:

Adaptability involves the flexibility to accommodate diverse needs and preferences. Youth-driven spiritual growth may lead to the development of flexible and inclusive programming that caters to a variety of learning styles, schedules, and interests. This adaptability ensures that the Church remains accessible and relevant to a broad spectrum of individuals.

H. Leadership in Change Management:
Youth who undergo spiritual growth in an environment that values adaptability become leaders in change management. They are equipped to navigate transitions, embrace innovation, and guide the Church through periods of transformation. This leadership style fosters a positive attitude toward change and positions the Church as a dynamic and forward-thinking community.

I. Encouraging a Growth Mindset:
Spiritual growth intertwined with adaptability nurtures a growth mindset within the Church community. This mindset encourages individuals to see challenges as opportunities for learning and growth. It fosters resilience in the face of change and promotes a culture where the Church community continuously seeks ways to improve and evolve.

Encouraging spiritual growth in a way that values the unique perspectives of youth contributes significantly to the adaptability and innovation of a Church community. This approach not only allows the Church to respond effectively to changing dynamics but also positions it as a dynamic and inclusive space that resonates with a diverse and evolving population.

6. Personal Development: Spiritual growth is often accompanied by personal development. Youth who engage in spiritual practices may experience increased self-awareness, emotional resilience, and a sense of purpose. These qualities contribute not only to their well-being but also to their ability to positively influence the wider Church community.

Encouraging spiritual growth in youth has far-reaching implications for their personal development, not only enriching their individual lives but also enhancing their capacity to contribute positively to the broader Church community. The intertwining of spiritual practices and personal development creates a transformative journey that influences various aspects of their well-being and interactions within the community. Here's an expansion on how spiritual growth contributes to the personal development of youth and its broader impact:

A. Increased Self-Awareness:

Engaging in spiritual practices often involves self-reflection and introspection. Youth, as they embark on their spiritual journey, develop a heightened sense of self-awareness. This involves an understanding of their values, beliefs, strengths, and areas for growth. This self-awareness becomes a foundation for personal development, guiding them in making choices aligned with their authentic selves.

B. Emotional Resilience:

Spiritual growth provides a source of emotional support and resilience. Youth, through their engagement in spiritual practices, learn coping mechanisms and gain a perspective that helps them navigate life's challenges. This emotional resilience not only contributes to their well-being but also equips them to support others within the Church community who may be facing difficulties.

C. Cultivation of Virtues and Values:

Spiritual practices often emphasise virtues such as compassion, empathy, humility, and gratitude. As youth incorporate these values into their lives, they undergo a process of character development. These virtues become integral aspects of their identity, shaping how they approach relationships, conflicts, and their roles within the Church community.

D. Formation of a Sense of Purpose:
Spiritual growth frequently leads to the discovery of a sense of purpose or calling. Youth, as they deepen their connection to their faith, may find meaning and direction in serving others, contributing to social justice, or engaging in mission work. This sense of purpose not only guides their individual choices but also inspires them to actively participate in the mission and activities of the Church community.

E. Enhanced Interpersonal Skills:
Spiritual growth involves relational aspects such as community engagement, fellowship, and shared worship experiences. Through these interactions, youth develop enhanced interpersonal skills. They learn to communicate effectively, listen empathetically, and collaborate with others. These skills contribute to their ability to build positive relationships within the Church community and beyond.

F. Formation of a Moral Compass:
The exploration of spiritual values and ethical principles in the process of spiritual growth helps youth form a strong moral compass. This moral foundation guides their decision-making, leading to

ethical choices in various aspects of their lives. As individuals with a well-defined moral compass, they become positive influencers within the Church community, contributing to a culture of integrity and moral responsibility.

G. Development of a Balanced Life Perspective:
Spiritual growth encourages individuals to view life holistically, considering the spiritual, emotional, and physical dimensions. This holistic perspective contributes to the development of a balanced and integrated life approach. Youth who undergo spiritual growth are more likely to prioritise their well-being, manage stress effectively, and maintain a healthy balance between various aspects of their lives.

H. Positive Influence on Peers:
Youth who experience personal development through spiritual growth become positive role models for their peers. Their self-awareness, emotional resilience, and commitment to moral values inspire others within the Church community to embark on their own journeys of spiritual and personal growth. This ripple effect contributes to the overall positive culture within the community.

I. Leadership Potential:
The personal development fostered through spiritual growth enhances the leadership potential of youth. As they cultivate qualities such as self-awareness, emotional intelligence, and a sense of purpose, they become effective leaders within the Church community. This leadership extends beyond formal

roles, influencing others through their example, encouragement, and willingness to serve.

In summary, the connection between spiritual growth and personal development is a transformative process that shapes the well-being and character of youth. The qualities developed through this journey not only contribute to their individual flourishing but also position them as positive influencers within the wider Church community. As youth engage in spiritual practices, they become valuable contributors to the overall health and vibrancy of the community, fostering a culture of personal development and mutual support.

7. Global Perspective: Encouraging spiritual growth can also foster a global perspective. Many churches engage in mission work and outreach beyond their local communities. As youth become more spiritually mature, they may develop a sense of responsibility for addressing global issues and participating in efforts to promote justice, peace, and compassion on a broader scale.

Encouraging spiritual growth in youth within the context of a global perspective is a powerful way for churches to instill a sense of responsibility and compassion that extends beyond local boundaries. This approach not only enriches the spiritual development of individuals, but it also aligns with the broader mission of many churches to contribute positively to the well-being of the global community. Here's an expansion on how fostering a global perspective through spiritual growth can influence youth and their engagement with global issues:

A. Exposure to Global Missions:

Churches often engage in mission work beyond their local communities, providing opportunities for youth to witness firsthand the challenges faced by individuals in different parts of the world. Participation in global missions exposes youth to diverse cultures, socioeconomic conditions, and global realities, fostering a broader understanding of the interconnectedness of humanity.

B. Cultivation of Empathy and Compassion:
Spiritual growth emphasises values such as empathy and compassion. As youth engage with global issues, they develop a heartfelt connection to the struggles and triumphs of people in different parts of the world. This heightened empathy becomes a driving force for action, motivating them to seek ways to alleviate suffering and contribute to positive change on a global scale.

C. Awareness of Social Justice and Equity:
The process of spiritual growth encourages a deeper reflection on issues of social justice and equity. Youth, as they mature spiritually, become more attuned to systemic injustices and disparities that affect communities globally. This awareness compels them to advocate for fairness, equity, and human dignity, aligning their actions with the principles of justice promoted by their faith.

D. Recognition of Shared Humanity:
Fostering a global perspective through spiritual growth reinforces the concept of shared humanity. Youth come to understand that, despite cultural, geographical, or socioeconomic differences, there are

common threads that connect all people. This recognition fosters a sense of solidarity and a commitment to working collaboratively toward the well-being of humanity as a whole.

E. Commitment to Peace-building:

Spiritual maturity often involves a commitment to peace-building and conflict resolution. Youth who undergo spiritual growth may feel a responsibility to contribute to global efforts to promote peace and reconciliation. This commitment extends beyond individual conflicts to a broader understanding of the interconnectedness of peace on a global scale.

F. Participation in Global Advocacy:

As youth become more spiritually mature, they may actively engage in advocacy efforts addressing global issues. This involvement can take various forms, including participating in campaigns for environmental sustainability, advocating for the rights of marginalised groups, and supporting initiatives that promote access to education and healthcare on a global level.

G. Environmental Stewardship:

A global perspective cultivated through spiritual growth includes a heightened awareness of environmental issues. Many faith traditions emphasise the responsibility of humans to care for the earth. Youth, as stewards of the environment, may engage in activities and initiatives that promote sustainability, conservation, and responsible stewardship of natural resources on a global scale.

H. Cross-Cultural Collaboration:

Fostering a global perspective encourages youth to engage in cross-cultural collaboration. This might involve forming partnerships with communities in different parts of the world, participating in exchange programs, or collaborating on projects that address global challenges. These cross-cultural interactions contribute to the development of a more interconnected and understanding global community.

I. Encouragement of Global Learning and Exploration:

Spiritual growth involves a continuous process of learning and exploration. Encouraging youth to explore global issues, learn about different cultures, and stay informed about international events broadens their perspectives. This ongoing exploration contributes to a mindset that seeks to understand and engage with the complexities of a globalised world.

Encouraging a global perspective through spiritual growth equips youth with the awareness, empathy, and sense of responsibility needed to engage with the challenges and opportunities present on a global scale. By fostering a commitment to justice, peace, and compassion, youth can become active participants in global initiatives that align with the principles of their faith, contributing to positive change and making a meaningful impact on a broader stage.

8. Cultural and Diversity Appreciation: A focus on spiritual growth can encourage an appreciation for cultural and religious diversity. Youth who engage in learning about different faith traditions and cultural practices may develop a more inclusive world-view, contributing to the Church's ability to connect with and welcome a diverse range of individuals.

Emphasising spiritual growth within the context of cultural and diversity appreciation is a transformative approach that not only enriches the individual journeys of youth but also contributes to the overall inclusivity and welcoming nature of the Church community. By encouraging youth to explore and appreciate various cultural and religious traditions, the Church fosters an environment where diversity is celebrated and valued. Here's an expansion on how this focus on cultural and diversity appreciation through spiritual growth can positively impact youth and the broader Church community:

A. Interfaith Exploration:

Spiritual growth involves an exploration of faith and belief systems. Encouraging youth to learn about different religious traditions fosters an environment of interfaith dialogue and understanding. This exploration not only broadens their knowledge but also promotes respect for diverse ways of approaching spirituality. It contributes to the development of individuals who appreciate the richness of religious diversity within and beyond the Church community.

B. Cultural Education and Awareness:

Spiritual growth can go hand in hand with cultural education and awareness. Youth, as they delve into their faith journeys, may be encouraged to learn about various cultural practices, traditions, and customs associated with different communities. This cultural education contributes to a more informed and respectful approach to engaging with people from diverse backgrounds.

C. Celebration of Religious Festivals:
Engaging youth in spiritual growth can involve the celebration of religious festivals from various traditions. This hands-on experience allows them to appreciate the significance of different cultural and religious celebrations. It promotes a spirit of inclusivity and shared joy within the Church community, fostering an atmosphere where individuals from diverse backgrounds feel acknowledged and welcomed.

D. Inclusive Worship Practices:
Spiritual growth can influence worship practices to become more inclusive of diverse cultural elements. This might involve incorporating music, art, or rituals from different cultural and religious traditions into worship services. Such inclusivity enhances the worship experience for all members of the Church community, creating a space where everyone can find resonance and connection.

E. Building Bridges Across Differences:
Encouraging an appreciation for cultural and religious diversity builds bridges across differences. Youth who undergo spiritual growth develop the skills and mindset to engage with individuals from diverse backgrounds in a spirit of openness and curiosity. This attitude fosters connections and friendships that transcend cultural and religious divides within the Church community.

F. Promoting Language and Communication Inclusivity:

Cultural appreciation involves recognising the diversity of languages and communication styles. Youth engaged in spiritual growth may be encouraged to learn about and appreciate different languages spoken by members of the Church community. Promoting language inclusivity contributes to a sense of belonging for individuals whose primary language may be different from the dominant language of the community.

G. Fostering a Global Perspective:

Cultural and diversity appreciation within the context of spiritual growth contributes to the development of a global perspective. Youth become more attuned to the interconnectedness of cultures and traditions worldwide. This global mindset positions the Church community as one that recognises and values the contributions of individuals from diverse cultural backgrounds.

H. Creating Inclusive Community Events:

Spiritual growth can inspire the creation of inclusive community events that celebrate cultural diversity. Whether through cultural festivals, potluck dinners featuring diverse cuisines, or collaborative artistic performances, these events provide opportunities for the Church community to come together in a spirit of appreciation and unity.

I. Empowering Culture

Youth who develop an appreciation for cultural and religious diversity can become cultural ambassadors within the Church community. They may actively contribute to initiatives that promote inclusivity, organise educational sessions on different cultures, and serve as bridges between individuals from diverse backgrounds. This empowerment of cultural ambassadors enriches the overall cultural fabric of the Church community.

J. Enhancing Cross-Cultural Competence:
As youth engage in spiritual growth with a focus on cultural and diversity appreciation, they naturally develop cross-cultural competence. This competence involves the ability to navigate and communicate effectively in multicultural settings. It prepares them to be leaders and contributors in an increasingly diverse and interconnected world.

Integrating cultural and diversity appreciation into the framework of spiritual growth creates a Church community that values and celebrates the uniqueness of each individual. This approach not only enriches the personal journeys of youth, but also positions the Church as a welcoming and inclusive space, where people from diverse cultural and religious backgrounds can find a sense of belonging and contribute to the collective spiritual tapestry.

In summary, encouraging spiritual growth in youth within a Church community can have far-reaching positive impacts, influencing the future of the Church, fostering community, promoting service and outreach, developing critical thinking, inspiring innovation, facilitating personal development, nurturing a global perspective, and fostering appreciation for diversity.

Chapter 3: Creating a Welcoming Environment

This chapter dives into the biblical underpinnings that govern the reevaluation of conventional Church practises and provides an in-depth analysis of those grounds. In order to inform the design of inclusive places and programmes, it strives to take inspiration from the ageless wisdom that is enshrined in the Scriptures. It is possible for the Church to actively participate in the construction of bridges of relevance, understanding, and acceptance if it responds appropriately to the call to comprehend and cater to the specific requirements of the youth.

It is essential for believers to recognise the ongoing transformation of socioeconomic and cultural landscapes in order to maintain a healthy perspective within the ever-changing fabric of the Church's existence. As a living organism, the Church has a responsibility to be adaptable and sensitive to the various requirements of each new generation that it wants to incorporate. The younger generations, who will be the leaders of the Church in the years to come, are receiving the ecclesiastical body's undivided attention at this time more than at any other. In order to properly value the contributions that young people offer to society, we must make concerted efforts to cultivate an atmosphere that not only recognizes but also rejoices in the unique views and difficulties that characterise today's youth.

The narrative of the biblical text emphasises, again and time again, how important it is to be flexible and attentive to the ever-changing requirements of the people. The preacher in Ecclesiastes 3:1 says, "For everything there is a season, and a time for every purpose under heaven" (WEB). This insight encapsulates the divine invitation to discern the times and change the Church's approach accordingly; read it both ways and you'll get the full picture. The young people, who are currently at the beginning of their spiritual journeys, demand a Church that speaks the language of their hearts, has a pace that matches their experiences, and understands the complexities of the difficulties they face.

When we turn our attention to the teachings of Christ, we discover a striking example of flexibility in Matthew 19:14, where Jesus says, "Allow the little children, and don't forbid them to come to me; for the Kingdom of Heaven belongs to ones like these" (WEB). In this verse, Jesus is referring to the fact that the Kingdom of Heaven belongs to those who are like children. This profound remark urges the Church to rethink any obstacles that may exist, whether they be institutional, cultural, or in any other form, that prevent the youth from fully interacting with the Kingdom of God. These obstacles could be cultural, but they could also be institutional. The way in which Christ interacted with children is a timelessly relevant illustration of the significance of cultivating an atmosphere in which young people not only feel welcome but also treasured.

The youth, who are armed with their own distinctive collection of cultural, technological, and societal lenses, are urging the Church to engage on a journey of self-reflection and adjustment. According to the advice that Paul gives in 1 Corinthians 9:22 (WEB), "I have become all things to all men, that I may by all means save some." The words of the Apostle encourage the Church to adopt a posture that is flexible and transcends generational divides, in order to effectively preach the unchanging message of the Gospel.

The narrative of the Bible resounds with a call to unity despite the diversity that exists, calling believers to embrace inclusivity as an essential component of the Christian identity. In light of this reality, Galatians 3:28 (WEB) declares, "There is neither Jew nor Greek, there is neither slave nor free man, there is neither male nor female; for you are all one in Christ Jesus." This holy proclamation highlights the inherent value that each human possesses in God's eyes, and it urges the Church to mirror this unity in its social life and practises.

In addition, the story told in the Bible fosters the development of an atmosphere in which open communication can thrive. According to the Book of Proverbs 18:15 (AMP), "The mind of the prudent [always] acquires knowledge, And the ear of the wise [always] seeks knowledge." The Church encourages an environment of open communication, which provides a secure setting for young people to voice their questions and concerns about the Christian faith, as well as to participate in in-depth discussions about religious topics. A strategy along these lines parallels the lessons found in James 1:19 (WEB), which states, "So, then, my beloved brothers, let every man be swift to hear, slow to speak, and slow to anger."

The third topic that will be discussed in this chapter is the promotion of projects that are driven by young people. These initiatives should be motivated by the notion that younger people are in possession of special spiritual abilities and insights. In 1 Timothy 4:1 (WEB), the Apostle Paul gives the following advice to Timothy, a young leader: "Let no man despise your youth; but be an example to those who believe, in word, in your way of life, in love, in spirit, in faith, and in purity." This scriptural confirmation highlights the potential that is already present in young people, and it challenges the Church to equip and encourage young people so that they might fulfil their callings within the Body of Christ.

In a nutshell, the purpose of this chapter is to delve into the vast tapestry of biblical wisdom in order to enlighten and inspire the construction of an atmosphere within the Church that is inviting to young people. The Church actively participates in shaping a community in which the younger generation does not only feel acknowledged but also empowered to play an important role in the unfolding story of God's redemptive plan. This is accomplished by rethinking traditional practises, embracing inclusivity, fostering open dialogue, and encouraging youth-driven initiatives.

Rethinking Established Church Practices Encourages Greater Participation from Younger Generations:

Believers are urged to remain alert to the dynamic movement of God's Spirit by the consistent reiteration throughout the pages of Scripture of the biblical demand for creativity and adaptability within the context of the local Church. In the book of Isaiah chapter 43 verse 19 (WEB), the voice of God resounds with a prophetic declaration: "Behold, I will do a new thing. It springs out now. Don't you know it?" This profound phrase epitomises the divine invitation to accept change and regeneration, a theme that is profoundly pertinent to the shifting terrain of ministry, particularly in regard to the involvement of young people.

These statements, when interpreted within the context of the Church, are a call to Christians to reexamine long-standing practises that may unintentionally obstruct the path of progression for younger people. The directive to "do a new thing" hints at the divine expectation that the Church will be receptive to novel forms of worship, discipleship, and community that are in tune with the ever-evolving cultural context. This divine commandment confronts any tendency to hold firmly to traditions that, while valuable to one generation, may not be to another. Traditions that are meaningful to one generation may inadvertently alienate another.

In 1 Corinthians 9:22 (WEB), the Apostle Paul offers a concrete illustration of the use of this principle when he says, "I have become all things to all men, that I may by all means save some." This adaptable approach displays a thorough knowledge of the importance of contextualising the message of the Gospel without compromising its essence. Adaptability is a hallmark of this approach. In a similar vein, the Church is obligated to evaluate the techniques of engagement it uses, bearing in mind that strategies that were successful in reaching earlier generations may now require reevaluation, in order to continue being pertinent to the specific requirements and modes of communication utilised by the younger generation.

Some really practical responses to these passages could look like these ideas:

1. Dynamic Engagement with Culture: Rather than viewing cultural shifts as challenges to be resisted, the Church can actively engage with contemporary culture. This involves understanding the language, interests, and concerns of younger generations and incorporating relevant elements into worship and teaching.

2. Technology Integration: Recognising the role of technology in the lives of younger individuals, the Church can leverage digital platforms for outreach, communication, and discipleship. Online sermons, interactive apps, and social media can be powerful tools for fostering community and connection.

3. Participatory Worship: Move beyond traditional forms of worship to embrace more participatory and experiential approaches. Incorporate a variety of musical styles, interactive elements, and multimedia to create a dynamic worship experience that resonates with diverse preferences.

4. Mentorship and Relationship Building: Establish intentional mentorship programs that bridge the gap between older and younger generations. Encourage meaningful relationships in which experienced members can guide and support younger individuals in their faith journey.

5. Flexible Discipleship Models: Adopt flexible discipleship models that cater to the diverse learning styles and preferences of younger generations. This could include small group studies, mentor-led discussions, or even incorporating elements of gamification to make learning more engaging.

6. Community Outreach and Social Justice: Emphasise the Church's commitment to social justice and community outreach. Younger generations often resonate with causes that address societal issues. Involving the Church in relevant community projects can provide a sense of purpose and mission.

7. Inclusive Decision-Making: Actively involve younger members in decision-making processes within the Church. This not only empowers them, but also ensures that the Church's direction is shaped by the perspectives and aspirations of diverse age groups.

8. Cultivating a Culture of Questions: Create an environment where questions and doubts are not only tolerated but welcomed. Younger individuals often seek a space where they can explore their faith openly and have their inquiries addressed with respect and understanding.

9. Celebration of Diversity: Embrace diversity in all its forms—cultural, ethnic, and theological. Ensure that the Church is a place where individuals from different backgrounds feel valued and included.

10. Continuous Feedback Loop: Establish a system for ongoing feedback from the congregation, especially from younger members. This could involve regular surveys, focus group discussions, or open forums where ideas and concerns can be shared.

In essence, rethinking established Church practices involves an ongoing commitment to staying attuned to the needs and preferences of younger generations, while remaining grounded in the timeless principles of faith. It's a dynamic and adaptive process guided by the recognition that the "new thing" that God is doing may require a departure from familiar routines, to embrace the evolving landscape of ministry.

Jesus Himself utilised creative ways that were relevant to the culture at the time in order to communicate everlasting truths. His ability to engage with people in their everyday lives, as well as the use of parables and storytelling, demonstrated an approach that went beyond the traditional conventions of religious practise. Jesus presents a figurative insight that corresponds with the necessity for flexibility in service in the following verse from Mark 2:22 (WEB): "No one puts new wine into old wineskins; or else the new wine will burst the skins, and the wine pours out, and the skins will be destroyed; but they put new wine into fresh wineskins."

This metaphor highlights how important it is to adapt the technique to the message, as a means of ensuring that the transformational force of the Gospel is not confined by methods that are either outmoded or ineffectual.

The Church is charged with discerning the signs of the times and adopting a posture that is open to constant innovation. This call is made in the spirit of the proclamation made by Isaiah and the example given by Jesus and Paul. This needs a willingness to rethink practises, traditions, and techniques that have been in place for a long time, not just for the sake of change, but also with the purpose of ensuring that the Gospel continues to be a compelling force in the lives of young people. It is an acceptance of the fact that the eternal truths of Scripture can be expressed in a number of ways that are relevant to different cultures and generations.

Rethinking of conventional Church practises in order to better engage the youth is a biblical necessity that has its roots in the divine demand for renewal and adaptability. This proclamation by Isaiah serves as a timeless reminder that God is ever at work, bringing forth new expressions of His redeeming love. It is the responsibility of the Church, in its role as stewards of this holy message, to recognise and respond to the new moves of the Holy Spirit. This will ensure that the transformational force of the Gospel is not hampered by outmoded methods, but rather flows freely into the hearts and lives of each new generation.

In Matthew chapter 9 verse 17 (WEB), Jesus reveals a significant truth about the nature of His teachings, and the susceptibility of individuals who come into contact with them, by employing a powerful metaphor. He says, "Neither do people put new wine into old wine skins," which is an interesting fact. If that happens, the skins will burst, the wine will spill out, and the wineskins will be damaged. This striking parallel conveys a message that is relevant even today: it urges believers to assess whether or not the message of Christ is compatible with the receptacles, sometimes known as vessels, into which it is poured.

In the context of this metaphor, wine represents the transformational and life-giving message of the Gospel, while the wineskins symbolise the structures, traditions, and procedures utilised to deliver and contain that message. The incapacity of the old wineskins to expand and make room for the fermentation process of the new wine is the source of the inherent risk that comes with pouring new wine into older wineskins. The consequence is a catastrophe, including broken skins, lost wine, and broken vessels.

This image serves as a powerful reminder that the message that Jesus brought is one that is dynamic, one that changes lives, and one that is constantly developing. The Gospel is not a fixed entity but rather a dynamic, active force that engages in conversation with the many contexts and cultures into which it is brought. As a result, the tactics and methods that the Church uses to transmit this message need to have a similar adaptability. They need to be able to resonate with the ever-changing dynamics of society, which include the distinct viewpoints and issues that are encountered by the youth.

The understanding that the unchanging message needs to be presented in ways that are relevant and meaningful to each generation is the motivation for the call to adopt new methods and approaches. This appeal does not constitute a rejection of the eternal truths that are found in the Gospel. In 1 Corinthians 9:22 (WEB), the Apostle Paul reflects this sentiment when he says, "I have become all things to all men, that I may by all means save some." This malleable strategy places an emphasis on the significance of contextualising the message without compromising the message's core, in recognition of the fact that different vessels call for distinct modes of communication.

The young people, who are frequently characterised by a different collection of cultural norms, technology fluency, and distinctive social dynamics, demand an approach to the communication of the Gospel that is purposeful and intentional. The Church has a responsibility to adopt tactics that are able to appeal directly to the minds and hearts of the younger generation. Just as Jesus taught through metaphors and parables that connected with the everyday experiences of His audience, the Church must do the same.

The Church embraces a spirit of innovation and creativity when it adopts new methods and approaches. This is done in recognition of the fact that the truth that God reveals cannot be bound to a single manner of expression. This figurative appeal to use new wineskins is an invitation to explore diverse routes of communication, such as digital platforms, interactive debates, and manifestations of worship that are culturally relevant. It emphasises the significance of being attuned to the language and cultural subtleties of the youth, with the goal of ensuring that the everlasting message of the Gospel continues to be persuasive, compelling, and accessible across generations.

In essence, the metaphor of new wine in ancient wineskins encourages the Church to be both the keepers of tradition and the pioneers of relevance in their respective spheres of influence. It advocates striking a careful balance between retaining the unchanging essence of the Gospel and embracing new ways that are culturally appropriate and engage the youth where they are. This is a difficult balance, because the essence of the Gospel does not change. By doing so, the Church ensures that the message of Jesus, which may alter a person's life, is not constrained by practises that are out of date, but rather flows freely, like new wine, into the hearts and lives of each successive generation.

Developing Inclusive Spaces and Programs to Attract and Retain the Younger Generation:

The beat at the centre of the Gospel is intrinsically inclusive, and it is an echo of the invitation that God has issued to every single person on earth. The Apostle Paul says it best in Galatians 3:28 (WEB), when he writes, "There is neither Jew nor Greek, there is neither slave nor free man, there is neither male nor female; for you are all one in Christ Jesus." This verse captures the essence of the Christian faith brilliantly. This deep phrase serves as a cornerstone for comprehending the extreme inclusivity that is incorporated in the message of the Gospel. This radical inclusivity transcends societal barriers and ushers Christians into a shared identity in Christ.

The Church is being put to the test by the far-reaching implications of this simple fact, which requires it to demonstrate the unity that can only be found in Christ within its fundamental structure. The call is unmistakable: the community of believers is to be a manifestation of a diverse and peaceful community in which the divisions that frequently separate society—whether they be cultural, social, or gender-based—are eclipsed by the overarching unity that can be found in the person of Jesus Christ. This is the call that we have been given.

By creating venues and programmes that are welcoming to people of all backgrounds, the Church is embracing its role as a living manifestation of God's love and acceptance. These places evolve into more than merely physical locations; they become settings in which people of every background, ethnicity, socioeconomic level, and gender find themselves not only welcomed but also celebrated. In Romans 12:4-5 (WEB), the Apostle Paul provides a compelling analogy for the inclusive unity that exists within the Body of Christ. Paul writes, "For even as we have many members in one body, and all the members don't have the same function, so we, who are many, are one body in Christ, and individually members of one another."

In a more concrete sense, this inclusiveness calls for deliberate efforts to be made to guarantee that the Church is a place where diversity is not only tolerated but cherished as a reflection of God's creative design. This is a prerequisite for achieving true inclusivity. The Church thrives when individuals from a variety of backgrounds actively participate, bringing their unique abilities, views, and experiences into the common life of the Church. In the same way that a body functions smoothly when each part contributes according to its specific purpose, the Church also thrives when individuals from a variety of backgrounds actively participate.

When developing inclusive spaces, it is also necessary to examine the structures and programmes that are already in place to ensure that they are accessible to all members of the community, and that they are of use to the younger generation in particular. The local Church can serve as a venue for the removal of obstacles to participation and the cultivation of a sense of personal belonging. This could involve measures to address difficulties such as language obstacles, cultural insensitivity, or obsolete procedures that may accidentally exclude specific demographic groups from participation.

In addition, the Church's dedication to inclusiveness extends beyond its physical locations and into the larger community, as well as society as a whole. In the spirit of Jesus' teachings, particularly in the Parable of the Good Samaritan (Luke 10:25-37), the Church is challenged to stretch outside its bounds to embrace people on the fringes, exhibiting a radical love that defies the norms and expectations of society.

The creation of inclusive spaces and programmes inside the Church is not only a necessity from a pragmatic point of view, but it is also an imperative from a biblical point of view. The body of believers is challenged in Galatians 3:28 to reflect the oneness that can only be found in Christ, so transcending the divisions that so frequently plague the world. When a Church makes an intentional effort to be inclusive, it transforms into a shining example of God's love for all people. This attracts younger people and makes it possible for them to not only learn about the grace of God but actually feel it in the warmth of a community that is accepting of people from all walks of life.

In his letter to the Romans, the Apostle Paul offers a powerful metaphor that magnificently encapsulates the core of the process of cultivating cultures within the Church that celebrate diversity and recognise the unique contributions that each member makes. In Romans 12:4-5 (WEB), the Apostle says, "For even as we have many members in one body, and all the members don't have the same function, so we, who are many, are one body in Christ, and individually members of one another."

This metaphor paints a realistic picture of the human body, with all of its different organs and functions cooperating with one another to achieve a common goal. In the same manner, the Church, which is a representation of the Body of Christ, is made up of a wide variety of people, each of whom possesses distinctive gifts, abilities, and points of view. The idea that "each member belongs to all the others" is emphasised in this passage highlights the connectivity and dependency that exists among the members of the community of believers.

To begin the process of cultivating surroundings that honour diversity, one must first have a thorough appreciation of the worth that each individual offers to the overall body of the collective. The youth, with their novel viewpoints, vivid energy, and distinctive cultural experiences, become indispensable additions to the complex fabric that is the Church. This acknowledgment is not only a passive acknowledgment; rather, it is an active affirmation of the value and significance of each and every member, irrespective of their age, origin, or status.

In addition, the metaphor in Romans advocates a change in attitude, namely a transition away from viewing diversity as a difficulty and towards embracing it as a source of strength. In the same way that the many organs and limbs of the human body serve varied functions, the diverse skills and abilities that exist within the community of the Church serve to enrich, strengthen, and edify the entire body. Within the larger framework of the Church, the youth, with their one-of-a-kind insights and capabilities, become catalysts for innovation, creativity, and a fresh sense of purpose.

To put it into practise, the creation of environments that promote diversity means making deliberate efforts to establish venues where young people can showcase their skills and abilities. This may include opportunities for leadership, participation in worship, input into decision-making processes, and participation in outreach projects that resonate with the individual's particular passions. The local Church evolves into a setting in which the abilities of the younger generation are not only acknowledged but also actively developed and put to use for the advancement of the community as a whole and the accomplishment of the Church's mandate.

This passage from Romans presents a challenge to the Church to build an atmosphere of inclusivity, one in which the various contributions of the youth are not merely valued but actively sought for. It fosters a culture of mutual support in which every member, regardless of age or background, is given the opportunity to flourish and contribute in accordance with the one-of-a-kind design that God has bestowed upon them.

In conclusion, the knowledge imparted in Romans 12:4-5 serves as an evergreen guidance for the Church in establishing environments that appreciate difference, particularly in the context of the youth. The Church is encouraged to recognise the intrinsic importance of each member by adopting the metaphor of the body. This helps to cultivate a sense of belonging and unity within the congregation. A lively and dynamic community forms as the unique gifts of the young are affirmed and actively integrated into the life of the Church. This community reflects the splendour of God's creative design and the unity that can be found in Christ.

Encouraging Open Dialogue and Creating Opportunities for Youth-Driven Initiatives:

The timeless words of Proverbs 27:17 (WEB) ring with profound insight: "Iron sharpens iron; so a man sharpens his friend's countenance." This potent metaphor embodies the transformative nature of relationships, by highlighting the mutual influence and progress that occurs when individuals participate in meaningful conversation. This is a powerful metaphor that encapsulates the transformative nature of relationships. This principle, which has its origins in the biblical canon, has major bearing on the development of open communication within the context of the Church, particularly as it relates to the younger generation.

The encouragement of open communication is not just a practical requirement; it is also in line with the fundamental teachings of the Bible, which emphasise the significance of true connections and the expansion of the community as a whole. As a community of believers, the Church has a responsibility to fulfil the role of a forum in which members of the community, especially young people, are free to voice their opinions, queries, and worries within the context of reverence, comprehension, and candour.

The image of one object honing another alludes to a dynamic process of progression towards greater perfection. In the context of open conversation within the Church, this suggests that individuals, both young and old, can have their understanding of faith sharpened and refined via the sharing of ideas, viewpoints, and experiences, so enriching their spiritual journey. This is true for both young people and older people.

To foster a culture of discourse, it is necessary to designate specific areas for talk, places in which young people's contributions to the discussion are not only tolerated but also sought for. This may include platforms for group debates, mentoring programmes, or regular get-togethers at which individuals can discuss their experiences and offer their perspectives. Through the provision of these possibilities, the Church transforms into a setting that fosters the development of trusting connections, which in turn fosters the growth of a robust sense of community.

Furthermore, open communication helps to cultivate an atmosphere of transparency and authenticity, which enables the youth to bring their true selves into the life of the Church and allows the Church to better serve them. By recognising and responding to the questions and concerns raised by the younger generation, the Church demonstrates its dedication to accompanying them on the path of faith that they are travelling. This is consistent with the admonition that the Apostle Paul gives in Ephesians 4:15, where he emphasises the significance of proclaiming the truth in love and growing together as a unified body.

The benefits of open discourse extend beyond the individual growth of each participant to include the overall enrichment of the congregation as a whole. Through conversation, individuals are able to share their unique viewpoints, life experiences, and unique insights, all of which lead to a more holistic understanding of both the Bible and the myriad of ways in which God works in the lives of those who follow Him. When this happens, it turns into a two-way street in which the more experienced members and the younger members contribute to each other's spiritual growth.

The words of wisdom given in Proverbs 27:17 act as a guiding principle for the Church to follow in order to encourage open communication, particularly with the younger generation. By accepting this biblical concept, the local Church is able to create an atmosphere in which true connections can be developed, questions can be asked, and faith may be strengthened through the communal refining of one another. The Church grows into a vibrant and dynamic community as it actively develops a culture of discourse. This community reflects the transformational power of mutual involvement and the common quest of a deeper understanding of God's truth, which causes the Church to become more vibrant and dynamic.

In Acts 2:17–18 (WEB), the Apostle Peter reveals a fundamental truth about the pouring out of the Holy Spirit, by referencing the Prophet Joel. This is a pivotal moment in the history of the Church. According to these Scriptures, "It will be in the last days,' says God, ' that I will pour out my Spirit on all flesh. Your sons and your daughters will prophesy. Your young men will see visions. Your old men will dream dreams. Yes, and on my servants and on my handmaidens in those days, I will pour out my Spirit, and they will prophesy.'"

This prophetic announcement is resonant with an eternal truth; the Holy Spirit of God is not bestowed only upon those of a certain age, but is poured out on all people, with a particular emphasis placed on the prophetic potential that is present in those of younger generations.

This verse is a potent reminder to the Church of the spiritual talents and imaginative potential that are innately present in young people. It portrays a picture of a generation that is in a unique position to receive and convey divine revelations, visions, and dreams. This generation is wonderfully positioned. In light of the fact that young people have the potential to be prophets, the Church has a responsibility to make sure that young people have many opportunities to articulate, develop, and apply the abilities that God has given them.

The conviction that the younger members of the Body of Christ are conduits, through which the Holy Spirit actively works, can find a concrete manifestation in the act of making room for initiatives pushed by younger people. This demands more than a superficial acknowledgment of the youth's presence; rather, it calls for a sincere understanding of the worth, insights, and new points of view that they bring to the table. It is possible for the Church to become a fertile field in which the seeds of the Holy Spirit that have been planted inside the hearts of young people are given the opportunity to grow and develop.

In a practical sense, offering possibilities for youth-driven initiatives can take on a variety of forms. For instance, giving them the authority to lead worship, organise events, participate in community outreach, or contribute to decision-making processes inside the Church are all examples of these forms. By doing so, the Church is able to not only capitalise on the potential of the younger generation but also cultivate a culture of empowerment, thereby confirming that the younger generation is an active participant in the larger purpose of the Church.

The potential for prophecy that is emphasised in Acts 2:17–18 draws attention to the fact that young people are not passive recipients of the Gospel but rather active participants in the proclamation of it. The Church fosters an atmosphere in which the youthful vitality and visionary potential of its younger members can contribute to the general vitality and efficiency of the Body of Christ, by providing opportunities for those younger members to express the spiritual gifts that God has given them.

Furthermore, this verse confronts any age-related biases that may exist within the Church, by reminding Christians that the Holy Spirit is poured forth on all people without regard to age, gender, or societal standing. It eliminates obstacles and encourages an all-encompassing acceptance of the myriad of channels via which God chooses to work through His people in the world.

Acts 2:17-18 provides a scriptural basis for gaining an awareness of the prophetic potential that exists within the younger generation. Not only does the Church recognise and honour this divine potential, but it also takes an active role in the formation of leaders, visionaries, and prophetic voices among its younger members by making chances for youth-driven initiatives available. When all of the Church's members, both young and old, are given the opportunity to participate in the intricate web that is God's plan for redemption, the Body of Christ, which is the Church, thrives.

To summarise, the endeavour to establish an environment inside the Church that is open to young people is not only a matter of practicality; rather, it is a strong biblical mandate. This imperative derives from the core values that are embedded in the Scriptures. These principles urge believers to adapt, embrace diversity in an inclusive manner, and foster open discourse, in order to ensure that younger generations are not only acknowledged but also actively nourished and empowered within the Body of Christ.

The idea that God is a living, active force that is constantly producing new things originates from the biblical text, and it is from this idea that the invitation to reassess long-standing practises originates. In the book of Isaiah chapter 43 verse 19 (WEB), God says, "Behold, I will do a new thing. It springs out now. Don't you know it?" This heavenly declaration puts the Church under the obligation to study and modify its practises in order to bring them into alignment with the ever-evolving requirements and viewpoints of the younger generation. The Church may ensure that the unchanging message of the Gospel is still relevant and accessible across generations by embracing creative techniques. This lays the foundation for a robust and healthy community.

In addition, the biblical principle of inclusion, which is demonstrated in Galatians 3:28, implores the Church to reflect the unity found in Christ by actively pursuing inclusivity in its spaces and programmes. This implores the Church to reflect the unity found in Christ in a way that is consistent with the teachings of the Bible. In Romans 12:4-5, the author uses the metaphor of the body to illustrate this concept, putting an emphasis on the connectivity and interdependence of every member. Not only does the Church adhere to the tenets of the Bible when it recognises and appreciates the distinctive contributions made by its younger members, but it also transforms into an accurate representation of the Kingdom, which is a diverse yet cohesive body in which every member plays an essential part.

The biblical perspective of relationships, as represented by Proverbs 27:17 (WEB), has a deep and profound influence on the encouraging of open discussion. The idea that one person's words can sharpen another's skills is the central theme of the proverb "iron sharpens iron," which emphasises the reciprocal learning and improvement that results when people have meaningful conversations with one another. The Church may become a place where true relationships are created, where questions are encouraged, and where faith is developed when a culture of open dialogue is fostered within the institution. This is consistent with the admonition given in the Bible to tell the truth in love, and it contributes to the formation of an environment in which persons, particularly young people, are encouraged to communicate their ideas, inquiries, and worries in a manner that exemplifies reverence and comprehension for one another.

In light of the fact that Acts 2:17-18 calls attention to the prophetic potential that resides within the younger generation, the necessity for the Church to actively provide chances for youth-driven initiatives becomes even more pressing. When the Church does this, it is able to make use of the spiritual gifts and potential for visionary work that are present in the younger members of the Body of Christ. This not only accords with the biblical understanding of the different distribution of spiritual gifts, but it also positions the youth as active participants in the unfolding story of God's redeeming plan, the biblical concept of the diverse distribution of spiritual talents.

In conclusion, cultivating an environment that is inviting to younger generations is not merely a recommendation; rather, it is a biblical necessity that requires reconsidering established practises, fostering inclusivity, supporting open discourse, and seeing and affirming the prophetic potential that exists within the younger generation. The Church actively engages the youth by adopting these principles, ensuring that they not only feel appreciated and heard, but that they are also equipped to contribute meaningfully to the rich tapestry of the Body of Christ. This is done by ensuring that the youth are actively engaged in the life of the Church. By doing so, the Church represents the nature of God's love, which is that it is inclusive and transforming, and it creates a space in which every generation can find a place to call home within the developing narrative of religion.

Chapter 4: Providing a Tool for the Job

Outlining Alpha as a Key Tool for Change:

There is no silver bullet to answer all the issues and challenges that have been highlighted in the first three chapters. As demonstrated, it requires a balance of scriptural knowledge, cultural understanding, and ultimately the work of God, for us to really meet the needs for these generations. However, there is one tool which meets a large amount of the needs; in reality, if one was to create a bespoke tool to meet the needs of this generation, you would come up with something very similar. That tool is Alpha.

Alpha is known for its open and inclusive approach. It provides a non-judgmental space where participants can explore their faith, ask questions, and express their opinions. This inclusivity aligns with the values of many in Generations Z and Alpha, who often prioritise diversity and acceptance. Generations Z and Alpha tend to respond well to interactive and engaging learning formats. The Alpha Course incorporates discussions, videos, and group activities, making it more dynamic and appealing to a generation that values participation and collaboration.

The Alpha Course has adapted to the digital age by offering online resources and virtual sessions. Generations Z and Alpha are known for their digital fluency and comfort with online platforms, making it easier for them to access and engage with the course content. Younger people are characterized by a diverse range of beliefs and a tendency to explore spirituality in non-traditional ways. The open and exploratory nature of the Alpha Course may resonate with individuals who are seeking spiritual meaning and understanding.

The small group format of the Alpha Course fosters a sense of community and allows participants to build relationships with others who are also exploring their faith. This can be particularly appealing to a generation that often seeks authentic connections.

Allow me to share my personal story of Alpha with you to put this into perspective.

During the day, I worked in retail, and at night, I was a nightclub bouncer. However, I only accepted these positions to support my cocaine habit. The situation was intense, and as a bouncer, I had to be prepared for anything. I would endure constant mistreatment while standing at the door, having pizzas thrown at me by individuals I refused entry to a club for being intoxicated.

There was a lot of banter of between the bouncers at the night club. We aimed to motivate each other to be the funniest, or strongest, fastest, and even most aggressive. Boasting about being able to knock someone out without being caught on camera was a common occurrence. This led to a peculiar combination of street fights and waking up in nearby parks.

This situation led me to consume more and more alcohol and drugs to hide from
who I was becoming. It felt like a never-ending cycle, and I ended up getting lost. One evening, overwhelmed by everything, I ended up by myself and took too much cocaine.

Yet, at that instant, I cried out a prayer. I didn't want to die.

On the following day, I woke up with a strong determination to never touch cocaine again. I attributed this to my own strength due to my self-obsessed nature. However, there was a change.

I encountered Christians frequently, which was unusual given my profession. There was a woman named Fiona who worked at the store where I was employed during the day. She shared her Christian faith, which caught my attention. I interrogated her with questions.

Instead of becoming irritated, she purchased a Bible for me and recommended that I give it a read. I developed feelings for her and invited her out on several occasions, but she consistently said no.

Fiona based her actions on the Bible, and I hoped to find support for our relationship within its pages. As I read it, I started to understand that a God had been at work in my life: helping me conquer my cocaine addiction, bringing certain individuals into my life, and guiding me through the teachings of the Bible.

That's when I asked Fiona to take me Church. Prior to that, I had never attended a Church service. I wasn't sure what to anticipate. One vivid recollection from Church involves accidentally melting my new boots on a heater under the pews.

I went and heard that Alpha was beginning. I had no reservations and decided to investigate.

Upon reflection, my initial impression was the warm reception I received from everyone. Meeting others who were pondering similar questions was a great experience that got me reflecting on faith. How can I be absolved for all my past actions? How could God possibly forgive someone like me?

As we all grew closer over the weeks, a strong sense of family emerged within our group. It was truly remarkable. We enjoyed meals and shared laughter during our discussions, which truly strengthened our bond. These individuals significantly altered my perspective on Christians through the message of Jesus they conveyed.

Alpha revealed the true essence of Christianity to me. It transformed my doubts about the existence of God into a conviction that God is concerned about me. I transformed from a violent, loveless drug addict to a happily married man filled with love. Fiona and I tied the knot and are now raising a family.

Transitioning from an Alpha guest, to serving as a group helper, then stepping into the role of a group leader, and eventually becoming a host shaped my discipleship journey and laid the foundation of my early faith journey.

Engaging in numerous courses across various contexts with diverse individuals has been instrumental in shaping my perspective on Alpha as a catalyst for change in contemporary society.

It just works.

Understanding the Key Dynamics of Alpha for These Generations:

The course discusses topics like purpose, identity, and the nature of God, which may resonate with the concerns of this generation. The discussion is centred especially around foundational questions about life, faith, and meaning, which can be relevant to individuals in Generations Z and Alpha who are navigating the challenges and complexities of the modern world. This flexibility allows churches, organizations, or individuals to tailor the course to the needs and preferences of Generations Z and Alpha, whether in a formal Church setting, a small group, or an informal gathering.

1. Digital Engagement:

In recognising the digital landscape of contemporary times, the integration of Alpha into Church frameworks represents a pivotal step towards embracing the evolving needs and preferences of today's learners. The importance of Alpha lies not only in its adaptability to modern tools and technology but also in its transformation of traditional educational paradigms into dynamic, digitally-immersive experiences.

One of the key aspects underscoring the significance of Alpha is its ability to transcend physical boundaries and seamlessly transition into the digital realm. This evolution is not merely about incorporating technology for the sake of novelty but is rather a strategic response to the changing nature of communication, collaboration, and information consumption. By doing so, Alpha not only keeps pace with the fast-paced advancements in technology but also positions itself as a trailblazer in education, by catering to the tech-savvy minds of Generation Z and Generation Alpha.

The shift towards a digital space ensures that the course is not confined to a specific location or time, making education more accessible than ever. Virtual platforms serve as a bridge between students and information, fostering a global community of learners who can engage in discussions, share ideas, and collaborate irrespective of geographical constraints. This inclusivity is especially crucial in an era where connectivity is a driving force, and educational opportunities should be extended beyond traditional boundaries.

Furthermore, the incorporation of interactive content and multimedia elements within the Alpha course enhances its relevance and resonance with the digital natives. Recognizing that contemporary learners often prefer visual and interactive stimuli, these features cater to diverse learning styles, ensuring a more engaging and effective educational experience. This shift from static, text-based learning materials to dynamic, multimedia-rich content not only captures the attention of the audience but also promotes deeper understanding and retention of the subject matter.

In essence, Alpha's embrace of the digital landscape signifies a commitment to providing an education that aligns with the evolving needs of today's learners. By creating a synergistic blend of modern tools, virtual platforms, interactive content, and multimedia elements, Alpha not only prepares students for the challenges of the digital age, but it also sets a precedent for the future of education—one that is dynamic, inclusive, and responsive to the ever-changing technological landscape. As we navigate an era of constant innovation, Alpha stands as a testament to the transformative power of adapting and leveraging technology to enhance the educational experience for generations to come.

2. Inclusivity:

The Alpha course's commitment to inclusivity goes beyond its non-denominational and open approach; it actively seeks to create a welcoming environment that resonates with the values of younger generations. In today's diverse and interconnected world, where individuals often find themselves amidst a tapestry of cultural, religious, and personal backgrounds, the importance of fostering inclusivity cannot be overstated.

The non-denominational aspect of Alpha serves as a bridge, allowing individuals to come together in a shared exploration of faith without being confined by the traditional boundaries of a specific denomination. This approach acknowledges the evolving landscape of spirituality and religious identity, acknowledging that people may not fit neatly into preestablished categories. By transcending denominational boundaries, Alpha invites participants to focus on the core principles of faith, creating a space where theological differences take a back seat to the shared journey of discovery.

The openness of the Alpha course plays a pivotal role in ensuring that diverse voices are not only heard but celebrated. It recognizes that everyone's spiritual journey is unique, and by providing a non-judgmental platform, it encourages individuals to express their beliefs, doubts, and questions without fear of exclusion. This inclusivity extends beyond the confines of religious identity to encompass a broader spectrum of diversity, including race, ethnicity, socio-economic background, and more.

The significance of this inclusivity becomes particularly pronounced when considering the demographics of Generation Z and Generation Alpha. These younger generations are characterized by a strong desire for authenticity, transparency, and social justice. They are more likely to engage with institutions and communities that reflect and embrace diversity. The Alpha course's commitment to inclusivity aligns seamlessly with these values, creating an environment where participants feel not only welcomed but understood.

In a world where divisive forces often dominate the narrative, the Alpha course becomes a beacon of unity. It fosters a sense of belonging among participants, irrespective of their backgrounds or beliefs. This sense of belonging is a powerful antidote to the feelings of isolation that some individuals may experience in a rapidly changing and sometimes fragmented society.

The inclusivity of the Alpha course reflects a broader trend in religious and spiritual communities, by recognizing the importance of embracing diversity. By dismantling barriers and promoting open dialogue, Alpha contributes to the creation of a global community where people can come together, learn from one another, and grow in their understanding of faith and spirituality. In doing so, it not only meets the needs of younger generations but also sets a positive example for the broader religious landscape, emphasizing the universal values that unite humanity.

3. Flexibility and Adaptability:

The adaptable nature of the Alpha Course is a testament to its recognition of the diverse and ever-changing preferences of Generation Z and Generation Alpha. In a world where individuality and personalization are highly valued, the Alpha Course stands out by offering a flexible framework that accommodates the unique characteristics of these generations.

Understanding that a one-size-fits-all approach is no longer effective in engaging today's youth, the Alpha Course embraces the desire for flexibility and customization. This adaptability is not merely a response to a trend but is a strategic acknowledgment of the dynamic nature of the younger demographic. It is an approach that goes beyond surface-level adjustments, delving into the very core of the course content and structure to ensure relevance and resonance.

The customization options provided by the Alpha Course allow for tailoring the experience to the specific needs and preferences of participants. Whether it's adapting the delivery style, incorporating diverse perspectives, or utilizing multimedia formats, the course empowers facilitators to create an environment that speaks directly to the interests and concerns of the younger generations. This approach not only fosters a more inclusive atmosphere but also ensures that the message remains relatable and impactful.

In a rapidly evolving cultural landscape, where trends and preferences can shift swiftly, the Alpha Course's commitment to adaptability is a strategic advantage. By staying attuned to the evolving expectations of younger participants, the course remains dynamic, avoiding the risk of becoming outdated or disconnected. This continuous responsiveness to the changing needs of Generation Z and Generation Alpha ensures that the course remains a relevant and influential force in the realm of spiritual exploration and personal development.

Furthermore, the adaptable nature of the Alpha Course extends beyond content alone. It permeates the very structure of the program, allowing for variations in duration, frequency, and format. This recognition that learning and growth occur in diverse ways and at different paces is a crucial element of the course's success. It accommodates the varied lifestyles and schedules of participants, making it more accessible and appealing to a broader audience.

In conclusion, the adaptable nature of the Alpha Course is a strategic and intentional response to the desire for flexibility and customization that characterizes Generation Z and Generation Alpha. By recognizing that one size does not fit all, and by embracing the dynamic nature of youth culture, the Alpha Course ensures that it remains not only relevant but also influential in the lives of those seeking spiritual exploration and personal growth in a rapidly changing world.

4. Authenticity:

Authenticity, as a core value, lies at the heart of the Alpha Course, creating an immersive and meaningful experience for participants. This experience especially resonates with the authenticity-seeking mindset of younger generations such as Generation Z and Generation Alpha. This fundamental principle is intricately woven into the very fabric of the course, influencing its structure, content, and overall approach.

One of the key ways in which authenticity manifests within the Alpha Course is through the emphasis on personal testimonies. Participants are not merely presented with theoretical concepts or abstract ideas; instead, they are invited to engage with real-life stories of individuals who have navigated their own spiritual journeys. These personal narratives bring a genuine and relatable dimension to the course, allowing participants to connect with the material on a deeply personal level.

Moreover, the course design prioritizes genuine conversations. Rather than presenting a one-sided narrative, the Alpha Course encourages open dialogue and exploration. Participants are invited to share their thoughts, ask questions, and engage in meaningful discussions. This approach fosters a sense of community and trust, creating an environment where individuals feel comfortable expressing their authentic selves without fear of judgment.

The transparency of the course content is another crucial element contributing to its appeal. The materials presented are not sugar-coated or artificially enhanced; instead, they are presented in an honest and straightforward manner. This transparency cultivates a sense of trust of the course for its participants, reinforcing the authenticity that is so vital for the younger generations.

In a world inundated with information and virtual connections, the Alpha Course stands out as a beacon of authenticity. It recognizes and embraces the fact that genuine spiritual exploration requires more than surface-level engagement. By weaving authenticity into its core, the course meets the yearning of Generation Z and Generation Alpha for real, unfiltered experiences and connections. This authenticity is not just a buzzword but a guiding principle that shapes the entire journey, making the Alpha Course a compelling and relevant experience for those seeking a genuine connection with spirituality in the contemporary landscape.

5. Community Connection:

The emphasis on community-building within the Alpha Course is a finely-tuned response to the prevalent yearning for meaningful connections and a profound sense of belonging, which is particularly prevalent among younger generations. In an age dominated by digital interactions and virtual relationships, the Alpha Course emerges as a haven for authentic, face-to-face connections, breathing life into the essence of community and forging bonds that extend beyond the confines of physical gatherings.

In a world where social media and online platforms often mediate human interactions, the Alpha Course stands as a refreshing departure. It recognizes the intrinsic human need for genuine connection and belonging, offering participants a tangible space to engage with one another in real-time. By facilitating in-person interactions, the course becomes a catalyst for authentic relationships, where participants can share experiences, exchange perspectives, and develop a sense of camaraderie that transcends the boundaries of the program.

The concept of community within the Alpha Course extends far beyond the duration of individual sessions. It is not confined to the physical gathering space but permeates the lives of participants, creating a ripple effect that fosters lasting connections. This emphasis on community is not a mere addendum but a fundamental aspect woven into the fabric of the course, influencing the design and execution to ensure that every participant feels seen, heard, and valued.

Moreover, the community-building aspect of the Alpha Course aligns seamlessly with the evolving social landscape. Younger generations, characterized by a digital existence, often grapple with a paradoxical sense of hyper-connectivity and isolation. The course becomes a counterbalance, offering a sanctuary for genuine, face-to-face interactions that fulfill the deep-seated human need for authentic relationships.

Practical Insights into the Reasons Why Alpha Works:

In essence, the Alpha Course becomes a catalyst for a transformative experience that goes beyond the acquisition of knowledge. It becomes a platform where individuals not only explore their spirituality but also find a supportive community that echoes their quest for authenticity and connection. By prioritizing and nurturing this sense of community, the Alpha Course becomes a beacon of genuine human connection in an era where such experiences are increasingly valued and sought after by younger generations.

1. Authentic Connection:

At the heart of Alpha's efficacy lies the profound impact of fostering genuine connections within the intimate confines of a small group setting. The peer-to-peer relationships cultivated within this framework serve as the cornerstone for creating an environment where participants not only feel welcomed but are also inclined to freely express their thoughts, uncertainties, and inquiries.

Within the sanctum of these authentic connections, a rich tapestry of dialogue unfolds, driven by openness and honesty. This candid exchange becomes the catalyst for unlocking a deeper comprehension of the course material. As participants engage in meaningful conversations, they embark on a journey of exploration, collectively unraveling complexities and grasping nuanced concepts that might otherwise remain elusive in a more impersonal educational setting.

Moreover, the authentic connection established within the small group setting transcends the mere exchange of academic ideas. It becomes a powerful force, fostering a profound sense of belonging among participants. As individuals share their unique perspectives, experiences, and challenges, a sense of unity and camaraderie naturally emerges. This sense of belonging is not only instrumental in enhancing the overall learning experience but also in creating a supportive community that encourages personal and intellectual growth.

In essence, the small group setting acts as a crucible for the transformative power of authentic connection. It goes beyond the traditional boundaries of education, nurturing an environment where participants not only absorb knowledge but also forge enduring bonds. They find a place where their voices are not just heard but valued—a space where the seeds of understanding and belonging are sown and allowed to flourish.

2. Shared Journey:

The peer-to-peer approach within the Alpha Course serves as a powerful catalyst, reshaping the entire experience into a collaborative odyssey. Here, participants no longer solely receive guidance, but actively engage as co-navigators, led by their peers through the labyrinthine avenues of faith exploration, leadership insights, and personal development.

This transformative journey embodies a collective pilgrimage where individuals, spurred by their peers' perspectives and shared experiences, embark upon a profound expedition into the realms of faith and self-discovery. As each participant contributes their unique insights and perspectives, the fabric of the course weaves itself with threads of diversity, fostering a rich tapestry of collective wisdom and understanding.

This shared expedition extends beyond the confines of scheduled sessions, forging unbreakable bonds among participants. The connections birthed during the Alpha Course transcend its temporal boundaries, blossoming into enduring relationships steeped in mutual respect, empathy, and understanding.

The essence of this shared experience lies not only in the acquisition of knowledge but in the cultivation of a supportive community. Participants become pillars for each other, offering unwavering support and encouragement, nurturing an environment where growth and vulnerability intertwine harmoniously.

In this symbiotic ecosystem, the peer-to-peer approach not only enriches the Alpha Course but lays the groundwork for a network of enduring connections. It fortifies the course's impact, empowering individuals not just to traverse their personal paths but to collectively illuminate the journey for others, fostering a legacy of shared growth and enduring camaraderie.

3. Relational Learning:

In contrast to conventional top-down educational approaches, Alpha embraces the transformative concept of relational learning, fostering an interactive and dynamic educational experience. Rather than relying solely on the expertise of an instructor, Alpha emphasizes the collaborative exchange of knowledge among participants. This innovative approach transcends traditional hierarchical structures, encouraging a horizontal flow of insights and experiences.

Within the Alpha framework, the learning process becomes a communal endeavor, with participants actively engaging with one another to construct a collective understanding of the course material. This collaborative spirit not only enriches the educational environment but also cultivates a sense of shared responsibility for the learning journey.

The horizontal exchange of knowledge within Alpha results in a diverse tapestry of perspectives, creating a vibrant and inclusive learning ecosystem. Participants bring a myriad of backgrounds, expertise, and life experiences to the table, contributing to a holistic comprehension of the subject matter. This diversity of viewpoints serves as a catalyst for critical thinking and broadens the intellectual landscape, promoting a more comprehensive and nuanced understanding of the course content.

Moreover, Alpha recognizes that learning is not confined to a unidirectional flow but is a multidimensional and reciprocal process. Participants not only receive knowledge from their peers but also actively contribute their own insights, fostering a sense of empowerment and ownership over their learning experience. This bidirectional exchange of information establishes a dynamic and adaptive learning community, where the collective wisdom of the group propels everyone forward.

In the Alpha model, the role of the instructor evolves into that of a facilitator and guide, steering the collaborative learning process while empowering participants to take the lead in their educational journey. This shift in dynamics cultivates a culture of autonomy and self-directed learning, where individuals are not merely passive recipients of information but active contributors to the co-creation of knowledge.

Ultimately, Alpha's commitment to relational learning transcends the limitations of traditional educational paradigms. By harnessing the collective intelligence of its participants, Alpha creates a transformative and empowering educational experience that goes beyond the confines of a classroom, paving the way for a new era of collaborative and interconnected learning.

4. Mutual Support:

Within the Alpha Course, the cultivation of peer-to-peer relationships serves as a dynamic force that not only expands but also deepens the bonds within the community. These connections form an intricate web of support that becomes a crucial aspect of the participant's journey through the complexities of faith, leadership, and personal development.

The essence of these peer-to-peer relationships lies in the shared experience of navigating the intricate path of self-discovery and spiritual exploration. As participants engage in open and honest conversations, they find a unique understanding and empathy from their peers, who are also on a similar journey. This shared vulnerability forms the basis of a culture of mutual support that goes beyond mere camaraderie—it becomes a source of strength.

In the context of faith, peers provide a safe space for participants to share their doubts, ask questions, and explore their beliefs without judgment. This open dialogue fosters a culture of acceptance and understanding, enabling individuals to grow in their spirituality at their own pace. The shared exploration of faith not only strengthens individual convictions but also creates a sense of unity within the group.

Leadership within the Alpha Course takes on a collaborative dimension through these peer-to-peer relationships. Participants learn from one another, sharing insights and experiences that contribute to the collective wisdom of the community. As individuals take on leadership roles, they do so with the backing of a supportive network that encourages them to step into their potential. The leadership journey becomes a shared endeavor, with each member contributing to the growth and wellbeing of the community.

Personal development, with its inherent challenges and triumphs, finds a fertile ground for exploration within the supportive framework of peer relationships. The understanding and encouragement offered by peers become a cornerstone for resilience. Participants can lean on each other during times of difficulty, drawing strength from the shared narratives of overcoming obstacles. This safety net of support provides a buffer against the inevitable setbacks and a catalyst for personal growth.

As these peer connections deepen, the Alpha Course evolves into more than just a program—it becomes a community of individuals committed to each other's well-being and growth. The bonds forged through mutual support transcend the duration of the course, extending into the participants' lives beyond the formal sessions. The impact of these relationships ripples through the community, creating a lasting legacy of interconnectedness and shared growth.

In essence, the Alpha Course becomes a fertile ground where peer-to-peer relationships flourish, contributing to a culture of mutual support that permeates every aspect of the participants' journeys. These relationships transform the challenges of faith, leadership, and personal development into opportunities for collective resilience and individual and communal growth.

5. Inclusive Environment:
The peer-driven nature of Alpha goes beyond merely fostering inclusivity; it actively cultivates an environment where participants, irrespective of their background or prior knowledge of Christianity, discover themselves standing on equal footing. This inclusive atmosphere serves as a catalyst for vibrant interactions, creating a space where individuals feel not only welcomed but empowered to engage in meaningful dialogue.

Within the Alpha community, diversity is not just acknowledged; it is celebrated. The varied backgrounds, experiences, and perspectives of participants become threads woven into a rich tapestry that reflects the beauty of pluralism. This diversity becomes a source of strength, as each individual brings a unique set of insights and questions to the table, enriching the collective exploration of faith and spirituality.

In this inclusive setting, the emphasis is not placed on hierarchy or predetermined knowledge but rather on the shared journey of discovery. Participants find themselves liberated from the constraints of predefined roles, creating an egalitarian platform where everyone's voice is not only valued but actively sought out. This democratic exchange of ideas fosters a sense of community where mutual respect and understanding flourish.

Active participation is not just encouraged; it is integral to the Alpha experience. The environment nurtures a culture where individuals feel comfortable expressing their thoughts, asking questions, and sharing their doubts without fear of judgment. This openness not only breaks down barriers but also ensures that the collective exploration benefits from the diverse perspectives of the entire group.

The inclusivity of Alpha extends beyond the intellectual realm; it permeates the emotional and spiritual dimensions as well. Participants feel a sense of belonging that transcends any differences they may have, creating a supportive community where genuine connections are forged. As individuals engage in conversations about faith, they discover commonalities that bind them together, fostering a shared sense of purpose and understanding.

In essence, the peer-driven nature of Alpha transcends the conventional boundaries of educational settings or religious discussions. It creates an environment where the richness of diversity is not only acknowledged but actively embraced, leading to a dynamic and inclusive space where everyone, regardless of their background, finds a place at the table of dialogue and exploration. Through this inclusive approach, Alpha becomes a microcosm of a world where unity is built on the foundation of understanding, respect, and the shared pursuit of spiritual discovery.

6. Leadership Emergence:

The peer-to-peer dynamic, inherent in the Alpha context, operates as a fertile soil for the emergence and maturation of leadership qualities. In the intimate setting of small-group discussions, the intricacies of individual personalities and strengths unfold, paving the way for natural leaders to rise to the forefront. This organic process is a testament to the profound and empowering nature of peer-to-peer relationships.

In the crucible of collaborative exchange, individuals within the Alpha context find themselves in a unique position to showcase their abilities and contribute meaningfully to the collective dialogue. As discussions unfold, certain individuals naturally step into roles of facilitation, possessing an innate ability to guide conversations and steer the group towards productive outcomes. This fluidity in leadership roles is not dictated by hierarchical structures, but rather arises spontaneously from the collective synergy of the participants.

The empowering nature of peer-to-peer relationships lies in the mutual respect and recognition of each member's unique strengths and perspectives. Within the Alpha context, individuals are not constrained by traditional top-down leadership models; instead, they are free to express themselves, take initiative, and assume leadership roles based on their expertise and influence.

Moreover, the peer-to-peer dynamic fosters a sense of shared responsibility and accountability. As individuals engage in meaningful discussions, they become stakeholders in the collective success of the group. This shared commitment amplifies the impact of leadership emergence, as individuals are not only leading by example but also inspiring others to actively contribute to the group's objectives.

In this context, leadership is not confined to a singular figure at the helm but is distributed among those who naturally excel in guiding discussions, motivating others, and navigating complex challenges. This decentralized approach to leadership is a hallmark of the Alpha environment, where the collective intelligence and diverse talents of the group are harnessed to their fullest potential.

Ultimately, the peer-to-peer dynamic within the Alpha context transforms the conventional notion of leadership development. It emphasizes the fluid and adaptive nature of leadership, proving that true leaders can emerge from any corner of the group, driven by a genuine passion for collaboration and a commitment to the shared goals of the community. This breeding ground for leadership not only enriches the Alpha experience but also exemplifies the strength and resilience of a community that values and empowers each individual within its midst.

7. Relational Discipleship:
In its pinnacle form, Alpha transcends the conventional boundaries of traditional education and blossoms into a dynamic platform for relational discipleship. At its zenith, Alpha doesn't merely serve as an informational conduit for participants to learn about the Christian faith; rather, it evolves into a vibrant ecosystem where individuals engage in a profound journey of spiritual growth, guided by the lived experiences and genuine embodiment of Christian principles by their peers.

Within the context of Alpha, participants are not passive recipients of knowledge but active witnesses to the transformative power of faith unfolding in the lives of those around them. The essence lies not only in the theoretical understanding of doctrines but in the vibrant tapestry of real-life narratives woven by the individuals who have embraced and internalized these principles.

The transformative journey within Alpha becomes a testament to the vitality of lived experiences, creating a fertile ground for spiritual maturation. As participants navigate through the course, they don't merely accumulate theological knowledge; they embark on a relational odyssey where the authenticity of their peers becomes a mirror reflecting the profound impact of faith on day-to-day living.

This relational discipleship extends beyond the structured sessions, permeating the very fabric of participants' lives. It is not confined to the classroom or designated meeting times but is a continuous, immersive experience. The power of this approach lies in the organic and authentic nature of the relationships forged within the Alpha community.

The lived experiences shared within the Alpha community become a powerful testimony, illuminating the transformative potential of faith in the crucible of real-world challenges. Participants witness resilience in adversity, grace in moments of trial, and love manifested in tangible, everyday actions. These narratives serve as beacons, guiding each participant on their spiritual journey, as they draw inspiration from the lived examples of their peers.

In this pinnacle form, Alpha becomes a catalyst for a deeper understanding of faith through the lens of relational interconnectedness. The community becomes a living embodiment of the Christian principles, fostering an environment where individuals not only learn about faith but actively participate in its unfolding narrative. The relational influence of peers within Alpha becomes a guiding force, shaping the spiritual trajectory of each participant and cultivating a community where faith is not just professed but lived out in the richness of daily life.

8. Emotional Resonance:
Peer-to-peer relationships form the foundation of a profound and transformative Alpha experience, going beyond the realms of mere intellectual exchange to infuse emotional resonance. In this dynamic space, participants connect on a deeper level, fostering an environment where vulnerabilities are not only acknowledged but embraced. The essence of these connections lies in the shared human experience, transcending the boundaries of traditional information-sharing and venturing into the realm of empathy and understanding.

The emotional depth woven into peer-to-peer relationships adds a layer of authenticity to the Alpha experience. It transforms the interactions from sterile exchanges of information into a rich tapestry of shared emotions and experiences. Participants find themselves not just engaged intellectually but also emotionally invested in the conversations, creating a unique synergy that transcends the confines of a typical learning or collaborative environment.

Within this emotionally charged space, individuals feel empowered to open up about their fears, uncertainties, and aspirations. Their shared vulnerabilities become the building blocks of trust, creating a strong foundation for meaningful connections. As participants reveal their authentic selves, a sense of camaraderie emerges, allowing for the cultivation of genuine relationships that extend beyond the duration of the Alpha experience.

Empathy flourishes in this environment, as participants not only understand each other's perspectives but actively embrace and support one another. The shared emotional journey fosters a sense of community, where individuals feel seen, heard, and valued. In turn, this emotional connection enhances the overall learning and collaborative process, as it becomes deeply rooted in the human experience.

The transformative power of these emotional connections is evident in the lasting impact they have on participants. Beyond the acquisition of knowledge or the completion of tasks, the Alpha experience becomes a catalyst for personal and collective growth. Participants emerge with a profound sense of self-awareness, having navigated the complexities of human connection and gained a deeper understanding of themselves and their peers.

In essence, the infusion of emotional resonance into peer-to-peer relationships within the Alpha experience elevates it from a conventional learning or collaborative endeavor to a journey of personal and collective transformation. It transcends the boundaries of conventional information-sharing, creating a space where the richness of human connection becomes the driving force behind innovation, understanding, and growth.

9. Sustainable Community:

A common description of the peer-to-peer model embedded within the Alpha Course highlights the strength and resilience that emerges from a community-driven approach to spiritual exploration and growth. The emphasis on collective engagement, shared experiences, and mutual support creates a dynamic and self-sustaining ecosystem that distinguishes the Alpha Course from more traditional programs.

The decentralized nature of the peer-to-peer model is particularly noteworthy. By eschewing reliance on a central figure, the community becomes more adaptable and enduring. The diversity of perspectives and experiences among participants contributes to the richness of the tapestry of relationships, fostering a sense of interconnectedness that extends beyond the structured course meetings. This approach not only deepens individual understanding but also forges bonds that transcend the confines of the educational program.

The community's strength lies in its ability to provide ongoing support and encouragement. Participants not only become fellow learners but also pillars of support for one another, creating a network that becomes a source of strength for spiritual growth. The absence of a singular central figure empowers individuals to contribute authentically, fostering a sense of ownership and shared responsibility for the community's wellbeing.

The portrayal of the Alpha Course as a living organism that evolves and adapts to the needs of its members emphasizes its dynamic and organic nature. The peer-to-peer model goes beyond being a mere educational program; it becomes a source of inspiration and strength for those involved. The interconnected and resilient network ensures that the community remains robust in the face of challenges, providing a testament to the enduring power of authentic human connections in the pursuit of spiritual growth and community support.

10. Cultural Relevance:

The peer-to-peer approach, embedded at the core of the Alpha Course, serves as a cultural bridge in today's interconnected society. This methodology is not merely a pedagogical tool but a reflection of the collaborative spirit inherent in contemporary communities. Its adaptability is evident in its capacity to traverse generational and cultural divides, creating a shared space where diverse individuals can engage in meaningful dialogue and discovery.

In its optimal manifestation, Alpha, fueled by the dynamics of peer-to-peer relationships, transcends the traditional boundaries of educational frameworks. It evolves into a living, breathing entity—a dynamic and inclusive journey that extends beyond the mere dissemination of information about the Christian faith and leadership. At its heart, Alpha becomes a transformative experience, one where participants not only absorb knowledge but also immerse themselves in the profound impact of authentic connections with their peers.

These relationships, fostered within the Alpha community, possess a unique power. They are more than conduits for the transfer of information; they are catalysts for personal, communal, and spiritual flourishing. The peer-to-peer model transforms the Alpha Course into an incubator for personal growth and a crucible for communal bonds. Participants, regardless of their background or beliefs, find themselves woven into a tapestry of shared experiences and shared understanding.

In this context, Alpha's zenith is marked by the synergy of learning and relationship-building. The transformative power of genuine connections amplifies the educational journey, elevating it to a level where the impact resonates not only intellectually but also emotionally and spiritually. The peer-to-peer dynamics create an environment where individuals feel heard, understood, and supported—a fertile ground for the seeds of personal and communal development to take root and flourish.

As the Alpha Course unfolds within the framework of peer-to-peer relationships, it embodies the essence of collaboration, adaptability, and inclusivity. It becomes more than a course; it becomes a living testament to the interconnected nature of human experience, where the journey of faith and leadership intertwines with the tapestry of diverse lives, creating a mosaic that reflects the richness and beauty of shared humanity.

Alpha at its best, driven by peer-to-peer relationships, transcends the conventional boundaries of educational models. It becomes a dynamic, inclusive, and transformative journey where participants not only learn about the Christian faith and leadership but also experience the profound impact of genuine connections with their peers. The power of these relationships elevates the Alpha Course to its zenith, making it a catalyst for personal, communal, and spiritual flourishing.

In summary, the Alpha Course proves to be an invaluable asset in the realm of personal and leadership development, boasting a multifaceted and dynamic structure that caters to a diverse range of individuals. Its richness lies not only in its curriculum but also in its dedicated focus on leadership development, fostering a comprehensive approach to growth that extends beyond mere theological exploration.

One of the course's standout features is its emphasis on small group dynamics, providing a conducive environment for meaningful discussions, shared experiences, and genuine connections among participants. This communal aspect enhances the learning process, allowing individuals to not only deepen their understanding of faith but also to develop crucial interpersonal skills essential for effective leadership in various aspects of life.

The incorporation of an engaging film series adds a unique and compelling dimension to the course, offering visual and narrative elements that resonate with participants on a deeper emotional level. This multimedia approach not only makes the learning experience more immersive but also caters to different learning styles, ensuring a well-rounded and inclusive educational journey.

Furthermore, the Alpha Course distinguishes itself through its flexibility and adaptability, allowing it to seamlessly integrate into diverse cultural contexts and respond to the evolving needs of participants. This adaptability is a key factor in its resonance with Generation Z and Generation Alpha, aligning with their values and preferences in terms of interactive and dynamic learning experiences.

Ultimately, the Alpha Course transcends conventional educational frameworks. It stands as a transformative journey that invites participants to explore the profound depths of faith, cultivate essential leadership skills, and authentically connect with others in a community that goes beyond the constraints of time and tradition. It is not merely a course; it is a living, breathing platform for personal and communal growth, reflecting the evolving dynamics of faith and leadership in the contemporary world.

Chapter 5: Youth Leadership Empowerment

We discover significant direction in the ageless wisdom of the Scriptures when diving into the areas of young leadership development. This investigation is based on recognising youth potential, implementing mentorship programmes, and encouraging intergenerational collaboration, all of which are anchored in biblical allusions that illustrate the route to a healthy and powerful Church community.

Exploring the areas of young leadership empowerment within the context of biblical wisdom is a journey that pulls from the reservoir of eternal truths found in the Scriptures. This investigation is founded on a comprehensive awareness of the youth's potential, guided by the establishment of mentorship programmes, and powered by the vibrant energy of intergenerational partnership. Let's unpack each aspect of this investigation by delving deeper into biblical allusions.

1. Recognising the Potential of Youth:
The biblical narrative is replete with examples of people who, despite their childhood, were selected and anointed for important roles in God's divine purpose. The story of David, a youthful shepherd chosen by God to become a powerful king (1 Samuel 16:113), is a compelling illustration. Recognising potential in adolescents links the Church with the divine idea that God frequently goes past outer appearances and sees the heart. This recognition not only empowers the youth, but it also symbolises God's inclusion and unlimited grace.

2. Creating Mentorship Programmes:
Relationships such as that of Elijah and Elisha, Moses and Joshua, and Jesus and His disciples are examples of

mentorship in the Bible. The mentorship interaction is more than just knowledge transfer; it is an intimate sharing of life, faith, and experience. Jesus' investment in the Twelve is a powerful model for mentorship, emphasising the necessity of guiding young leaders in spiritual growth as well as practical leadership (Matthew 28:19-20). By implementing mentorship programmes, the Church follows the divine pattern of investing in the next generation, insuring the Gospel message's continuance.

3. Promoting Intergenerational Cooperation:

The biblical invitation for intergenerational partnership is based on the recognition that each generation brings something unique to the Body of Christ. Titus 2:35 emphasises the need for older generations to teach and mentor the younger generations, so forming a community in which wisdom is shared and absorbed across age levels. Proverbs continually extols the importance of seeking advice from the wiser and older, emphasising the idea that a plethora of counsellors leads to success (Proverbs 15:22). Fostering intergenerational partnership in the Church not only enhances the community's spiritual fibre but also represents the unity and variety inherent in the body of believers.

In summary, the journey into young leadership empowerment is a profound and transforming investigation based on the knowledge of the Scriptures. It entails recognising youth potential, implementing mentorship programmes based on biblical patterns, and encouraging intergenerational partnership as a reflection of Christ's diverse and undivided body. This strategy lays the groundwork for a thriving and empowered Church community, in which each generation contributes to and learns from the other in the common pursuit of God's Kingdom.

Recognising the Leadership Potential of Young People and Empowering Them to Play Active Roles:

A strong and enduring message reverberates within the hallowed pages of the biblical narrative—age is not a factor of one's aptitude for influential leadership. This fundamental truth, as exemplified by the Apostle Paul's advice to his young protégé Timothy in 1 Timothy 4:12, serves as a beacon defying conventional norms and expectations. Paul, aware of the prevalent belief that youth casts doubt on one's legitimacy as a leader, presents a moving exhortation to Timothy, encouraging him not to be discouraged by his age but to rise beyond societal expectations.

In this scriptural instruction, Paul encourages Timothy to overcome the restrictions that age frequently imposes and to embody virtues that transcend chronological considerations. The mandate to set an example in speech, conduct, love, faith, and purity is more than just a list of virtues; it is an invitation to live the transformational power of a Christ-centred life. It is a call for Timothy to demonstrate moral maturity and faith depth that go beyond the limitations imposed by youth.

Examining Paul's advice reveals a theological depth—a knowledge that effective leadership is not dependent on one's age. It is rather about one's character, behaviour, and the manifestation of Christlike attributes in one's life. Paul proposes a paradigm shift in the notion of leadership by asking Timothy to emulate these traits. It is not a domain destined for the elderly only but a summons to all people, regardless of age, to radiate the transformational force of a life devoted to Christ.

Timothy's story becomes a living testament to the unlimited potential contained in young people's hearts. Instead of succumbing to cultural misgivings about his youth, Timothy is empowered to be a trailblazer, proving that youth and great spiritual maturity may coexist. This scriptural episode serves as a ringing statement of the unlimited grace and potential bestowed upon the young, reminding the Church that age does not restrict God's power to employ individuals for His holy purposes.

In light of this fact, the Church is challenged to rethink its approach to leadership and to see that God frequently chooses the unexpected to confuse the wisdom of the world. The charge to Timothy goes beyond a personal exhortation to the Church as a whole to nurture and empower the youth in its midst. It is an invitation to foster a climate in which the younger generation is not marginalised or undervalued, but rather viewed as vessels of great potential capable of influencing, leading, and changing the world for Christ.

The biblical narrative sends a clear message: age is not a barrier to effective leadership. Paul's advice to Timothy transcends its historical setting, resonating as a timeless theological truth. It calls on the Church to welcome and empower youth, recognising that they are not only tomorrow's leaders but also important participants to God's transformative work now. In doing so, the Church embraces the fundamental reality that God's call knows no age, and that His transformative power is not bound by cultural expectations.

When one dissects Paul's advice, it becomes clear that what he supports is more than just an acknowledgement of chronological age; rather, it is a call to embrace the unique talents and strengths fundamentally contained within the younger generation.

Paul, conscious of the transforming potential resting in the hearts of the young, sees adolescence as a pool of untapped virtues waiting to be unearthed, rather than as a period of life. Paul offers a comprehensive image of leadership by pushing Timothy to set an example in speech, conduct, love, faith, and purity. It is a dynamic and diversified manifestation of character and faith that transcends temporal considerations, rather than a one-dimensional paradigm defined by age.

We find a theological perspective in this dissection that pushes the Church to go beyond prejudices and preconceived conceptions about the potential of youth. It is an invitation to recognise and value the unique gifts that young people contribute to the community—a plea to recognise that their contributions go well beyond their years. Timothy is urged to demonstrate not merely a checklist of virtues, but a total embodiment of Christ's transformative power in the context of his youth, by providing an example in various facets of life.

The challenge Paul delivers to Timothy reverberates through the ages, reaching every part of the Church. It is a call for the Church to be intentional in its approach to youth leadership—to look beyond the obvious and tap into the immense potential that exists inside the hearts of today's kids. It is a call for the community to recognise the particular abilities, views, and passion that youngsters contribute, recognising that their endowments are not supplementary but essential to the whole body's thriving.

This appreciation for the special features of youth is a practical call to action, not just a theoretical concept. It obligates the Church to provide an environment that encourages the development of these inherent strengths. It is a call to invest in the mentorship and direction that allows youth to thrive and in turn become catalysts for positive change in the community.

In essence, Paul's wisdom invites the Church to be careful cultivators of potential, recognising that youth leadership is a present reality rather than a future prospect. By valuing the unique characteristics of the younger generation, the Church participates in a richer, more vibrant expression of leadership—one that embraces the diverse tapestry of the entire body, allowing each member, regardless of age, to contribute authentically to the shared journey of faith.

In the story of David, a shepherd destined for royalty, the biblical narrative unfolds one of its most engaging chapters, a tale that serves as a poignant illustration of the transformational power buried in recognising and fostering adolescent leadership potential (1 Samuel 16:1-13). This drama, inspired by divine revelation, carves a profound image in the tapestry of biblical history, defying traditional assumptions and redefining the bounds of leadership.

Samuel, the elderly prophet, appeared before Jesse's sons in Bethlehem, seeking the one anointed by God to be the future king. According to cultural conventions, the eldest, strongest, and most visibly imposing would be the expected pick. However, God's ways are not constrained by human expectations. When Samuel first saw David, the youngest son and a shepherd in the hills, he experienced a seismic shift in his idea of leadership.

The anointing of David as the future king demolished preconceived notions based on age or physical height. The condition of his heart, not his external look, indicated his worthiness. God's choice of David became an imprint—a declaration that leadership capacity transcends external characteristics. The true compass directing God's choice revealed as the heart, the epicentre of one's faith, courage, and humility.

This story contradicts the widely held belief that leadership is equated with age or outward grandeur. It transforms leadership from an external presentation to an inward, spiritual reality. David's youth did not decrease his merit; rather, it served as a blank canvas for God to paint a story of exceptional leadership.

The emphasis on attributes such as faith, courage, and humility emphasises a key truth: these virtues are not limited to age or experience. In his youth, David displayed a profound and steadfast faith in God, showed courage in the face of adversity, and demonstrated humility even in the face of kingship. This heart-centred style of leadership set the tone for a reign of devotion, victory, and even vulnerability.

David's journey from shepherd to king becomes a model for the Church—an eternal lesson in the transforming power of identifying and fostering young leadership potential. It invites the community to see past the surface, to recognise the intrinsic traits that distinguish true leadership. David's story becomes a living monument to the fact that, regardless of age or cultural expectations, God calls and prepares individuals for significant roles in His divine purpose.

In modern circumstances, this story resonates as a call to identify potential where others may miss it, to cultivate the attributes that genuinely characterise leadership, and to recognise that, like David, adolescents may be vessels of tremendous impact when guided by a surrendered heart to God. It is a living monument to the concept that true leadership is a matter of the heart—a divine appointment that reveals the transformational power of youth.

David's story goes beyond simply recognising teenage leadership potential; it unfolds as a conscious and intentional nurture of that ability. David's path from poor shepherd to anointed king of Israel contains a divine tale characterised by God's nurturing touch, a journey that serves as a deep template for the Church. Examining David's path reveals the transforming impact that occurs when youth are not just recognised but also actively enabled to engage and lead in the community.

David's ascension to kingship was not an easy one; it was a narrative of challenges, triumphs, and divine sculpting. His time spent alone in the shepherd's fields was not wasted; rather, it served as a furnace for the development of his character and the strengthening of his faith in God. David's trust in God's providence and courage were developed through the hardships of encountering wild creatures and the solitude of keeping sheep.

The defeat of Goliath, David's anointing by Samuel, his tenure in Saul's court, and his years in exile all contributed to the shaping of a leader. It was a journey that included both successes and defeats, but throughout it all, God was actively at work, nurturing David's potential. This story serves as a beacon for the Church, demonstrating that the journey of youth leadership is not linear but dynamic, defined by growth, maturation, and divine intervention.

The Church is challenged to recognise this theological imperative, which is based on the biblical statement that God calls and equips individuals of all ages for significant roles in His divine design. David's narrative demonstrates that youth is not a barrier, but rather a blank canvas on which God can paint incredible stories of leadership. In order to intentionally cultivate youth leadership potential, the Church must be proactive in discovering, fostering, and creating opportunities for the expression of distinctive abilities and qualities inherent in the younger members.

When the Church embraces this need, it becomes a channel for revealing and celebrating divine appointments among its younger members. It evolves into a community where age is no longer a barrier, but rather a tribute to the numerous ways God works through His people. The Church is called to break down barriers and enable the youth to adopt active, transforming roles within the body of believers, just as David's youth did not hamper his anointing.

Empowerment is a deliberate investment in the development of young leaders, not a passive acknowledgement. It entails mentoring, guidance, and chances for active participation in various aspects of Church life. Recognising youth leadership potential becomes a rallying cry for the Church to create an environment in which the younger generation is not only welcomed but encouraged to flourish, giving their unique perspectives and abilities to the communal faith narrative.

In essence, David's journey serves as a long-term model for the Church, demonstrating the transforming impact of intentionally cultivating teenage leadership potential. It invites the community to actively participate in the divine process of creating leaders, recognising that youth have a pool of untapped potential waiting to be discovered and recognised.

Creating Mentorship Programmes to Help and Guide Emerging Leaders:

In the everchanging landscape of the world, the Church is called to raise and guide the next generation of leaders. This practical guide seeks to help churches establish mentorship programs specifically designed for Generation Z and Generation Alpha, drawing inspiration and guidance from biblical principles.

Step 1: Prayer and Discernment

Commence the journey of creating a mentorship program by grounding it in prayer and seeking divine discernment. James 1:5 (WEB) aptly directs us to approach this task with humility, acknowledging our need for God's wisdom: "But if any of you lacks wisdom, let him ask of God, who gives to all liberally and without reproach, and it will be given to him." This Scripture emphasises the importance of recognising our limitations and turning to God for the insight needed to understand the unique challenges and aspirations of Generation Z and Generation Alpha.

Proverbs 3:5-6 (WEB) reinforces the significance of relying on God's guidance: "Trust in Yahweh with all your heart, and don't lean on your own understanding. In all your ways acknowledge him, and he will make your paths straight." By starting with prayer, we acknowledge our dependence on God and affirm our trust in His wisdom to lead us in creating a mentorship program that aligns with His purposes.

During this prayerful stage, Church leaders and organisers should seek clarity on the specific needs, concerns, and aspirations of the emerging generation. Through prayer, God can reveal insights that might not be apparent through human understanding alone. This intentional seeking of divine guidance sets the foundation for a mentorship program that is not merely human-driven, but infused with spiritual discernment.

Here some practical actions to ground this into reality:

1. Organise Prayer Sessions: Set aside dedicated times for individuals involved in the mentorship program to come together in prayer. Seek God's guidance collectively and individually for wisdom, insight, and understanding.

2. Pray for the Emerging Generation: Specifically lift up the needs and challenges of Generation Z and Generation Alpha in prayer. Ask God to reveal His heart for these young individuals and guide the Church in effectively addressing their unique circumstances.

3. Create a Prayer Team: Establish a team committed to interceding for the mentorship program regularly. This team can serve as a spiritual anchor, continuously seeking God's direction as the program unfolds.

Remember, prayer is not just a preliminary step; it is an ongoing practice that should permeate every phase of the mentorship program, ensuring that it remains grounded in God's wisdom and aligned with His purpose for the next generation of leaders.

Step 2: Identify Mentors as Spiritual Guides

In the process of establishing a mentorship program for emerging leaders from Generation Z and Generation Alpha, the selection of mentors is a pivotal step. The guidance provided in 1 Timothy 4:12 (WEB) serves as a beacon: "Let no man despise your youth; but be an example to those who believe, in word, in your way of life, in love, in spirit, in faith, and in purity." This Scripture underscores the importance of mentors embodying qualities that set a positive example for the younger generation.

Qualities to Look for in Mentors:

1. Deep and Vibrant Faith:

Beyond a surface-level acknowledgment of faith, mentors should possess a deep and vibrant connection with God. This involves not only a commitment to regular spiritual practices but also an ongoing journey of seeking and growing in faith. Mentors become living testimonies to the transformative power of a profound relationship with Christ, inspiring mentees to pursue a dynamic and authentic faith journey.

2. Unconditional Love and Compassion:

Love, in the context of mentorship, extends beyond mere affection to embody the selfless, unconditional love exemplified by Christ. Mentors should demonstrate genuine care and compassion for their mentees, creating a safe and supportive environment. This includes a willingness to listen empathetically, an openness to understand diverse perspectives, and a commitment to stand by mentees through both triumphs and challenges. The mentor's love becomes a tangible expression of Christ's love, fostering an atmosphere of trust and growth.

3. Holistic Purity and Integrity:

The call to purity, as outlined in 1 Timothy 4:12, encompasses more than just moral integrity; it extends to the holistic purity of thoughts, intentions, and integrity in all aspects of life. Mentors should uphold a standard of purity in their personal and professional conduct, serving as role models for mentees. This involves transparency in decision-making, ethical behavior in all circumstances, and a commitment to upholding biblical principles in both public and private life. Mentors guide mentees towards a life characterized by integrity and purity, aligning their actions with the teachings of Christ.

4. Wisdom and Discernment:

A crucial quality in mentors is the possession of wisdom and discernment. Mentors should be individuals who can navigate the complexities of life with insight and understanding, drawing from both their experiences and a deep understanding of biblical principles. This wisdom enables mentors to provide thoughtful guidance, helping mentees make informed decisions and navigate challenges with a perspective grounded in faith.

5. Humility and Teachability:

While mentors are sources of guidance, they should also embody humility and a willingness to learn. Humble mentors recognize that they too are on a journey of growth and that mentorship is a reciprocal relationship. This quality fosters an environment where mentees feel comfortable sharing their thoughts and questions, creating a collaborative learning experience. It also models the humility required for a genuine pursuit of Christlikeness.

6. Resilience and Perseverance:

Life is filled with trials and setbacks, and mentors should exemplify resilience and perseverance in the face of challenges. By sharing their own stories of overcoming adversity with faith, mentors inspire mentees to face challenges with courage and endurance. This quality teaches mentees that setbacks are not roadblocks, but opportunities for growth and deeper reliance on God.

7. Commitment to Continued Learning:

A mentor's journey should be marked by a commitment to continued learning and growth. This involves staying current in their field of expertise, but more importantly, continually deepening their understanding of Scripture and their relationship with God. Mentors who prioritize lifelong learning inspire mentees to approach life with a similar mindset of curiosity, exploration, and a thirst for spiritual understanding.

8. Effective Communication Skills:

To effectively guide and mentor, individuals must possess strong communication skills. This includes the ability to articulate thoughts and ideas clearly, actively listen to mentees, and provide constructive feedback. Effective communication fosters a healthy mentor–mentee relationship, allowing for the free exchange of ideas, concerns, and insights.

In essence, mentors with qualities such as deep faith, unconditional love, holistic purity, wisdom, humility, resilience, commitment to continued learning, and effective communication skills contribute to a mentorship dynamic that goes beyond professional guidance, nurturing the spiritual and personal development of mentees.

Mentors as Spiritual Guides:

1. Living Examples of Faith:

Mentors, in their role as spiritual guides, must transcend theoretical teachings and become living embodiments of Christian principles. Their daily lives should mirror a deep commitment to prayer, regular immersion in Scripture, and unwavering obedience to God's Word. The guidance in Hebrews 13:7 serves as a directive to remember and emulate the leaders who have spoken the Word of God. Mentors, therefore, are entrusted with the responsibility to consider the outcomes of their way of life, recognizing that their actions speak louder than words and serve as a tangible manifestation of faith.

2. Prayer Warriors with Fidelity:

Beyond merely encouraging prayer, mentors should exemplify what it means to be faithful prayer warriors. Their individual prayer lives should be marked by consistency and authenticity, serving as a model for mentees to follow. Additionally, mentors should emphasize the collective power of prayer by engaging in corporate prayer, showcasing the transformative impact of seeking God's guidance, and relying on His strength in the face of life's challenges. In this way, mentors become not only instructors in prayer but living testimonies to its efficacy.

3. Intentional Biblical Discipleship:

Mentors, as spiritual guides, are called to engage in intentional discipleship rooted in biblical principles. Titus 2:7-8 underscores the importance of mentors embodying qualities such as integrity, seriousness, and soundness of speech. This involves not only imparting theoretical knowledge but actively guiding mentees in understanding and applying these principles in their daily lives. Mentors serve as navigators through the complexities of life, ensuring that their mentees develop a deep and nuanced understanding of the Scriptures, fostering spiritual growth that goes beyond surface-level understanding.

4. Cultivating Spiritual Depth:

The role of mentors extends beyond the transfer of knowledge; it involves cultivating spiritual depth within mentees. Mentors should inspire a hunger for spiritual growth, guiding their mentees to explore the richness of their faith through personal study, reflection, and contemplation. By encouraging a vibrant and personal relationship with God, mentors help mentees move beyond a superficial understanding of spirituality to a profound and transformative encounter with the Divine.

5. Modeling Resilience and Trust in God:

In the journey of spiritual guidance, mentors must model resilience and an unwavering trust in God's providence. Life is replete with challenges, and mentors, by facing adversity with faith and trust, become living illustrations of the steadfastness that comes from relying on God. Through their own experiences, mentors impart the invaluable lesson that faith is not immune to trials but is strengthened through them, providing a source of inspiration and encouragement for mentees navigating their own paths.

6. Encouraging a Lifestyle of Worship:

Mentors, as spiritual guides, should encourage a holistic lifestyle of worship beyond the confines of traditional religious practices. This involves guiding mentees to recognize the sacred in the ordinary and encouraging a posture of gratitude and reverence in all aspects of life. By demonstrating a life where work, relationships, and daily activities are offerings of worship, mentors instill in mentees a deep understanding that every facet of life can be lived in service to God.

In summary, mentors, as spiritual guides, play a transformative role by leading through example, emphasizing the power of prayer, engaging in intentional discipleship, cultivating spiritual depth, modeling resilience, and encouraging a lifestyle of worship. In doing so, they not only impart knowledge but also contribute to the holistic and profound spiritual development of the emerging leaders under their care.

Practical Moves:

1. Selection Criteria: Develop clear criteria for selecting mentors based on the qualities outlined in 1 Timothy 4:12. Consider personal interviews, recommendations, and a review of the potential mentor's spiritual journey.

2. Training and Equipping: Provide mentors with training that emphasises the significance of their role as spiritual guides. This training can include workshops, resources, and opportunities for mentors to grow in their own faith.

3. Regular Check-ins: Establish a system for regular check-ins and support for mentors. Recognise that they too need encouragement and spiritual nourishment to effectively guide the next generation.

By intentionally selecting mentors who embody faith, love, and purity, churches can ensure that the mentorship program becomes a transformative journey for emerging leaders, grounded in biblical principles and exemplified by the lives of their spiritual guides.

1. Comprehensive Selection Criteria:

The process of selecting mentors should be guided by a comprehensive set of criteria aligned with the qualities outlined in 1 Timothy 4:12. Develop a structured approach that may include personal interviews, recommendations from spiritual leaders, and a thorough review of the potential mentor's spiritual journey. Consider their commitment to prayer, engagement with Scripture, and a demonstrated track record of living out their faith. This meticulous selection process ensures that mentors not only possess the desired qualities but are also equipped to effectively guide and inspire the next generation.

2. Holistic Training and Equipping:

Recognizing the importance of the mentor's role as a spiritual guide, invest in a robust training program that goes beyond conventional mentorship training. Workshops and resources should emphasize the spiritual dimensions of mentorship, focusing on deepening the mentor's own faith. This may involve sessions on prayer practices, biblical discipleship, and cultivating a lifestyle that reflects Christ. By equipping mentors with the tools to navigate spiritual conversations and address the holistic development of mentees, the program ensures a transformative and spiritually enriching mentorship experience.

3. Regular Check-ins and Support:

Establish a systematic approach for regular check-ins and ongoing support for mentors. Acknowledge that mentors, despite their role as guides, also require encouragement and spiritual nourishment. Provide platforms for mentors to share experiences, seek advice, and participate in collective prayer. Recognize and celebrate their milestones, fostering a sense of community among mentors. By prioritizing the well-being of mentors, the program ensures that they remain spiritually grounded and motivated to effectively guide emerging leaders.

4. Peer Mentoring and Collaborative Learning:

Foster a sense of community among mentors by encouraging peer mentoring and collaborative learning. Create opportunities for mentors to share insights, challenges, and strategies with each other. This collaborative approach not only enriches the mentorship experience but also allows mentors to draw from each other's strengths and experiences. It creates a supportive network where mentors can collectively contribute to the spiritual growth of both mentees and themselves.

5. Spiritual Retreats and Reflection:

Incorporate spiritual retreats into the mentorship program, providing mentors with dedicated time for reflection, prayer, and renewal. These retreats offer a space for mentors to deepen their own connection with God, recharge spiritually, and gain fresh perspectives on their role as spiritual guides. By integrating moments of reflection and renewal, the program ensures that mentors remain attuned to their own spiritual journeys, fostering authenticity and depth in their mentorship relationships.

6. Continuous Feedback and Improvement:

Implement a feedback mechanism that allows both mentors and mentees to provide insights on the effectiveness of the mentorship program. Use this feedback to make continuous improvements and adaptations to better meet the spiritual needs of both mentors and mentees. An iterative approach ensures that the program remains dynamic and responsive to the evolving spiritual landscape, maximizing its impact on the development of emerging leaders.

7. Integration with Church Activities:

Integrate the mentorship program with existing Church activities and ministries. This alignment ensures that the spiritual growth facilitated through mentorship is complemented by broader Church community engagement. By intertwining the mentorship journey with the larger fabric of Church life, mentors and mentees can draw from the rich resources of the Church community, fostering a holistic and interconnected spiritual experience.

In summary, practical moves involve meticulous selection, holistic training, regular support, peer collaboration, spiritual retreats, continuous feedback, and integration with Church activities. These intentional steps contribute to the development of a mentorship program that not only imparts knowledge but also serves as a catalyst for profound spiritual growth and transformation in both mentors and emerging leaders.

Step 3: Establish Clear Goals Anchored in Scripture

Defining mentorship goals rooted in biblical principles is a foundational step in shaping a mentoring relationship that aligns with the teachings of Scripture. Ephesians 4:11-13 serves as a rich source of inspiration, emphasizing the equipping of the saints for the work of ministry, unity, and maturity in faith. To translate these profound principles into actionable and impactful goals, consider the following expanded and deepened steps:

1. Identify Individual Callings:

Scriptural Basis: Ephesians 4:11 mentions various roles within the body of believers.

Practical Action: Collaborate with mentees to delve into the exploration of their unique gifts, talents, and callings. Facilitate in-depth discussions and self-reflection to unveil the distinctive aspects of each mentee's spiritual identity. Develop goals that not only recognize but actively support mentees in understanding and fulfilling their specific roles in God's Kingdom. This may involve ongoing dialogue, spiritual assessments, and guidance on navigating their individual paths of service.

2. Promote Unity Within the Mentorship Relationship:

Scriptural Basis: Ephesians 4:3 encourages believers to maintain the unity of the Spirit.

Practical Action: Go beyond superficial connections and establish goals that nurture a deep sense of community and collaboration within the mentorship relationship. Encourage mentees and mentors to engage in open and honest communication, communal prayer, and mutual support. Plan joint activities or group sessions that not only impart wisdom but also strengthen the relational bonds between mentors and mentees, fostering an environment of unity that mirrors the harmony encouraged in Ephesians.

3. Cultivate Maturity in Faith:

Scriptural Basis: Ephesians 4:13 speaks of attaining the unity of the faith and maturity in Christ.

Practical Action: Set comprehensive goals that guide mentees in their spiritual growth journeys. Beyond the mere acquisition of knowledge, these goals should encompass a holistic approach, incorporating regular study of the Bible, active participation in spiritual disciplines such as prayer and fasting, and engagement in intentional discipleship activities. Encourage mentees to develop reflective practices that help them apply biblical teachings to the complexities of their daily lives, fostering a robust and enduring maturity in their faith.

4. Establish Measurable Milestones:

Scriptural Basis: Ephesians 4:12 highlights the purpose of equipping believers for ministry.

Practical Action: Break down overarching spiritual goals into smaller, achievable milestones. Define clear expectations and timelines, establishing a roadmap for spiritual development. Regularly assess progress in the context of these milestones, and be prepared to make necessary adjustments. This structured approach ensures that both mentors and mentees are actively contributing to the fulfillment of the established goals, aligning with the purpose of equipping believers for their unique ministries.

5. Encourage Accountability:

Scriptural Basis: The entire passage underscores the interconnectedness of believers in their spiritual journey.

Practical Action: Instill a culture of accountability within the mentorship relationship. Beyond mere goalsetting, establish regular check-ins, feedback sessions, and opportunities for mentees to share their experiences and challenges. True accountability goes beyond surface-level discussions and delves into the deeper aspects of spiritual growth. This ensures that mentees are not only setting goals but actively pursuing them, fostering a sense of responsibility and shared commitment to the spiritual journey.

6. Adapt Goals to Individual Needs:

Scriptural Basis: Ephesians 4 recognizes the diversity of spiritual gifts and callings.

Practical Action: Acknowledge and celebrate the diversity of each mentee's spiritual journey. Tailor goals to individual strengths, weaknesses, and circumstances. Be flexible in adapting goals as needed, recognizing that the path to maturity in faith is personal and may vary among individuals. This personalized approach ensures that mentorship is not a one-size-fits-all endeavor but a dynamic and responsive relationship that respects and nurtures the uniqueness of each mentee.

By thoughtfully implementing these practical actions, mentors can ensure that their goals are not only rooted in biblical principles but also serve as transformative guides, leading mentees toward profound spiritual growth, unity, and the fulfillment of their unique callings in Christ.

Step 4: Mentorship as Discipleship

In crafting an effective mentorship program for emerging leaders from Generation Z and Generation Alpha, it is essential to view the mentorship relationship through the lens of discipleship. This approach, inspired by the model set by Jesus in His relationship with His disciples, is grounded in the Great Commission found in Matthew 28:19-20 (WEB): "Go and make disciples of all nations, baptizing them in the name of the Father and of the Son and of the Holy Spirit, teaching them to observe all things that I commanded you. Behold, I am with you always, even to the end of the age."

Understanding Mentorship as Discipleship:

Mentorship and discipleship are two concepts that share some similarities but are often associated with different contexts and connotations.

Mentorship:

Mentorship is a professional relationship where a more experienced or knowledgeable person (the mentor) guides, supports, and shares their expertise with a less experienced or knowledgeable individual (the mentee). This relationship is often focused on career development, skill enhancement, and personal growth within a specific field or industry. Mentors provide advice, feedback, and encouragement to help mentees navigate their professional journeys.

Discipleship:

Discipleship, on the other hand, has a more religious or spiritual connotation. It refers to the process of following and learning from a teacher or leader, particularly in a religious or philosophical context. In Christianity, for example, discipleship involves followers learning from and emulating the teachings and example of Jesus Christ.

Understanding Mentorship as Discipleship:

While mentorship and discipleship may seem distinct, there are situations where the two concepts intersect, particularly in educational and philosophical contexts. Here are some points of connection:

1. Purposeful Relationship: A disciple-making mentorship program goes beyond a casual exchange of advice. It is a purposeful, intentional relationship where mentors guide and nurture mentees to become committed followers of Christ.

2. Teaching and Obedience: The emphasis on teaching and obedience in Matthew 28:19-20 underscores the transformative nature of discipleship. Mentors are not just sharing knowledge; they are guiding mentees in applying biblical principles to their lives and fostering a lifestyle of obedience to God's commands.

3. Multiplication Effect: Just as Jesus invested in a small group of disciples who, in turn, went on to impact the world, mentorship as discipleship has a multiplication effect. Mentees are empowered not only to grow personally but also to become influencers and mentors to others in the future.

It's important to note that the extent to which mentorship resembles discipleship may vary based on the cultural, religious, or philosophical context in which it occurs. While mentorship is generally seen as a secular and professional concept, the principles of guidance, learning, and personal development can be universal and may overlap with the tenets of discipleship in certain situations.

Practical Implementation:
Practically implementing the concept of Mentorship as Discipleship involves integrating mentorship principles with a focus on the four following principles:

1. Biblical Curriculum: Develop a curriculum that aligns with the teachings of Jesus. Include topics such as prayer, studying Scripture, servanthood, and the application of biblical principles in everyday life.

2. Life-on-Life Learning: Encourage mentors to engage in life-on-life learning experiences. This could involve shared activities, practical demonstrations, and joint service-projects, creating a holistic discipleship experience.

3. Accountability and Reflection: Integrate accountability into the mentorship program. Regularly schedule times for mentors and mentees to reflect on their spiritual growth, discuss challenges, and celebrate victories, fostering a sense of shared journey.

4. Encourage Service and Outreach: Emphasise the importance of service and outreach as integral components of discipleship. Engage mentors and mentees in joint community service projects, providing practical opportunities to live out the love and teachings of Christ.

Building a Discipleship Culture:

To complete the holistic design of this model, it is crucial that whilst implementing this strategy, the following points of culture are also set in place to allow the maximum of support and challenge for everyone involved.

1. Community Engagement: Foster a sense of community within the mentorship program. Acts 2:42-47 paints a picture of the early Church devoted to fellowship, breaking bread together, and growing in their faith. Create a similar environment within the mentorship circles.

2. Prayerful Atmosphere: Infuse the mentorship program with prayer. Acts 4:31 highlights the transformative power of collective prayer. Regular prayer sessions within mentorship groups deepen the discipleship experience.

3. Long-term Vision: Encourage mentors and mentees to embrace a long-term vision for discipleship. Just as Jesus invested in His disciples for an extended period, a discipleship-focused mentorship program aims for enduring impact, extending well beyond the immediate mentoring relationship.

By framing the mentorship program as a form of discipleship, churches can instill a strong foundation of faith, obedience, and community within the emerging leaders of Generation Z and Generation Alpha. This approach not only enriches the spiritual lives of individuals but contributes to the broader mission of making disciples who, in turn, make disciples.

Step 5: Biblical Training for Mentors

Equipping mentors with a solid biblical foundation is crucial for the success of any mentorship program. As outlined in 2 Timothy 3:16-17 (WEB), "Every Scripture is God-breathed and profitable for teaching, for reproof, for correction, and for instruction in righteousness, that each person who belongs to God may be complete, thoroughly equipped for every good work." This Scripture emphasises the centrality of the Bible in guiding and shaping the mentor's approach to teaching, correcting, and training mentees in the ways of righteousness.

Foundations of Biblical Training:

Understanding the foundations of biblical training extends beyond theological qualifications, recognizing that individuals throughout the Church spectrum play a crucial role. The following five principles are essential for mentors, forming the bedrock of effective guidance and discipleship:

1. Scripture as a Living Guide:

Mentorship goes beyond imparting information; it involves navigating life's complexities with the timeless wisdom found in Scripture. Mentors should be trained to view the Bible not merely as a reference book but as a dynamic guide, actively seeking its counsel for every facet of life and leadership. Encouraging mentors to draw on the living Word ensures that their guidance is rooted in enduring principles.

2. Teaching Competence:

Effectiveness in mentoring requires more than just biblical knowledge—it demands the ability to communicate that knowledge compellingly. Emphasize the importance of teaching competence, equipping mentors with tools and strategies to convey biblical truths in ways that resonate with the challenges faced by the emerging generation. This includes fostering engagement, relatability, and practical application in the mentor–mentee dynamic.

3. Rebuking with Love:

Acknowledge the necessity of correction within the mentorship relationship while emphasizing the biblical principle of rebuking with love. Galatians 6:1 serves as a guide, encouraging mentors to approach correction with humility and a genuine desire for restoration. Balancing correction with compassion allows mentors to foster an environment where mistakes are opportunities for growth, not condemnation.

4. Correction and Grace:

Training mentors to administer correction with a focus on grace is pivotal. By exemplifying the redemptive nature of correction, mentors mirror the forgiveness and grace extended to them by Christ. Colossians 3:13 underscores the importance of forgiveness in the mentoring relationship, reinforcing the transformative power of grace in shaping the character and conduct of mentees.

5. Training in Righteousness:

Beyond the transfer of knowledge, mentors play a crucial role in guiding mentees to live out biblical principles in their daily lives. This involves practical training in righteousness, helping mentees not only understand but also apply God's Word in their decisions and actions. Mentors serve as living examples, demonstrating how faith intersects with the challenges of everyday life.

In cultivating these foundations, mentors become instrumental in shaping the spiritual journey of those under their care. The goal is to create a mentorship environment where the transformative power of God's Word is not only understood but also actively lived out, fostering a community deeply rooted in biblical principles.

Practical Implementation:
The practical implementation of this training can generally be done in-house and doesn't require huge resources or overly qualified scholars. The basics that you should think about are as follows:

1. Biblical Seminars and Workshops: Organise seminars and workshops focused on specific biblical topics relevant to mentoring. This could include sessions on leadership, discipleship, character development, and navigating contemporary challenges from a biblical perspective.

2. Resource Libraries: Establish a library or online repository of resources that mentors can access. Curate materials such as books, articles, and videos that align with biblical principles and provide practical insights for effective mentoring.

3. Peer Learning Groups: Facilitate peer learning groups where mentors can come together to study and discuss relevant biblical passages and teachings. This collaborative approach fosters a community of

mentors who learn from one another's experiences and insights.

4. Mentor Training Retreats: Conduct retreats specifically designed for mentor training. These retreats can offer focused teaching sessions, group discussions, and practical exercises to enhance mentors' biblical knowledge and application.

Evaluation and Feedback:

To truly create transparency and authenticity for Generations Z and Alpha, we need to have clear accountability within our structures. This not only guarantees inclusivity, but it also guarantees accountability is being maintained to a high level.

1. Regular Assessments: Implement regular assessments to evaluate mentors' understanding and application of biblical principles. Provide constructive feedback and support to help mentors continually grow in their biblical competence.

2. Mentor Support Networks: Create networks or mentorship cohorts where mentors can share challenges and successes. This collaborative environment allows for ongoing learning and mutual support among mentors.

By prioritising biblical training for mentors, churches ensure that the mentorship program remains firmly rooted in the timeless truths of Scripture. This not only empowers mentors to guide emerging leaders effectively but also contributes to the spiritual growth and maturity of both mentors and mentees.

Step 6: Cultivate a Culture of Love and Encouragement

Creating a mentorship program that thrives on a culture of love and encouragement is foundational to the spiritual and personal growth of both mentors and mentees. Drawing inspiration from 1 Thessalonians 5:11 (WEB), which states, "Therefore exhort one another, and build each other up, even as you also do," this step emphasises the importance of fostering a supportive environment where positive affirmation and genuine care are at the core.

Essentials of a Culture of Love and Encouragement:

1. Affirmation and Positivity: Instill in mentors the power of positive affirmation. Encourage them to regularly affirm the strengths and potential of their mentees. Romans 15:2 (WEB) reminds us, "Let each one of us please his neighbor for that which is good, to be building him up."

2. Constructive Feedback with Compassion: Train mentors to provide constructive feedback with a spirit of compassion. Ephesians 4:29 (WEB) guides us, "Let no corrupt speech proceed out of your mouth, but only what is good for building others up as the need may be, that it may give grace to those who hear."

3. Embrace Diversity: Foster an inclusive culture that celebrates the diversity of backgrounds, experiences, and perspectives within the mentorship program. Galatians 3:28 (WEB) reminds us that in Christ, "There is neither Jew nor Greek, there is neither slave nor free

man, there is neither male nor female; for you are all one in Christ Jesus."

4. Cultivate a Listening Culture: Stress the importance of active and empathetic listening within the mentorship dynamic. James 1:19 (WEB) advises, "So, then, my beloved brothers, let every man be swift to hear, slow to speak, and slow to anger." Encourage mentors to create spaces where mentees feel heard and understood.

5. Nourish a Growth Mindset: Teach mentors to foster a growth mindset in their mentees, emphasizing the belief that abilities and intelligence can be developed through dedication and hard work. Philippians 4:13 (WEB) encourages this mindset: "I can do all things through Christ, who strengthens me." Help mentees see challenges as opportunities for growth.

6. Model Vulnerability: Encourage mentors to share their own struggles and challenges, fostering an environment where mentees feel safe to be vulnerable. This authenticity builds trust and a sense of unity. 2 Corinthians 12:9 reminds us that Christ's power is made perfect in weakness, encouraging openness about imperfections.

7. Promote a Culture of Gratitude: Emphasize the importance of expressing gratitude and appreciation within the mentorship relationship. Colossians 3:15 (WEB) encourages a heart of thankfulness: "And let the peace of God rule in your hearts, to which also you were called in one body, and be thankful." Gratitude enhances the sense of connection and support.

8. Encourage Continuous Learning: Instill a commitment to lifelong learning within the mentorship culture. Proverbs 18:15 (WEB) states, "The heart of the discerning gets knowledge. The ear of the wise seeks knowledge." Promote the idea that both mentors and mentees have valuable insights to offer and can learn from one another.

9. Establish Boundaries and Respect: Help mentors set clear boundaries while fostering an atmosphere of mutual respect. 1 Peter 2:17 (WEB) advises, "Honor all men. Love the brotherhood. Fear God. Honor the king."

10. Foster a Community of Support: Encourage mentors and mentees to connect with others within the mentorship program, creating a community of support. Ecclesiastes 4:9-10 (WEB) highlights the strength found in companionship: "Two are better than one, because they have a good reward for their labor. For if they fall, the one will lift up his fellow; but woe to him who is alone when he falls, and doesn't have another to lift him up."

In weaving these principles into the fabric of a mentorship program, one can create a culture of love and encouragement that not only benefits individual mentees and mentors but also contributes to the overall health and vibrancy of the community.

Practical Implementation

Regular Appreciation Moments:

In order to foster a culture of gratitude within the mentorship program, it is imperative to integrate moments of appreciation and acknowledgment seamlessly into the mentor–mentee dynamic. Beyond just occasional recognition, these instances should become an integral part of the program's structure. Regular meetings, carefully scheduled and thoughtfully conducted, serve as the perfect platform for mentors and mentees to not only share their individual accomplishments, but also to express heartfelt gratitude for each other's contributions. This practice not only uplifts spirits but also cultivates a sense of mutual respect and understanding, reinforcing the bond between mentor and mentee.

Encouragement Challenges:

Elevating the mentorship experience involves incorporating innovative elements, such as encouragement challenges, that actively prompt mentors and mentees to engage in uplifting activities. These challenges could take various forms, ranging from sharing motivational quotes to composing personalized notes of encouragement. By infusing an element of friendly competition, the mentorship relationship transforms into a dynamic, positive force. This approach not only strengthens the mentor–mentee connection but also encourages a proactive attitude toward seeking and providing support.

Celebrating Milestones:

Embracing the biblical wisdom of Hebrews 3:13, the mentorship program should go beyond routine acknowledgment and actively celebrate milestones, both individual and collective. Birthdays, personal achievements, and significant progress in the mentorship journey become not just events but opportunities for communal rejoicing. This celebratory spirit not only fosters a sense of shared accomplishment but also guards against the subtle erosion of enthusiasm and motivation. It reinforces the idea that each step forward, no matter how small, is a cause for celebration within the mentorship community.

Establishing a Support System:

Beyond the formal framework of mentorship, it is essential to cultivate an atmosphere where mentors and mentees feel not only comfortable but compelled to seek support from one another. Establishing a robust support system involves promoting open communication, empathy, and trust. This goes beyond the mentorship sessions; it's about creating a network where individuals genuinely care about each other's well-being. As Hebrews 3:13 suggests, the daily encouragement and support within this network act as a powerful antidote against the hardening influence of challenges and setbacks. In this environment, mentorship is not merely a one-way street, but a reciprocal exchange of strength and resilience.

The mentorship relationship should transform into a dynamic, nurturing community where appreciation, encouragement, celebration, and support are not just occasional features, but integral components of the mentor–mentee relationship. This holistic approach ensures that the mentorship experience becomes a source of enduring inspiration and growth for all involved.

Leadership by Example:

 1. Mentor Modelling: Encourage mentors to lead by example in creating a culture of love and encouragement. Their behaviour and attitudes set the tone for the entire mentorship program. 1 Corinthians 11:1 (WEB) reminds us to "Be imitators of me, even as I also am of Christ."

2. Open Communication Channels: Establish open channels of communication for mentors and mentees to express their needs, challenges, and successes. This transparency builds trust and fosters a culture where individuals feel heard and supported.

Mentor Modeling:

A. Authenticity in Leadership:

Encourage mentors to be authentic in their leadership. Authenticity fosters trust, as mentors share their personal journeys, challenges, and victories. This vulnerability creates a genuine connection between mentors and mentees.

B. Continuous Learning:

Emphasize the importance of mentors being committed to continuous learning. Demonstrating a growth mindset and a willingness to learn from mistakes sets a powerful example for mentees, encouraging them to embrace challenges and see failures as opportunities for growth.

C. Servant Leadership:

Inspire mentors to embody the principles of servant leadership. By prioritizing the needs of others, mentors demonstrate humility and a commitment to the well-being of their mentees. This approach mirrors Christ's teachings and reinforces a culture of selflessness.

D. Celebrating Diversity and Inclusion:

Mentor leaders should actively promote and celebrate diversity. By acknowledging and respecting differences, mentors demonstrate that a culture of love and encouragement extends to everyone, regardless of background or identity.

E. Empowering Others:

Encourage mentors to empower their mentees. Leadership isn't just about personal success; it's about lifting others up. Mentors can model this by actively supporting mentees' ideas, providing opportunities for growth, and fostering an environment where everyone feels valued.

Open Communication Channels:

A. Active Listening Skills:

Mentor leaders should prioritize developing active-listening skills. Actively listening to mentees demonstrates respect and empathy. It also allows mentors to better understand the unique needs and challenges faced by each mentee.

B. Conflict Resolution Training:

Provide mentors with training in conflict resolution. Open communication doesn't mean the absence of disagreements, but rather the ability to address conflicts constructively. Mentor leaders should model effective conflict resolution strategies, showcasing the importance of resolving issues peacefully.

C. Timely and Constructive Feedback:

Encourage mentors to provide timely and constructive feedback. This helps mentees understand their strengths and areas for improvement. Mentor leaders should model the art of giving feedback in a way that motivates and encourages growth.

D. Digital Communication Etiquette:

In today's digital age, mentor leaders should exemplify proper digital communication etiquette. This includes being responsive, clear, and respectful in all forms of communication, whether through emails, messaging platforms, or virtual meetings.

E. Cultivating a Safe Space:

Foster a culture where mentees feel safe expressing their thoughts and concerns. Mentor leaders should model vulnerability, sharing their own experiences and challenges, creating a nonjudgmental atmosphere that encourages open dialogue.

In essence, deepening leadership by example involves mentors embodying authenticity, continuous learning, and servant leadership. Open communication channels should extend beyond verbal exchanges, encompassing active listening, conflict resolution, and the cultivation of a safe and inclusive environment. By combining these elements, mentorship programs can truly become transformative spaces where individuals are inspired to follow the example of Christ in both their leadership and communication styles.

Valuation and Reflection: Nurturing a Culture of Love and Encouragement in Mentorship Programs

1. Regular Reflection Sessions:

Incorporating regular reflection sessions into the mentorship program serves as a cornerstone for fostering a culture of love and encouragement. These sessions provide a structured platform for participants to introspect on the impact of this intentional approach. During these sessions, mentors and mentees can delve into the nuances of their relationships, sharing insights into the ways love and encouragement have manifested.

Through guided discussions, participants can explore the transformative power of positive affirmation, constructive feedback, and genuine care. These reflections not only deepen personal awareness but also contribute to a collective understanding of the program's dynamics. The valuable insights gained from these sessions become a foundation for continuous improvement, allowing program organizers to tailor the mentorship experience to better align with the principles of love and encouragement.

2. Surveys and Feedback:

Supplementing regular reflection sessions, the incorporation of surveys and feedback mechanisms adds a quantitative dimension to the evaluation process. Periodic surveys distributed among mentors and mentees, as well as informal discussions, create a comprehensive feedback loop. These tools enable participants to articulate their experiences, providing organizers with tangible data to assess the program's effectiveness.

Surveys can be designed to gauge specific aspects of the mentorship experience, such as the perceived level of support, the effectiveness of communication, and the overall atmosphere of love and encouragement. By analyzing this feedback, program coordinators gain valuable insights into areas of strength and areas that may require adjustment. The dynamic nature of these assessments allows for timely interventions, ensuring that the mentorship program remains responsive to the evolving needs of its participants.

Cultivating a Culture of Love and Encouragement:

By intentionally infusing a culture of love and encouragement into the mentorship program, churches go beyond the conventional approach to mentorship. This deliberate focus aligns with the teachings of Christ, emphasizing the importance of love, compassion, and uplifting one another. The mentorship environment becomes a reflection of these principles, creating a nurturing space for personal and spiritual growth.

The ripple effect of this intentional culture extends beyond individual relationships, shaping the collective identity of the Church community. Participants find themselves not only supported in their personal journeys but also inspired to emulate these values in other aspects of their lives. The scriptural call to build each other up in faith and unity finds practical expression in the vibrant tapestry of mentorship relationships.

In conclusion, the valuation and reflection processes outlined above serve as integral components of a holistic approach to mentorship program management. By weaving love and encouragement into the very fabric of these programs, churches lay the groundwork for relationships that are not only transformative but also reflective of the profound love exemplified by Christ. Through continuous reflection and responsive adjustments, mentorship programs become dynamic laboratories for cultivating a culture that mirrors the essence of Christian teachings.

Step 7: Mentorship as Iron Sharpening Iron: An In-Depth Exploration

In delving into the profound concept of mentorship as "iron sharpening iron," we uncover a rich tapestry of principles that not only shape individuals but also cultivate a culture of continuous improvement within the mentorship dynamic. Drawing inspiration from Proverbs 27:17, which likens the interaction between mentors and mentees to the sharpening of iron, we unfold the essentials that contribute to a robust and transformative mentorship experience.

Essentials of Iron Sharpening Iron:

1. Mutual Growth:

Mentorship is a reciprocal journey of growth where both mentors and mentees contribute to the intellectual, emotional, and spiritual evolution of each other. Emphasizing the concept of mutual growth instills the understanding that wisdom is a two-way street. Mentors share their wealth of experience, while mentees offer fresh perspectives and innovative insights. This collaborative exchange creates a dynamic atmosphere where both parties actively engage in shaping and refining one another.

2. Constructive Challenge:

At the heart of "iron sharpening iron" lies the principle of constructive challenge. Mentors and mentees are encouraged to engage in thoughtful discourse, where questioning assumptions, providing alternative viewpoints, and challenging preconceived notions become integral to the mentorship process.

This approach not only stimulates intellectual growth but also fosters an environment of trust and openness. Through constructive challenge, mentorship becomes a crucible for refining ideas, beliefs, and actions, ensuring that both parties emerge sharper and more resilient.

3. Accountability:

Galatians 6:2 illuminates the significance of shared responsibility within the mentorship relationship. Establishing a culture of mutual accountability goes beyond mere mentor–mentee interactions; it forms the bedrock of a unified commitment to growth and development. When mentors and mentees carry each other's burdens, they not only fulfill the law of Christ but also create a supportive ecosystem where challenges are faced collectively. This shared accountability reinforces the idea that mentorship is not just about individual success; it is about the collective journey towards becoming better versions of ourselves.

4. Spiritual Transformation:

Beyond intellectual and emotional growth, mentorship as iron sharpening iron has profound implications for spiritual transformation. The mentorship relationship becomes a sacred space where spiritual insights are shared, and individuals are encouraged to deepen their understanding of faith. By integrating spiritual dimensions into the mentorship journey, mentors guide mentees in navigating life's challenges with resilience, compassion, and a sense of purpose. This spiritual synergy elevates the mentorship experience, fostering a holistic transformation that extends beyond the professional realm.

5. Legacy of Impact:

The metaphor of iron sharpening iron extends to the idea of leaving a lasting impact. Mentors, by investing in the growth of their mentees, contribute to a legacy that transcends individual accomplishments. Mentees, in turn, carry forward the lessons learned and become mentors themselves, perpetuating a cycle of positive influence. This legacy of impact echoes the ripple effect of mentorship, where the sharpened edge of wisdom extends far beyond the immediate mentor–mentee relationship, shaping communities and inspiring future generations.

In conclusion, embracing the concept of mentorship as iron sharpening iron involves recognizing the transformative power of collaboration, constructive challenge, mutual accountability, spiritual growth, and the enduring legacy of impact. As mentors and mentees actively engage in this process, they not only refine each other but also contribute to the continuous evolution of a vibrant and interconnected mentorship community.

Practical Implementation: Nurturing Growth Through Purposeful Actions

1. Goal Setting:

The collaborative setting of goals within a mentorship relationship serves as the compass guiding both mentors and mentees toward their desired destinations. This process involves a thoughtful exploration of individual aspirations, professional ambitions, and personal development areas. These mutually established goals act as beacons, not only illuminating the path forward but also fostering a shared sense of purpose. Regular revisitation and assessment of progress create a dynamic feedback loop, ensuring that the mentorship journey remains aligned with the evolving needs and aspirations of both parties. This iterative goalsetting process becomes a testament to the commitment to continuous improvement and the shared pursuit of excellence.

2. Challenging Discussions:

The essence of mentorship is often distilled in moments of challenging discussions that propel both mentors and mentees toward deeper levels of self-awareness and intellectual growth. Proverbs 27:9 beautifully captures the transformative power of open communication, likening it to the joy derived from perfume and incense. Encouraging mentors and mentees to engage in such discussions creates an environment where the exchange of heartfelt advice becomes the catalyst for profound personal and professional insights. These conversations, marked by candor and vulnerability, stimulate critical thinking, broaden perspectives, and cultivate a bond grounded in the mutual pursuit of wisdom. In the crucible of challenging discussions, individuals find not only guidance but also the fertile ground for personal reflection and growth.

3. Feedback Sessions:

The cornerstone of any thriving mentorship relationship lies in the deliberate cultivation of feedback sessions. These sessions serve as forums for constructive evaluation, where mentors and mentees offer insights, observations, and reflections on each other's journey. Feedback, presented with empathy and a commitment to growth, becomes a powerful tool for honing skills, addressing weaknesses, and amplifying strengths. By focusing on areas of improvement and acknowledging achievements, these sessions create a balanced and nuanced understanding of the mentorship dynamic. Through the mutual exchange of feedback, mentors and mentees contribute to a culture of continuous refinement, ensuring that the mentorship journey remains a dynamic and responsive process.

In weaving together the fabric of practical implementation, goal setting becomes the roadmap, challenging discussions the crucible, and feedback sessions the sculptor's chisel. Through these purposeful actions, mentors and mentees not only navigate the intricacies of their mentorship relationship but also co-create an environment where growth, learning, and meaningful connections flourish. The synergy between these elements amplifies the transformative potential of mentorship, turning it into a deliberate and intentional journey of self-discovery and shared advancement.

Leadership by Example: Nurturing Authenticity and Humility

1. Mentor Vulnerability:

In the tapestry of effective leadership, the thread of mentor vulnerability weaves a narrative of authenticity and shared humanity. Encouraging mentors to embrace vulnerability entails creating an environment where they feel not only empowered but compelled to share their own stories of trials, setbacks, and ongoing personal growth. This deliberate act of transparency serves as a powerful catalyst for connection, breaking down the barriers between mentor and mentee. As mentors reveal the chapters of their own journeys marked by challenges and failures, they cultivate a safe space—a crucible of understanding and empathy. In this vulnerable exchange, mentees find inspiration and reassurance, realizing that even leaders, with their wealth of experience, are not immune to the ebb and flow of life. The mentor's vulnerability becomes a beacon guiding mentees through the complexities of their own challenges, fostering a culture of openness and mutual support.

2. Humility in Leadership:

At the heart of impactful leadership lies the virtue of humility—a cornerstone echoed in the timeless wisdom of Philippians 2:34. The essence of this biblical guidance transcends the professional realm, underscoring the transformative power of humility in fostering genuine connections and effective leadership. Reminding mentors of the significance of humility serves as a compass guiding their actions and decisions. By avoiding selfish ambition and vain conceit, mentors create a leadership paradigm centered on valuing others above themselves. This selfless approach is not a relinquishment of authority but a deliberate choice to prioritize the collective interests of the team or mentee. Humility becomes the conduit through which leaders inspire trust, empower others, and cultivate a culture of collaboration. In the mentorship relationship, humility is not a sign of weakness but a source of strength—an acknowledgment that leadership is a shared journey where the mentor learns as much as they guide.

In the rich tapestry of leadership by example, the threads of mentor vulnerability and humility intertwine to form a fabric of authentic, transformative leadership. This approach transcends mere guidance; it becomes an invitation for mentees to embrace their own vulnerabilities, cultivate humility, and, in turn, inspire others. Through these intentional acts, mentors become not just leaders but stewards of growth, shaping a legacy that extends beyond professional achievements—an enduring testament to the transformative power of authentic, humble leadership.

Evaluation and Reflection: Nurturing Growth Through Continuous Assessment

1. Regular Check-ins:

In the intricate dance of mentorship, the rhythm of regular check-ins becomes the heartbeat, ensuring the vitality of the mentorship relationship. These intentional sessions serve as sacred moments where mentors and mentees converge to assess the evolving dynamics of their journey together. Beyond a mere formality, regular check-ins provide a dedicated space for open dialogue, allowing both parties to share experiences, articulate challenges, and collectively celebrate achievements. This ongoing dialogue not only reinforces the bonds of trust but also acts as a compass, guiding the mentorship relationship through the ever-changing landscapes of personal and professional development. Through these rhythmic check-ins, mentors and mentees engage in a collaborative symphony of growth, ensuring that the mentorship journey remains a dynamic and responsive force in both their lives.

2. Surveys and Reflection Exercises:

Elevating the assessment process to a higher plane, the use of surveys and reflection exercises becomes a deliberate act of introspection and refinement. Surveys, designed to capture nuanced feedback, and reflection exercises, crafted to prompt deeper contemplation, serve as mirrors reflecting the impact of the iron-sharpening dynamic. Administering these tools creates a structured approach to evaluation, offering mentors and mentees the opportunity to express thoughts, insights, and areas of improvement. This feedback becomes not just a collection of data but a narrative—a story that informs the ongoing evolution of the mentorship program. As churches embrace this evaluative framework, they engage in a continuous cycle of improvement, adapting the mentorship experience to meet the everchanging needs of the individuals involved. Through surveys and reflection exercises, the mentorship relationship becomes a canvas, constantly being painted and repainted with the strokes of collective wisdom and shared experiences.

By intertwining regular check-ins, surveys, and reflection exercises, churches cultivate a culture of continuous assessment—a commitment to the ongoing refinement of mentorship dynamics. This intentional approach aligns seamlessly with the biblical principle of iron sharpening iron, as it emphasizes not only individual growth but the collective enrichment of the entire community of faith. In this dynamic process of evaluation and reflection, mentorship transcends a mere exchange of guidance; it becomes a living testament to the transformative power of intentional, collective growth within the tapestry of a supportive and nurturing community.

Step 8: Incorporate Bible Study and Reflection

The inclusion of regular Bible study and reflection sessions stands as a pivotal and transformative element within the mentorship program. This step is not merely an addition but a cornerstone that firmly grounds the mentorship relationship in the illuminating power of God's Word. Psalm 119:105 (WEB) paints a vivid picture, declaring, "Your word is a lamp to my feet, and a light for my path." This image beautifully encapsulates the essence of this step, positioning Scripture at the epicentre of the mentorship journey. By doing so, both mentors and mentees are guided by divine wisdom, fostering spiritual growth, and aligning their trajectories with the purpose that God has set forth for their lives.

Essentials of Bible Study and Reflection:

1. Spiritual Alignment:

The mentorship dynamics must be deeply rooted in biblical principles, and Proverbs 3:6 (WEB) serves as a guiding light: "In all [our] ways acknowledge him, and he will make [our] paths straight." Emphasizing the importance of spiritual alignment ensures that both mentors and mentees continuously seek God's guidance in navigating their roles and relationships within the mentorship program. Regular Bible study becomes the compass by which they align their actions with God's divine plan.

2. Mutual Discovery:

Bible study within the mentorship context becomes a journey of mutual discovery. As mentors and mentees engage in the exploration of Scripture together, they unearth timeless truths that transcend individual lives and contribute to the deepening of bonds within the mentorship relationship. This shared exploration fosters a profound connection as they collectively glean wisdom, insights, and spiritual understanding from the Word of God.

3. Application in Daily Life:

The essence of Bible study extends beyond theoretical knowledge; it demands practical application. James 1:22 (WEB) echoes this sentiment, urging believers to be "doers of the word, and not only hearers." Encouraging mentors and mentees to apply biblical principles in their daily lives infuses authenticity into their faith. The mentorship program becomes a laboratory where the teachings of Christ are not only discussed but actively lived out. This application of biblical wisdom transforms abstract concepts into tangible actions, shaping character, and influencing decision-making in a manner that reflects the teachings of Christ.

In summary, the integration of Bible study and reflection into the mentorship program transcends routine religious practice; it becomes the lifeblood that nourishes and sustains a relationship deeply rooted in the transformative power of God's Word.

Practical Implementation:

1. Structured Bible Studies:

To ensure a robust integration of Bible study into the mentorship program, it is imperative to develop meticulously structured Bible-study plans or curriculum. These plans should be designed with a keen awareness of the specific goals and objectives of the mentorship journey. Thematic studies, for instance, can delve into topics such as resilience, integrity, or servant leadership, aligning closely with the values both mentors and mentees aspire to embody. Character studies could explore biblical figures, drawing lessons from their strengths and weaknesses. Additionally, delving into passages relevant to leadership and discipleship can provide a solid foundation for understanding the principles that guide effective mentorship. This structured approach ensures that each session contributes meaningfully to the overall spiritual and personal development of both mentors and mentees.

2. Reflection Journals:

Introducing reflection journals is a powerful way to foster individual growth and introspection within the mentorship program. These journals serve as personal repositories for mentors and mentees to document their spiritual journey. Encourage participants to record insights gleaned from Scripture, capturing moments of revelation or understanding. Reflections on mentoring experiences provide an opportunity for self-awareness and improvement, as mentors can evaluate their impact, and mentees can articulate their growth. Furthermore, these journals can be a sacred space for personal prayers, creating a tangible record of the ongoing dialogue between individuals and God. The act of journaling not only solidifies the impact of

Bible study, but also becomes a valuable resource for future reference and reflection.

3. Interactive Discussions:

Moving beyond passive engagement, the mentorship program should actively facilitate interactive discussions during Bible study sessions. This dynamic approach encourages mentors and mentees to actively participate, share their unique perspectives, ask probing questions, and collectively explore the practical applications of biblical principles. By creating an open forum for dialogue, participants can deepen their understanding of Scripture and its relevance to their lives. This interactive process also fosters a sense of community and shared learning, as individuals contribute diverse insights and experiences. Ultimately, these discussions become a breeding ground for practical wisdom, enabling mentors and mentees to collaboratively navigate the complexities of their personal and professional journeys guided by the timeless truths found in the Word of God.

Leadership by Example:

1. Mentor-Led Devotionals:

Elevate the mentorship experience by actively incorporating mentor-led devotionals into the fabric of your relationship. This goes beyond the traditional mentorship dynamic, transcending into a shared spiritual journey. Encourage mentors to lead devotionals during mentorship sessions, setting a profound and intentional spiritual tone for the relationship. This practice not only provides a structured space for biblical exploration but also allows mentors to authentically share their personal insights and experiences related to the chosen biblical passages. By weaving personal narratives into the discussion, mentors not only impart wisdom but also become relatable role models. This vulnerability fosters a deeper connection between mentors and mentees, creating a space where faith is not just taught but lived.

2. Integrate Prayer:

Infuse intentionality into the mentorship program by seamlessly integrating prayer into the fabric of Bible study. Philippians 4:6-7 (WEB) serves as a guiding principle: "And the peace of God, which surpasses all understanding, will guard your hearts and your thoughts in Christ Jesus." The act of combining Bible study with intentional prayer creates a holistic spiritual experience, fostering a deepened reliance on God's guidance. As mentors and mentees explore Scripture together, the inclusion of prayer becomes a vital component, inviting God into the dialogue and seeking His wisdom, understanding, and peace. This intentional alignment with prayer not only reinforces the transformative power of the Word but also acknowledges the importance of divine guidance in every facet of the mentorship journey. The result is a relationship that goes beyond mentorship—it becomes a shared spiritual pilgrimage where leaders not only lead by example but also lead in communion with God.

Evaluation and Reflection:

1. Feedback Surveys:

To comprehensively assess the impact of Bible study and reflection sessions, implement structured feedback surveys within the mentorship program. These surveys serve as valuable tools to gauge the effectiveness of the spiritual components in shaping the overall mentorship experience. Inquire about specific aspects such as the perceived impact on spiritual growth, the depth of relationship building fostered by these sessions, and the tangible application of biblical principles in real-life scenarios. By soliciting feedback, the mentorship program gains insights into the nuances of how these sessions contribute to the holistic development of individuals within the program. Additionally, this evaluative process enables program organizers to adapt and refine the structure of Bible study sessions to better meet the evolving needs of mentors and mentees.

2. Testimonials and Sharing:

Cultivate a culture of openness and shared experiences by actively encouraging mentors and mentees to articulate their reflections on the role of Bible study in their mentorship journey. Invite them to share testimonials that highlight personal transformations, pivotal insights gained, or moments of profound spiritual revelation. These testimonials serve as powerful narratives, not only inspiring others within the program but also acting as a testament to the transformative power of God's Word in the context of mentorship. By sharing these stories, mentors and mentees become ambassadors for the program's spiritual dimension, creating a ripple effect of motivation and encouragement. This collective sharing of experiences reinforces the idea that Bible study is not just a programmatic component but a lived reality that shapes and enriches the mentorship journey.

By anchoring the mentorship program in the regular evaluation and reflection of its spiritual components, churches ensure that the mentorship relationship is not merely a practical exercise but a profound spiritual journey guided by the illuminating wisdom of God's Word. This intentional approach aligns seamlessly with the foundational belief that Scripture is not only a source of wisdom but also a living guide for every aspect of life, ensuring that the mentorship program remains a dynamic and spiritually enriching experience for all participants.

Step 9: Celebrate Growth and Milestones

In the intricate tapestry of a mentorship program, the act of celebrating growth and milestones transcends mere ceremonial observance; it becomes a profound and spiritually rich practice that underscores the transformative influence of God in the lives of mentees. Anchored in the timeless wisdom of Philippians 1:6, this step echoes the confidence that the divine hand initiating a virtuous work within individuals will meticulously see it through to fruition until the day of Christ Jesus. To engage in the celebration of achievements is, therefore, more than a symbolic gesture—it is a resounding affirmation of the continuous and divine shaping of destinies.

Scriptural Guidance as a Foundation:

Philippians 1:6 serves as a guiding beacon, a lighthouse illuminating the path of mentorship. It encapsulates the belief that the transformative journey, initiated by God, is an ongoing narrative where growth and milestones become chapters chronicling His work. By turning to this verse, mentors and mentees are reminded that the celebration of achievements is not merely a human recognition but a divine acknowledgment of a celestial masterpiece in progress.

Essentials of Celebrating Growth:

1. God-Centered Recognition:

At the core of celebrating growth is a deliberate commitment to God-centered recognition. The resonance of Psalm 34:3 (WEB) permeates the atmosphere: "Oh magnify Yahweh with me. Let's exalt his name together."

The celebration becomes a communal act of glorifying God, recognizing that each milestone achieved is a manifestation of His faithfulness. It is an acknowledgment that the mentorship journey is a joint venture with the Divine, and the milestones are signposts of God's active involvement in shaping the mentee's character and purpose.

2. Encouragement for Perseverance:

Celebrations within the mentorship journey serve as not only markers of progress but also as powerful encouragement for sustained perseverance. The wisdom of Hebrews 10:36 (WEB) echoes in the mentorship space: "For you need endurance so that, having done the will of God, you may receive the promise." Each celebration becomes a testament to the endurance required in navigating the divine will, reinforcing the mentees' commitment to the path set before them. It is a reminder that the journey is as significant as the destination, and each step, celebrated or not, contributes to the fulfillment of God's promises.

In essence, Step 9 becomes a sacred pause, a deliberate moment to collectively recognize and honor the unfolding divine narrative in the lives of mentees. It is a celebration that transcends the tangible achievements, delving into the spiritual realm where growth is a reflection of God's ongoing masterpiece, and milestones are stepping stones toward the realization of His promises.

Practical Implementation:

1. Milestone Recognition Ceremonies:

Elevating the celebration of growth and milestones from a concept to a tangible experience, milestone recognition ceremonies become pivotal in the mentorship journey. These ceremonies are meticulously crafted events designed to honor and commemorate significant junctures in the mentees' paths. Whether it's the completion of a phase within the mentorship program, the realization of personal goals, or the manifestation of profound spiritual growth, each milestone becomes a stepping stone marked with reverence. These ceremonies serve not only as a testament to individual achievements but also as a collective affirmation of the divine narrative unfolding within the entire mentorship community. Through these intentional gatherings, mentors and mentees forge lasting memories that echo the celebratory nature of God's work in their lives.

2. Personalised Acknowledgments:

The art of mentorship lies not only in recognizing milestones but also in providing deeply personal acknowledgments for these accomplishments. Written notes, certificates, or symbolic gifts are carefully curated to reflect the unique journey and triumphs of each mentee. These personalized gestures go beyond a mere pat on the back; they become tangible expressions of the mentor's investment in the mentee's growth. Each acknowledgment is a tailored reminder of the mentee's significance and a testament to the intricate details of their transformative journey. In the realm of mentorship, these personal touches serve as beacons of encouragement, fostering a sense of individuality and purpose that extends far beyond the immediate celebration.

3. Group Celebrations:

The essence of mentorship transcends individual achievements, weaving a tapestry of interconnected lives. Group celebrations, in alignment with the spirit of Galatians 6:2, become the heartbeat of a thriving mentorship community. These collective moments of joy and recognition form the bedrock of a supportive atmosphere, where mentees not only share in their own triumphs but also bear witness to the victories of their peers. Through group celebrations, the mentorship community fulfills the law of Christ, becoming a tangible embodiment of shared burdens and shared joys. The bonds forged in these communal celebrations become a source of strength, fortifying mentees for the continued journey ahead. In this collaborative spirit, mentorship evolves into a collective pilgrimage, and each celebration becomes a testament to the power of unity in Christ.

Leadership by Example:

1. Mentor Testimonials:

At the heart of leadership by example lies the power of narrative—the stories that unfold within the mentorship relationship. Mentor testimonials become the living, breathing testament to the transformative journey of mentees under their guidance. Encouraging mentors to share these testimonials is more than a recounting of achievements; it is a profound invitation into the tapestry of God's ongoing work. These testimonials, crafted with sincerity and humility, become a beacon of inspiration for the entire mentorship community. They showcase not only the mentees' growth but also the impact of God's grace in shaping lives. As mentors unveil the narratives of transformation, they create a ripple effect, inspiring others to recognize the divine potential within their own mentorship journeys. In this way, leadership by example becomes a narrative leadership—a storytelling of God's redemptive and guiding hand.

2. Express Gratitude:

Leadership is not only about steering the ship but also about recognizing the divine privilege embedded in the journey. Expressing gratitude becomes a cornerstone of leadership by example. Drawing inspiration from 1 Thessalonians 5:18 (WEB), where believers are urged to "In everything give thanks, for this is the will of God in Christ Jesus toward you," leaders within the mentorship program cultivate an attitude of thankfulness. Gratitude is expressed not just for the successes but for the privilege of witnessing God's transformative work in the lives of mentees. It is an acknowledgment that leadership is a sacred trust, a divine appointment where leaders are coparticipants in God's redemptive plan. This expression of gratitude deepens the sense of God's presence and guidance, infusing every leadership action with humility and a profound awareness of the higher purpose at play. It becomes a spiritual discipline that radiates through the mentorship program, shaping a culture of appreciation and humility that mirrors the heart of Christ.

In essence, leadership by example becomes a symphony of stories and gratitude—a harmonious blend of shared narratives that illuminate the transformative power of God's love. Through mentor testimonials and expressions of gratitude, leaders not only guide the path but also inspire others to embrace the profound responsibility of mentoring, with a heart attuned to the divine rhythms of growth and thanksgiving.

Evaluation and Reflection:

1. Impact Assessments:

Delving into the realm of evaluation and reflection, the first facet involves conducting thorough impact assessments of the celebratory elements within the mentorship program. These assessments go beyond the surface-level recognition of achievements; they seek to understand the profound influence of celebrations on the overall well-being and motivation of mentees. Through thoughtful examination, mentors and program leaders aim to discern how the joyous acknowledgment of milestones contributes to the creation of a positive and encouraging mentorship environment. This process involves measuring the tangible outcomes, such as increased self-esteem and motivation, as well as the intangible aspects, such as a deepened sense of purpose and belonging. The impact assessment becomes a tool for refining and optimizing the celebratory practices, ensuring that they align seamlessly with the transformative objectives of the mentorship journey.

2. Feedback Sessions:

Intertwining celebration with introspection, the second dimension of evaluation and reflection unfolds through purposeful feedback sessions. These sessions, embedded within the regular mentorship framework, become spaces for mentees to express the intricacies of their experiences with recognition. Mentees are invited to articulate how the celebratory moments have influenced their sense of achievement and motivation to continue growing. This dialogue goes beyond quantitative data; it delves into the qualitative dimensions of the mentorship journey, unraveling the nuanced impact of celebrations on the mentees' emotional and spiritual landscapes. By integrating feedback sessions, the mentorship program embraces a culture of open communication and mutual understanding, fostering an environment where the celebratory elements are tailored to resonate with the unique needs and aspirations of each mentee.

By actively celebrating growth and milestones, churches ensure that the mentorship program is not a mere passage of time but a purposeful journey marked by the joyous acknowledgment of God's continuous work in the lives of mentees. This intentional practice transcends the individual milestones and becomes a collective symphony, resonating with the heartbeat of a supportive and thriving mentorship community. The process of evaluation and reflection emerges as a compass, guiding the program toward a deeper understanding of the transformative dynamics at play and paving the way for an even more impactful and God-honoring mentorship experience.

Step 10: Continual Evaluation and Adjustment

Recognizing that a mentorship program is a dynamic and evolving initiative, Step 10 underscores the profound significance of continual evaluation and adjustment in the pursuit of fostering growth and wisdom. Proverbs 19:20 serves as a timeless beacon of wisdom, advising that embracing counsel and discipline leads to a culmination where one is counted among the wise. In the context of mentorship programs within churches, this biblical wisdom becomes a guiding principle for ensuring the ongoing relevance and effectiveness of the mentorship journey.

Essentials of Continual Evaluation:

2. Flexible Program Design:

   Acknowledge that the mentorship program design should be fluid and adaptable, mirroring the everchanging dynamics of the Church community and its members. Regularly assess whether the program's structure, goals, and methods align harmoniously with the evolving needs, aspirations, and challenges faced by both mentors and mentees. A flexible design allows for the organic growth and customization required to address the diverse and dynamic nature of individual spiritual journeys.

2. Feedback-Driven Improvements:

Place a premium on the continual collection of feedback from both mentors and mentees, recognizing it as a vital source of information for program enhancement. Actively seek insights into their lived experiences, challenges encountered, and constructive suggestions for improvement. This iterative feedback loop transforms the mentorship program into a living, breathing entity that evolves based on the real-time experiences and needs of its participants. By embracing a culture of openness and responsiveness, the program can make informed adjustments that resonate with the unique dynamics of each mentoring relationship.

3. Holy Spirit Guidance:

Elevate the importance of seeking guidance from the Holy Spirit throughout the entire evaluation and adjustment process. Proverbs 16:3 reminds believers to commit their endeavors to the Lord, with the assurance that He will establish their plans. Trusting in the leading of the Holy Spirit becomes the anchor that ensures adjustments are made, not only in response to feedback and observations but also in alignment with the divine will. This spiritual dimension adds depth and purpose to the evaluation process, instilling confidence that the mentorship program is not just a human endeavor but a divinely guided initiative.

In essence, Step 10 underscores the transformative power of continuous refinement, echoing the biblical principle that wisdom is cultivated through a humble openness to counsel, a commitment to disciplined growth, and a steadfast reliance on the guidance of the Holy Spirit. Through these essentials of continual evaluation, mentorship programs within churches can truly become dynamic platforms for nurturing spiritual maturity and fostering lasting connections within the body of believers.

Practical Implementation:

1. Regular Review Meetings:

In establishing a robust framework for the mentorship program, the significance of regular review meetings cannot be overstated. These gatherings serve as dynamic forums where program organizers, mentors, and mentees converge to delve into the nuanced facets of the mentorship journey. By fostering an environment of open dialogue and collaborative decision-making, these meetings become pivotal moments for collective reflection and strategic planning. Discussions can span from assessing the alignment of program goals to realigning strategies based on the evolving dynamics within the Church community. Through these meetings, the mentorship program becomes a living entity that responds effectively to the everchanging landscapes of individual spiritual needs and collective growth aspirations.

2. Surveys and Assessments:

The implementation of periodic surveys and assessments becomes the pulse-check mechanism for the mentorship program. These tools delve beyond mere quantitative metrics, delving into the qualitative dimensions of the mentorship experience. Crafted with intentionality, these surveys inquire about the profound impact of the program on spiritual growth, the depth of interpersonal relationships cultivated, and the successful attainment of set goals. By soliciting candid feedback from both mentors and mentees, the program gains insights that transcend numbers, offering a rich tapestry of narratives that illuminate the transformative power of mentorship. This data-driven approach empowers program organizers to make informed decisions, identify areas of strength, and address potential challenges with precision and purpose.

3. Adaptive Curriculum:

The mentorship journey, akin to a dynamic voyage of growth, demands an adaptive curriculum that mirrors the ever-evolving needs of its participants. Embracing a proactive stance, program organizers integrate new insights, relevant topics, and innovative approaches into the curriculum. This integration is not merely a reaction to feedback but a deliberate response to the changing landscape of spiritual development and leadership emergence. By staying attuned to the pulse of the mentorship community, the program's curriculum becomes a reservoir of wisdom, continuously enriched by the collective experiences and aspirations of mentors and mentees. This adaptability ensures that the mentorship program remains a relevant and potent catalyst for spiritual maturation, equipping emerging leaders to navigate the complexities of their individual journeys with resilience and purpose.

In essence, the practical implementation of regular review meetings, surveys, and an adaptive curriculum transforms the mentorship program into a dynamic and responsive ecosystem. It thrives on the synergy of collaborative evaluations, candid reflections, and intentional adjustments, creating an environment where mentorship becomes a transformative force, shaping not only individual destinies but also the collective tapestry of spiritual growth within the Church community.

Leadership by Example:

1. Organisational Flexibility:

Exemplifying leadership by example entails going beyond rhetoric and embracing a culture of organizational flexibility. Leaders become torchbearers of adaptability, showcasing a profound openness to change. In the context of a mentorship program, this means modeling a proactive willingness to adjust and refine the program dynamically. Leaders demonstrate that the program is not a static entity but a living, breathing initiative responsive to the evolving needs of participants. By weaving the principle of flexibility into the organizational fabric, leaders create an environment where change is not perceived as a disruption but as an opportunity for growth. This exemplification becomes a visible testament to the belief that true leadership embraces the fluidity of circumstances and actively seeks improvement, guided by both insightful evaluation and the discernment of the Holy Spirit.

2. Transparent Communication:

At the heart of leadership by example is transparent communication. Leaders become architects of trust, cultivating an environment where openness is not just a virtue but a guiding principle. When it comes to the evaluation process and subsequent adjustments, transparent communication becomes the linchpin. Leaders share the intricacies of the evaluation process, articulating the reasons behind every adjustment made to the mentorship program. This transparency goes beyond the surface level, delving into the underlying motivations, lessons learned, and the broader vision for program enhancement. Through clear and authentic communication, leaders ensure that participants comprehend the purpose and benefits of ongoing improvements, fostering a sense of collective ownership and engagement. The narrative woven by transparent communication transforms adjustments from arbitrary changes into purposeful steps toward an enriched and more effective mentorship experience.

In essence, leadership by example is a dynamic interplay of organizational flexibility and transparent communication. Leaders, as living embodiments of the values they espouse, set the tone for a culture where adaptability is not just encouraged but expected. They navigate the delicate balance of steering the ship toward improvement while anchoring decisions in a foundation of trust. By embracing flexibility and communicating transparently, leaders pave the way for a mentorship program that transcends its functional aspects, becoming a beacon of inspiration and a catalyst for holistic growth within the organization.

Evaluation and Reflection:

1. Assessment Metrics:

To embark on a journey of meaningful evaluation, it is crucial to establish well-defined assessment metrics that serve as the compass for gauging the success of the mentorship program. These metrics go beyond mere numerical values; they encapsulate the essence of spiritual growth, the sustainability of connections, and the overall satisfaction experienced by participants. Spiritual growth indicators may encompass deepened prayer life, increased biblical knowledge, and a heightened sense of purpose. Retention rates illuminate the program's ability to keep participants engaged and committed. Satisfaction metrics delve into the qualitative dimensions, capturing the emotional resonance of the mentorship experience. By comprehensively defining and measuring these metrics, the evaluation process transcends the surface, providing a nuanced understanding of the program's impact and effectiveness in nurturing the spiritual development of emerging leaders.

2. Post-Program Reflection:

Beyond the structured assessment metrics lies the invaluable practice of post-program reflection. This reflective process, undertaken after each cycle of the mentorship program, serves as a crucible of learning and improvement. It involves a meticulous examination of the adjustments made during the cycle, analyzing their impact on the mentorship journey. It is an opportunity to celebrate successes, acknowledge challenges, and identify areas ripe for further refinement in subsequent iterations. The post-program reflection delves into the collective experiences of mentors and mentees, extracting insights that go beyond numerical metrics. It is a narrative exploration, capturing the stories of transformation, the bonds forged, and the challenges overcome. This introspective exercise not only informs future adjustments but also becomes a source of inspiration, reinforcing the purpose and impact of the mentorship program.

By committing to continual evaluation and adjustment, churches go beyond a mere administrative obligation; they signify a profound commitment to excellence in their mentorship programs. This iterative approach, inspired by the wisdom of Proverbs 19:20 and guided by the leading of the Holy Spirit, ensures that the mentorship journey is not a static experience but a dynamic and responsive process. It remains relevant, impactful, and finely attuned to the evolving needs of emerging leaders from Generation Z and Generation Alpha, fostering a transformative environment where mentorship becomes a catalyst for sustained spiritual growth and leadership development.

Promoting Intergenerational Learning and Collaboration within the Church Community:

Promoting intergenerational learning and collaboration within a Church community is a powerful strategy for building strong bonds, fostering understanding, and creating a supportive environment. Here's a more detailed exploration of each suggested initiative:

Intergenerational Bible Study Groups:
Create a structured program of small Bible-study groups that deliberately include members from different age groups.

Encourage participants to engage in open discussions, share their unique perspectives, and collectively explore the teachings of the Bible. This approach not only deepens spiritual understanding but also provides a platform for the exchange of life experiences and wisdom.

Workshops and Seminars:
Organise a series of workshops and seminars that cater to the diverse needs and interests of different age groups within the Church. Topics could range from parenting and marriage to navigating faith in the workplace and utilising technology responsibly. This initiative promotes cross-generational dialogue, creating an environment where everyone feels heard and valued.

Intergenerational Worship Services:
Design worship services that intentionally incorporate elements appealing to all age groups. Blend traditional and contemporary music, prayers, and sermons that address the challenges and joys experienced by different generations. This inclusive approach ensures that every member of the Church community feels a sense of belonging during worship.

Family Events:
Plan and organise family-oriented events such as picnics, potlucks, or game nights, to bring together members of different generations in a relaxed and informal setting. These events provide opportunities for organic interactions, fostering the development of meaningful relationships within the Church community.

Storytelling Sessions:

Host dedicated storytelling sessions where older members can share their personal stories of faith, challenges, and triumphs. Use various formats such as panel discussions, interviews, or written narratives to convey these stories. This initiative not only preserves the rich history of the Church but also creates a sense of continuity and shared experience among its members.

Service Projects:
Engage the Church community in collaborative service projects that require teamwork and cooperation. This could involve participating in local community initiatives or organising projects specific to the needs of the congregation. Working together towards a common goal fosters a sense of unity and shared purpose among members of different ages.

Skill Sharing Workshops:
Arrange skill sharing workshops where individuals can impart practical skills to others. This might include cooking classes, gardening tips, or technology tutorials. This initiative not only facilitates the exchange of knowledge but also promotes a sense of interdependence among generations within the Church community.

Intergenerational Prayer Partnerships:
Establish prayer partnerships between individuals from different generations. Encourage these pairs to regularly pray for each other's specific needs and share their prayers during Church gatherings. This initiative fosters a sense of spiritual connection and support across age groups.

Special Events:

Celebrate special events, such as milestone birthdays or anniversaries, as a Church community. Use these occasions to recognise and honour the unique contributions of individuals from different generations. This initiative strengthens a sense of community and appreciation for the diversity within the Church.

Technology Training Sessions:
Facilitate technology training sessions where younger members can share their technological expertise with older members, and vice versa. This not only bridges the generation gap but also empowers everyone with valuable skills, promoting a culture of continuous learning and mutual support.

Feedback and Planning Sessions:
Include members from various age groups in the planning and decision-making processes of the Church. This ensures that diverse perspectives are considered when shaping the future direction of the Church community. Regular feedback sessions provide a platform for open communication and foster a culture of inclusivity and collaboration.

By implementing these initiatives, your Church community can create an inclusive and vibrant environment where members of all ages feel valued, connected, and actively engaged in the shared journey of faith.

As churches embark on the journey of mentoring emerging leaders from Generation Z and Generation Alpha, let the Bible be the guiding light. Through prayer, biblical principles, and intentional discipleship, the Church can play a vital role in nurturing the next generation of leaders who will impact the world for Christ.

Promoting Intergenerational Learning and Collaboration within the Church Community:

In the culmination of our exploration into youth leadership empowerment, we find ourselves standing on the solid ground of theological principles deeply embedded in the sacred text. This theologically robust approach is a deliberate journey into the heart of biblical truths, unveiling a roadmap that not only empowers the youth but also fortifies the entire body of believers.

Recognising the Potential within the Youth:

At the core of this theological framework is the recognition that the potential for leadership transcends age. The Scriptures, as our guide, affirm the intrinsic value and capabilities of the youth. Drawing inspiration from 1 Timothy 4:12 and the story of David, the Church embraces a perspective that looks beyond societal expectations, acknowledging the unique qualities and gifts that the youth bring to the tapestry of the community. By recognising the potential within the youth, the Church becomes a conduit for the manifestation of God's diverse and manifold grace.

Establishing Mentorship Programs:

Mentorship, as modelled by figures like Elijah and Elisha and exemplified in Jesus' relationship with His disciples, stands as a cornerstone of this theological approach. By creating mentorship programs, the Church aligns itself with the biblical mandate to pass on not only knowledge but the essence of faith and practical leadership skills. The intentional investment in the younger generation becomes a living testimony to the enduring principle of discipleship, perpetuating a legacy of wisdom and faith that spans generations.

Fostering Intergenerational Collaboration:

The beauty of intergenerational collaboration emerges as a key theme woven into the fabric of this theological approach. Rooted in Titus 2:35 and echoed in the wisdom literature of Proverbs, the Church actively promotes a synergy where the experience of the older generation converges with the vigour and innovation of the youth. This intentional collaboration creates a rich tapestry of shared wisdom, mutual learning, and dynamic growth. The community, in embracing this interconnectedness, becomes a living testament to the unity and diversity inherent in the Body of Christ.

The Strengthening of the Entire Body:

In the final analysis, this theologically robust approach serves as a holistic strategy for the empowerment of youth leadership. By recognising, mentoring, and fostering collaboration, the Church not only nurtures future leaders but also strengthens the entire body. Every generation becomes a vital contributor to the community, bringing forth diverse gifts, insights, and experiences that enrich the collective journey of faith. The Church, as a dynamic and vibrant entity, becomes a microcosm of the Kingdom of God—embracing the call to empower and uplift all its members, irrespective of age or background.

A Community Thriving on Diverse Gifts:

In essence, this approach culminates in the creation of a community that thrives on the diverse gifts and insights of every generation. The youth, equipped and empowered, emerge as leaders with a deep understanding of their calling and a commitment to the timeless truths of the Scriptures.

The Church, in turn, becomes a living testament to the transformative power of biblical principles, radiating a vibrancy that draws people in and reflects the glory of God.

In the tapestry of youth leadership empowerment, woven with the threads of recognition, mentorship, and collaboration, the Church stands as a testament to the enduring wisdom encapsulated in the Scriptures. This theological approach is not merely a strategy; it is a sacred commitment to shaping a community that mirrors the beauty of God's diverse creation—a community where every member, young and old, contributes to the symphony of faith, creating a harmonious melody that resounds through the corridors of time.

Chapter 6: Embracing Technology and Innovation

In an era defined by rapid technological advancements and constant connectivity, the Church must adapt to meet the spiritual needs of Generation Z and Generation Alpha. This chapter delves into the multifaceted realm of technology and innovation, exploring how these tools can be harnessed to create a more inclusive and engaging space for the youth within the Church.

The Digital Landscape as a Mission Field:

In the tapestry of the digital age, where screens illuminate our lives and information flows ceaselessly, the very essence of communication and connection has been redefined. For Generation Z and Generation Alpha, born into a world where smartphones are not just tools but extensions of self, technology is not a peripheral convenience but an intricate thread woven into the fabric of their identity. Recognising this profound integration is not merely an acknowledgment of contemporary trends; it is a vital recognition of the evolving mission field that exists within the digital realm.

The traditional notion of a mission field often conjures images of physical places, distant lands where missionaries embark on journeys to share the Gospel. However, the mission field of the 21st century extends far beyond geographical boundaries; it permeates the digital landscape that Generation Z and Generation Alpha inhabit. To effectively engage with these generations, the Church must not only embrace the advancements of the digital era but also perceive the screens, networks, and virtual spaces as sacred ground for spiritual cultivation.

Understanding the Language of the Digital Pilgrimage:

To navigate this digital mission field, the Church must become fluent in the language spoken in the realms of social media, video content, and interactive platforms. It is a language that transcends words and encompasses visual narratives, memes, emojis, and the shared experiences that unfold in the online sphere. This digital pilgrimage requires the Church to become adept at storytelling in a world dominated by fleeting attention spans and scrolling timelines.

Just as missionaries historically learned the native languages and customs of the people they sought to reach, the Church must learn the digital dialects that resonate with the hearts and minds of the younger generations. It involves adapting the timeless message of faith to the digital vernacular, using mediums that resonate with the ways Generation Z and Generation Alpha process information and build connections.

Becoming fluent in the language of social media, video content, and interactive platforms involves a strategic and intentional approach. Here are practical steps the Church can take to navigate this digital landscape and effectively communicate with younger generations:

1. Digital Literacy Training:
- Provide training sessions for Church leaders and staff on digital literacy. Ensure they are familiar with various social media platforms, video content creation tools, and interactive technologies.
- Encourage continuous learning about emerging trends and features within popular platforms to stay relevant.

2. Youth Involvement:

- Involve young members of the Church in decision-making processes related to digital communication. Seek their input on content ideas, platform preferences, and communication styles.
- Create a dedicated team or committee responsible for managing the Church's digital presence, consisting of individuals who understand the language and preferences of the younger demographic.

3. Engage in Social Listening:

- Monitor social media platforms for conversations related to faith, spirituality, and relevant cultural topics. Use social listening tools to understand the concerns, questions, and interests of the community.
- Respond thoughtfully to comments and messages, fostering a sense of connection and engagement within the online community.

4. Create Visual Content:

- Invest in creating high-quality visual content, including images, infographics, and videos. Visual content tends to capture attention more effectively than text alone.
- Utilise tools like Canva or Adobe Spark for creating visually appealing graphics, and consider hiring or involving individuals with design skills.

5. Tell Compelling Stories:

- Train Church leaders and members to be effective storytellers. Share personal stories of faith, transformation, and community impact through various mediums, including written narratives, podcasts, and video testimonials.
- Connect biblical teachings with real-life experiences to make the message relatable and accessible.

6. Leverage Memes and Emojis:

- Embrace humour and relatability by incorporating memes and emojis into digital communication. Use them thoughtfully to add a personal touch to posts and messages.
- Be aware of current meme trends and adapt them to convey relevant spiritual messages or encourage engagement.

7. Interactive Campaigns:

- Plan and execute interactive campaigns, challenges, and contests that encourage participation. This could include photo contests, hashtag challenges, or collaborative projects.
- Regularly assess the success of these campaigns and adapt future initiatives based on the feedback and engagement metrics.

8. Consistent Branding:

- Establish a consistent visual and messaging style across all digital platforms to create a cohesive brand identity. This helps in building recognition and trust among online followers.
- Ensure that the Church's branding aligns with the cultural aesthetics of the digital age.

9. Utilise Live Streaming:

- Embrace live streaming for virtual events, sermons, and interactive sessions. Platforms like Facebook Live, Instagram Live, or YouTube Live can facilitate real-time engagement with the audience.
- Schedule regular live sessions to maintain a consistent online presence and encourage active participation.

10. Adapt Content for Each Platform:

- Tailor content for the specific features and audience of each platform. For example, content on Instagram may differ from content on Twitter or TikTok.
- Keep up with algorithm changes and platform updates to maximise visibility and engagement.

11. Digital Discipleship:

- Integrate digital discipleship programs that leverage technology for Bible study, prayer groups, and spiritual mentorship.
- Explore platforms like YouVersion, Bible apps, or online study groups to facilitate digital discipleship initiatives.

12. Seek Professional Assistance:

- If resources allow, consider hiring or consulting with professionals in digital marketing, content creation, or social media strategy to ensure a strategic and effective approach.

By taking these practical steps, the Church can navigate the digital landscape adeptly, speaking the language of social media, video content, and interactive platforms fluently. This approach not only enhances engagement with the younger demographic but also fosters a digital presence that reflects the authentic and dynamic nature of the Church in the 21st century.

Creating Meaningful Connections Amidst the Virtual Congregation:

The concept of a congregation is no longer confined to physical pews within a brick-and-mortar Church. In the digital mission field, the congregation is dispersed across online communities, social media groups, and virtual gatherings. To create meaningful connections, the Church must transcend the limitations of physical proximity and embrace the boundless possibilities offered by the digital landscape.

The Evolution of Congregation in the Digital Era:

In the vast tapestry of technological innovation and cultural transformation, the traditional concept of a congregation has undergone a profound metamorphosis. No longer confined to the rigid contours of physical pews within the walls of a brick-and-mortar Church, the congregation has transcended spatial limitations to become a dynamic and dispersed community across the digital mission field.

Dissolving Physical Boundaries:

The advent of the digital era has ushered in an unprecedented era of connectivity. Congregants are no longer bound by the constraints of physical proximity; instead, they navigate a virtual landscape where geographical distances fade into insignificance. The Church, once tethered to the locality of its physical building, now exists in a boundless realm of possibilities where the faithful gather in online communities, social media groups, and virtual gatherings.

Online Communities as Sacred Spaces:

In the digital mission field, online communities serve as sacred spaces where believers congregate to share, learn, and connect. These communities transcend the limitations of time zones and cultural boundaries, creating a global congregation that is diverse, dynamic, and interconnected. Whether through forums, chat groups, or dedicated platforms, the Church becomes a living, breathing entity in the online realm—a congregation that thrives beyond the confines of physical structures.

Social Media as the Pulpit of the Digital Age:

Social media platforms emerge as the modern-day pulpit, where the message of faith is disseminated, discussed, and lived out. The congregation, once defined by faces in a crowd, now extends its reach through likes, shares, and comments. The digital landscape becomes a canvas for expressions of spirituality, a place where believers engage in meaningful conversations, share personal testimonies, and find common ground in their collective journey of faith.

Virtual Gatherings as Communal Worship:

Gone are the days when congregational worship was solely an in-person experience. Virtual gatherings, facilitated by video conferencing platforms, enable believers to come together in shared moments of worship, prayer, and fellowship. These gatherings transcend the physical constraints of a sanctuary, allowing the congregation to assemble in the comfort of their homes while fostering a sense of unity that transcends the limitations of physical distance.

Transcending Temporal Barriers:

The digital mission field not only transcends spatial barriers but also dismantles temporal constraints. The congregation is no longer bound by the rigid schedule of Sunday services; rather, believers engage in spiritual discussions, reflections, and interactions at any time that suits their individual rhythms. The

Church becomes a continuous presence in the lives of its members, offering support, guidance, and community across the entire spectrum of their daily experiences.

Embracing Boundless Possibilities:

To create meaningful connections in this digital landscape, the Church must embrace the boundless possibilities offered by technology. It involves not just adapting to the online realm but actively participating in shaping a vibrant and inclusive digital community. The Church becomes an architect of virtual spaces, curating environments that foster connection, understanding, and shared spiritual growth.

In this digital evolution, the congregation is not diminished; it is liberated from the constraints of physicality. The Church becomes a beacon that extends its light into the vast expanse of the digital mission field, inviting believers to gather, commune, and grow in ways that were once unimaginable. As the Church embraces the opportunities afforded by the digital landscape, it charts a course towards a future where the congregation is not confined by walls but exists boundlessly in the hearts and minds of the faithful across the digital spectrum.

Embracing the Digital Mission Field with Biblical Wisdom:

In delving into the concept of the Church as a participant in the digital mission field, a biblical lens provides profound insights, drawing parallels with the missionary endeavours of the past and recognising the evolving nature of outreach in the digital age.

Building Relationships in the Virtual Vineyard:

In the biblical narrative, missionaries sought not only to disseminate the Gospel but to build relationships within the communities they served. The Apostle Paul, for instance, immersed himself in the cultures he encountered, adapting his message to resonate with the specific needs and understanding of diverse audiences. Similarly, in the digital mission field, the Church is called to foster a sense of belonging and shared purpose within the virtual congregation.

Drawing inspiration from 1 Corinthians 9:22 (WEB), where Paul says, "I have become all things to all men, that I may by all means save some," the Church is invited to actively engage with the digital conversations of the youth. This involves more than mere broadcasting of messages; it's about entering into the virtual spaces where the younger generations gather, participating in their discussions and embracing their questions, doubts, and celebrations.

Virtual Spaces as Mission Fields:

Just as missionaries set out to foreign lands, the Church is called to recognise the digital landscape as a mission field. In the biblical context, the Great Commission in Matthew 28:19-20 (WEB) charges believers to "go and make disciples of all nations." In the digital era, this command extends to the vast nations of online communities, social media platforms, and interactive spaces where Generation Z and Generation Alpha dwell.

The virtual mission field is not a separate realm; it's an intersection of the sacred and the secular, where the Church is called to navigate with grace and relevance. The Parable of the Sower in Matthew 13 illustrates the scattering of seeds in various soils, emphasising the adaptability required to effectively communicate the message of the Gospel in diverse contexts. In the same way, the Church in the digital age must plant seeds of faith in the varied virtual soils where the youth are sowing their thoughts, questions, and experiences.

A New Kind of Missionary Journey:

The call to recognise the digital landscape as a mission field is an invitation for the Church to embark on a new kind of missionary journey. Drawing from the imagery of Ephesians 6:10-18, where believers are encouraged to put on the armour of God, this journey includes not only the traditional wisdom found in Scripture but also a proficiency in the language of the digital realm.

The armour of the digital missionary includes the ability to speak the language of social media, to understand the nuances of online communication and to navigate the ever-changing landscapes of digital platforms. It involves a discerning spirit to recognise the genuine needs and concerns of the virtual congregation and respond with empathy and wisdom.

Transforming Screens into Sacred Spaces:

Ultimately, the aim is to transform screens into sacred spaces, where the digital realm becomes a conduit for the sacred encounter with the Divine. Just as the Tabernacle in the Old Testament was a space for encountering God, the Church in the digital age seeks to create virtual sanctuaries where the Gospel is not only accessible but also deeply relevant to the evolving identities and spiritual quests of the youth.

By integrating biblical wisdom with digital fluency, the Church can echo the words of Paul in 1 Corinthians 9:23 (WEB), "Now I do this for the sake of the Good News, that I may be a joint partaker of it." The blessings of the Gospel, when shared in the digital mission field, have the potential to resonate with the hearts and minds of the younger generations, fostering a transformative encounter that transcends the boundaries of physical structures and permeates the digital spaces where the youth journey in the pursuit of faith.

Virtual Communities and Online Fellowship:

In navigating the ever-expanding landscape of digital interconnectedness, the concept of fellowship undergoes a profound metamorphosis. The Church, once constrained by the geographical boundaries of brick-and-mortar structures, now stands at the forefront of a global renaissance, where virtual communities emerge as dynamic hubs of spiritual connection and shared purpose.

In this digital age, the dissolution of once-formidable geographical distances is not a mere byproduct; it is a transformative alchemy occurring within the pixels and data streams of virtual spaces. The advent of video conferencing platforms, online forums, and social media groups has ushered in an era where believers can unite seamlessly across continents, redefining the very essence of fellowship. This technological evolution transcends convenience; it is a sacred shift that transmutes physical limitations into opportunities for a richer, more diverse tapestry of fellowship.

Virtual Sanctuaries of Global Communion:

As steward of this transformative potential, the Church has the capacity to leverage virtual platforms, creating global sanctuaries of communion. Video conferencing becomes more than a tool; it transforms into a sacred space where faces, once separated by vast distances, can now gather in real-time communion. The virtual sanctuary transcends physical constraints, allowing believers to participate in worship, prayer, and fellowship as if they were side by side, fostering a profound sense of interconnectedness and unity.

Exchange Sites on the Internet:

In this digital age, online groups change into lively digital exchanges. Not only are these places to talk, but they are also busy hubs where people from all over the world share ideas, religious insights, and personal stories. Believers from all over the world have deep conversations with each other, helping each other on their spiritual paths through the collective knowledge of a global congregation. People can talk about religion and share their own stories in the digital agora, which turns into a marketplace of ideas where people can understand each other and help each other.

Crossing Cultural Boundaries in Cyberspace:

The digital mission field, manifested in virtual communities, provides a unique opportunity for the Church to bridge cultural gaps. As believers from different corners of the world converge in cyberspace, cultural boundaries dissolve, and a shared spiritual language emerges. The Church, as a facilitator of this global conversation, can encourage a celebration of diversity within the unity of faith. Through intentional efforts to understand and appreciate various cultural expressions, the digital community becomes a tapestry where different threads interweave to form a beautiful and harmonious whole.

Fostering Authentic Connections:

Virtual communities and online fellowship are not a substitute for physical gatherings but an augmentation of the Church's reach. In these digital spaces, the Church has the responsibility to foster authentic connections. This involves more than superficial engagement; it requires intentional efforts to nurture relationships, provide pastoral care, and create spaces for genuine vulnerability and support.

Empowering Believers for Global Impact:

The Church, by embracing virtual communities, empowers believers for global impact. Through shared online experiences, believers gain exposure to diverse perspectives, cultural nuances, and global challenges. This exposure serves as a catalyst for collaborative initiatives, humanitarian efforts, and collective prayer for global issues. The virtual community becomes a training ground for a generation of believers who are not just locally rooted but globally aware and engaged.

In essence, the concept of virtual communities and online fellowship is a paradigm shift in how the Church perceives and facilitates fellowship. It is an acknowledgment that the digital realm is not a diminished or secondary space but a frontier for profound spiritual connection. As the Church harnesses the potential within these virtual spaces, it becomes a catalyst for a global renaissance of fellowship, breaking down geographical barriers and fostering a sense of unity that transcends physical limitations.

Fostering Deeper Connections in the Digital Sanctuary:

In the virtual realm, the Church has the power to redefine the traditional notion of fellowship. It's not merely about physical presence but about the shared heartbeat of believers resonating through the digital ether. Video conferencing is not just a tool for communication; it's a portal to a shared sacred space where believers can see, hear, and support one another in their respective journeys of faith.

Online forums, far from being mere discussion boards, become vibrant marketplaces of thought, where the currency is not just ideas but empathy, encouragement, and understanding. Social media groups cease to be echo chambers and instead evolve into dynamic ecosystems where diverse voices contribute to a harmonious symphony of spiritual exploration.

Facilitating Spiritual Growth Beyond Borders:

The virtual fellowship transcends the limitations of physical proximity, but its impact extends far beyond the convenience of connectivity. It becomes a powerful catalyst for spiritual growth and mutual edification. Bible studies, once confined to local gatherings, now span time zones and cultures, enriching the collective understanding of Scripture.

Prayer sessions, conducted through the digital medium, become intercontinental prayer chains, weaving a tapestry of collective intercession that blankets the globe. The Church, by embracing these virtual spaces, not only facilitates fellowship but becomes a facilitator of a global spiritual awakening, where believers from every corner of the world contribute to the vibrant mosaic of a unified faith.

Transcending Cultural Barriers, Celebrating Diversity:

In the dynamic realm of virtual communities, the Church not only navigates but actively transcends cultural barriers, ushering in an era where the rich tapestry of diversity within the body of believers is celebrated. The digital fellowship becomes a vibrant melting pot, a sacred space where the myriad cultural expressions of faith blend into a harmonious chorus. Here, believers from varied backgrounds share the beauty of their unique perspectives, collectively fostering a deeper understanding of the universal truths that bind them together in a shared spiritual journey.

Cultural Fusion in Digital Fellowship:

In the virtual embrace of the digital mission field, the Church becomes a catalyst for cultural fusion. Different worship styles, theological perspectives, and spiritual practices coalesce in an intricate dance, creating a mosaic that reflects the multifaceted nature of the global Body of Christ. This fusion is not a dilution of cultural identity but a celebration of the diverse ways that believers express and experience their faith. The digital fellowship becomes a canvas where the colours of various cultures blend, giving rise to a tapestry of worship and community that transcends geographical and cultural confines.

Facilitating Cross-Cultural Dialogue:

Virtual communities, as hubs of cross-cultural interaction, facilitate meaningful dialogue among believers from diverse backgrounds. The Church, recognising the value of this intercultural exchange, actively encourages conversations that delve into the nuances of different traditions, customs, and spiritual journeys. Through intentional efforts to listen and learn from one another, virtual spaces become incubators for mutual respect and appreciation, fostering a spirit of unity amid diversity.

Understanding Universal Truths:

In the midst of cultural diversity, the Church, in virtual communities, guides believers to a profound understanding of universal truths. The shared foundation of faith provides a common ground where cultural nuances become a source of enrichment rather than division. The teachings of Christ, echoed in the universal language of love, grace, and redemption, serve as the unifying force that transcends cultural variations, emphasising the essential bond that believers share despite their diverse backgrounds.

Empowering Cultural Ambassadors:

Virtual communities empower believers to become cultural ambassadors within the global Body of Christ. Individuals, equipped with the ability to share their cultural insights and practices, become agents of understanding and bridge-builders across digital divides. This empowerment fosters a sense of responsibility to represent and honour one's cultural heritage while engaging in a spirit of humility and openness to the diverse expressions of faith within the virtual congregation.

Inclusion as a Pillar of Virtual Fellowship:

As the Church navigates the digital landscape, the principle of inclusion becomes a foundational pillar of virtual fellowship. Recognising the importance of creating spaces where believers from all walks of life feel valued and heard, the Church actively promotes a culture of inclusivity. This involves intentional efforts to ensure that voices from every cultural background are not only welcomed but actively sought out and celebrated within the virtual community.

In conclusion, the emergence of virtual communities as conduits of fellowship represents a paradigm shift in the way the Church engages with its members. It is an invitation to not only transcend the confines of physical space but to actively celebrate the diversity that enriches the global Body of Christ. The digital fellowship becomes a testament to the beauty of cultural fusion, cross-cultural dialogue, and the power of shared universal truths that bind believers together in the digital age—a global perspective that resonates with the timeless echoes of a shared faith.

Navigating the Digital Landscape with Authenticity:

In the ever-evolving digital landscape, authenticity becomes the Church's compass, guiding its narrative through the vast and dynamic realms of social media. It is an acknowledgment that, in an era of fleeting attention spans and incessant content, the transformative force of storytelling holds the potential to captivate the hearts of Generation Z and Generation Alpha.

Social Media as Canvases for Authentic Narratives:

Social media platforms cease to be passive channels; instead, they transform into dynamic canvases for the brushstrokes of authentic narratives. The Church recognises these platforms not as mere information conduits but as sacred spaces for the genuine expression of faith. In utilising social media as story-sharing spaces, the Church steps into the role of a digital storyteller, using every post, image, and video as brushstrokes to paint a vivid portrait of faith.

Bridging the Gap with Unfiltered Testimonies:

The narratives crafted are not just stories; they are unfiltered testimonies etched with the raw emotions of the human experience. They traverse the landscape of struggle, doubt, perseverance, and triumph, creating a mosaic that resonates with the core of the human condition. By sharing these testimonies, the Church weaves a tapestry of faith that transcends the barriers of religious jargon and doctrinal intricacies, making the timeless truths of Christianity tangible and relatable.

Emotionally Charged Storytelling:

Authentic storytelling delves beyond the surface, tapping into the emotionally charged currents of lived experiences. It goes beyond the polished presentations of curated content, embracing the messiness and beauty of real-life journeys. By infusing emotion into the narratives, the Church creates a resonance that goes straight to the hearts of the digital audience. These are not sanitised tales but narratives that evoke empathy, understanding, and connection.

Humanising the Digital Experience

A Compass in the Sea of Digital Noise:

Within the vast sea of digital noise, authenticity serves as a navigational compass, directing the Church through the complex currents of online communication. It is a recognition that amidst the constant influx of information, the genuine and authentic stories stand out as beacons of connection. The Church, armed with authenticity, charts a course that humanises the digital experience, creating a space where meaningful connections can thrive.

Stories Beyond Distance and Inaccessibility:

The narratives woven by the Church cease to be distant or unattainable tales. Instead, they become tangible, real, and relatable stories that bridge the perceived gaps between the digital realm and the human experience. By bringing forth the imperfect yet sincere journeys of individuals navigating faith, the Church dismantles the barriers that might make it seem like a distant institution. The digital space transforms into a virtual town square where faith is not an abstract concept but a lived experience, accessible to all who seek a genuine connection.

A Community of Real and Relatable Journeys:

In embracing authenticity, the Church metamorphoses into a community where the raw and genuine aspects of faith take centre stage. The digital landscape becomes a gathering place where individuals share their stories of struggle, doubt, growth, and perseverance. It's not a curated display of perfection but a genuine portrayal of the human experience within the context of faith. This authenticity establishes the Church as a living, breathing community where everyone, regardless of background or circumstance, can find resonance in the shared narratives.

Accessibility to All Seekers:

Authentic storytelling renders faith accessible. It removes the perception of exclusivity and opens the doors wide to all who seek a genuine connection with matters of spirituality. By humanising the digital experience, the Church becomes an inclusive space where individuals, irrespective of their digital literacy or familiarity with religious language, can engage with faith on a personal level. The digital realm transforms into a welcoming environment, inviting seekers to explore the richness of a genuine and lived faith experience.

A Departure from Distant Institutionality:

Gone are the days of a distant and imposing institution. The Church, through authentic storytelling, sheds the cloak of formality and invites individuals into an intimate space where vulnerability is celebrated, doubts are acknowledged, and growth is shared openly. It becomes a living testament to the fact that faith is not a remote and unapproachable concept but a dynamic journey that is embraced collectively.

Connecting Through Shared Humanity:

Humanising the digital experience is not just about presenting stories; it's about forging connections through shared humanity. The Church's narratives become threads in a tapestry woven with universal emotions, experiences, and aspirations. This shared humanity creates a powerful bond that transcends the digital divide, fostering a sense of kinship among diverse individuals navigating their unique paths of faith.

Fostering a Culture of Genuine Connection:

In the digital community shaped by authentic storytelling, a culture of genuine connection blossoms. It's a culture that values authenticity over perfection, celebrates the diversity of individual journeys, and encourages open dialogue. The Church becomes a facilitator of these connections, recognising that the digital experience is not just a transaction of information but an opportunity for individuals to connect at a deeply human level.

In conclusion, humanising the digital experience through authenticity is an intentional and transformative act. It positions the Church as a guide, companion, and fellow traveler in the digital journey of faith. By making faith relatable, accessible, and deeply human, the Church not only survives in the digital noise but thrives as a beacon of genuine connection in the vast seas of online interaction.

Creating Resonance Across Generations

Authentic Narratives as Timeless Echoes:

The authenticity embedded in the Church's storytelling doesn't exist in a temporal vacuum; it resonates as timeless echoes that reverberate through the corridors of history. These narratives become threads woven into the fabric of a collective human experience. They transcend the immediate digital audience, reaching backward and forward in time, creating a bridge between the experiences of today's youth and the stories of those who walked the path of faith before them.

A Living Connection to Historical Faith:

The Church, through its authentic narratives, evolves into a living connection to historical faith. It becomes a guardian of stories that have weathered the tides of time, carrying the wisdom, struggles, and triumphs of generations past. As today's narratives echo the sentiments of ancient believers, the Church embraces its role as a custodian of a sacred legacy, ensuring that the digital era is not a departure from tradition but a continuation of a timeless journey.

Navigating the Interplay of Tradition and Innovation:

Creating resonance across generations involves navigating the delicate interplay of tradition and innovation. The Church, in telling authentic stories on digital platforms, recognises the need to balance the timeless truths of the Gospel with the evolving language and challenges of each generation. It acknowledges that while the medium may be modern, the essence of faith remains a perennial source of guidance and inspiration for all ages.

Bridging the Generation Gap:

The power of authentic storytelling becomes a bridge spanning the generation gap. It dispels the notion that the digital age and historical faith are disparate realms. Instead, it shows that the core experiences of faith—struggle, doubt, joy, and perseverance—are constants that transcend time. The Church becomes a meeting ground where the wisdom of age converges with the energy of youth, fostering a harmonious exchange that enriches the spiritual journey for all.

Digital Narratives as Contemporary Psalms:

In the tradition of the Psalms, which encapsulate the varied emotions of humanity in poetic form, digital narratives become contemporary Psalms. They express the highs and lows, the doubts and certainties, the celebrations and lamentations of a generation. By echoing the emotional landscape of contemporary believers, these narratives join a chorus that resonates with the Psalms of old, creating a harmonious blend of ancient wisdom and modern expression.

The Church as a Living Storybook:

As the Church embraces the role of a storyteller in the digital age, it transforms into a living storybook. Each authentic narrative becomes a page turned by today's readers and tomorrow's custodians. The stories told in the digital realm become chapters that connect the dots between historical narratives and the unfolding tales of future believers. The Church becomes a dynamic repository, ensuring that the resonance of faith endures as a living and breathing testament across the ages.

Passing Down a Spiritual Inheritance:

Authentic storytelling is not just about the present; it's about passing down a spiritual inheritance. The Church, through its narratives, ensures that the richness of faith is handed from one generation to the next. In creating resonance across generations, it becomes a beacon that illuminates the spiritual path, guiding the footsteps of those who follow in the footsteps of their spiritual ancestors.

In conclusion, the power of authentic storytelling lies not only in its impact on the current digital audience but in its ability to create a lasting legacy that transcends time. The Church, through these narratives, becomes a timeless storyteller, weaving a narrative tapestry that unites the diverse threads of historical and contemporary faith into a harmonious and enduring melody.

Inviting Dialogue and Connection

The Dynamics of Interactive Engagement:

Authentic storytelling on social media transforms the Church's communication from a one-way street into a bustling intersection of ideas, experiences, and shared faith. It transcends the boundaries of a monologue, inviting individuals to actively participate in the ongoing narrative. The Church, aware of the dynamic nature of digital engagement, becomes a facilitator of a two-way dialogue where every narrative shared is an invitation for others to join the conversation.

Encouraging Personal Story Contributions:

The power of authenticity extends beyond the stories told by the Church; it includes the narratives contributed by the digital community. The Church actively encourages individuals to share their own stories, doubts, and triumphs. Social media platforms become not just stages for the Church's storytelling but canvases where every participant can add their strokes to the collective masterpiece. By fostering a culture of openness, the Church transforms into a space where every voice is valued, and every story contributes to the richness of the ongoing dialogue.

Facilitating Sacred Conversations:

The Church becomes a facilitator of sacred conversations within the digital community. These are more than casual exchanges; they are moments of shared vulnerability, mutual support, and collective growth. The shared narratives serve as conversation starters, sparking discussions that delve into the nuances of faith, doubt, and the diverse ways in which spirituality is experienced. In these conversations, the Church embraces its role as a guide, fostering an environment where individuals can explore, question, and deepen their understanding of faith.

Transforming Passive Observers into Active Participants:

Authentic storytelling shifts the digital audience from passive observers to active participants. The Church recognises that engagement is not a one-sided transaction but a collaborative effort. Every like, comment, and share become a form of active participation in the ongoing narrative of the Church. By encouraging interaction, the Church ensures that the digital space is not a mere platform for consumption but a dynamic arena where individuals actively contribute to the collective understanding of faith.

Building a Collective Understanding of Faith:

In the space of shared authenticity, the Church contributes to building a collective understanding of faith. It becomes a repository of diverse perspectives, experiences, and interpretations of spirituality. The digital community becomes a tapestry woven with threads of various narratives, creating a rich and textured depiction of faith. Through ongoing dialogue, the Church fosters an environment where individuals learn from one another, challenge assumptions, and collectively deepen their grasp of the profound and multifaceted nature of faith.

Nurturing a Culture of Openness and Inclusivity:

Authentic storytelling nurtures a culture of openness and inclusivity. The Church becomes a safe space where individuals feel empowered to share their stories without fear of judgment. It actively dismantles barriers that might hinder open dialogue, creating an environment where diverse voices, perspectives, and even doubts are welcomed. In this culture of openness, the Church not only captures attention but builds genuine connections that transcend the digital realm.

An Ongoing Narrative of Faith:

In conclusion, the power of authentic storytelling on social media is not confined to crafting compelling narratives but extends to creating an ongoing narrative of faith. The Church becomes a living story, ever-evolving and enriched by the contributions of the digital community. As individuals actively participate in this sacred dialogue, the authenticity of faith resonates with the deepest yearnings of the human soul, inviting them into a narrative that is not just heard but actively co-created. In embracing this transformative force, the Church doesn't just capture attention; it becomes a living and breathing testament to the dynamic and profoundly human nature of faith in the digital age.

Humanising the Message of Christianity

Unveiling Imperfect Yet Sincere Journeys:

The heart of engaging narratives is in the revelation of imperfect yet sincere journeys. The Church, through authentic storytelling on social media, unveils the raw and genuine experiences of individuals navigating their faith. These narratives are not carefully curated tales of perfection but honest depictions of the struggles, doubts, and triumphs encountered in the journey of belief. By sharing these unfiltered stories, the Church fosters an environment where authenticity takes precedence over idealised portrayals.

A Departure from Pulpit-Centric Communication:

The message of Christianity transcends the confines of traditional pulpits. In the digital age, it unfolds in the everyday lives of believers, shared authentically and vulnerably on social media platforms. The Church acknowledges that the digital sphere is a dynamic landscape where the message is not confined to formal sermons but is woven into the fabric of everyday existence. This departure from pulpit-centric communication allows Christianity to be a living, breathing force that permeates the diverse aspects of life.

Breaking Down Perceived Barriers:

Authentic storytelling becomes a tool for breaking down the perceived barriers of an unapproachable institution. By showcasing the genuine humanity of believers, the Church communicates that Christianity is not a distant and untouchable concept. It is a lived experience, entwined with the daily struggles and joys of real people. The digital narrative becomes an open invitation for individuals to engage with Christianity on a personal level, dismantling preconceived notions of exclusivity.

Presenting Christianity as a Lived Experience:

Christianity is no longer a distant set of doctrines; it becomes a lived experience, authentically portrayed in the stories shared on social media. The Church, through its narratives, illustrates that faith is not relegated to grandiose moments but is interwoven into the mundane, the messy, and the beautiful aspects of life. By presenting Christianity as a lived experience, the Church invites individuals to see it not as a set of rules but as a dynamic relationship with the Divine that is relevant to the complexities of contemporary existence.

Redefining the Church's Image:

In the digital sphere, where skepticism and authenticity hold significant value, the Church seizes the opportunity to redefine its image. It transforms from an institution of perfect saints to a community of real people grappling with faith in a broken world. This redefinition is a powerful acknowledgment that Christianity is not about having all the answers but about the journey of seeking, questioning, and growing. It positions the Church as a relatable companion in the struggles of life, resonating deeply with the inherent humanity of every individual.

Vulnerability Resonating with Younger Generations:

The vulnerability displayed in authentic storytelling resonates profoundly with Generation Z and Generation Alpha. In a world saturated with curated content, these younger generations yearn for genuine connections and relatable role models. The Church's willingness to showcase the imperfections of its members communicates authenticity. It becomes a space where young individuals see not flawless figures but fellow travelers on a spiritual journey, navigating the complexities of faith in a way that aligns with their own experiences and struggles.

An Opportunity to Redefine Christianity's Image:

In conclusion, humanising the message of Christianity through authentic storytelling is more than a communication strategy; it's an opportunity to redefine the image of Christianity in the digital age. By unveiling imperfect yet sincere journeys, breaking down perceived barriers, and presenting Christianity as a lived experience, the Church becomes a beacon of authenticity. In a world hungry for genuine connections, the vulnerability showcased in these narratives not only captures attention but opens doors for meaningful engagement, resonating with the evolving spiritual quests of the younger generations.

Establishing Relatability and Approachability

Engaging Narratives Foster Relatability:

Engaging narratives foster relatability, creating an environment where the message of Christianity is not distant theology but a living, breathing reality. By sharing stories that address the nuances of doubt, the complexities of spiritual journeys, and the beauty of redemption, the Church establishes itself as a relatable companion in the varied landscapes of life.

Engaging narratives often evoke emotions, making the content more relatable. When a narrative is approachable, it means that the audience feels a sense of connection, either through shared experiences or empathetic understanding. This emotional connection can be a powerful tool for building rapport.

Approachability is woven into the fabric of authenticity. As the Church embraces the imperfections and victories of its members, it becomes a safe space where individuals from diverse backgrounds can see themselves reflected in the collective narrative. This approachability dismantles the perception of an exclusive club and invites all, regardless of their past or present, to partake in the transformative power of faith.

In conclusion, the marriage of engaging narratives and authenticity on social media transcends the realm of mere communication; it becomes a sacred dialogue that bridges the ethereal and the earthly. It transforms the message of Christianity from an abstract doctrine to a living, breathing force, embedded in the stories of individuals. As the Church embraces this narrative-driven approach, it not only captures the attention of the younger generations but also invites them into a journey of faith that is vibrant, authentic, and profoundly human.

Interactive Campaigns and Challenges

The Dynamics of Digital Participation:

In the era of likes, shares, and swipes, static content often struggles to capture the attention of the youth. Interactive campaigns and challenges, however, transcend the passive consumption of information. They invite the youth to be active participants in the narrative of faith, transforming the act of engagement from a mere observation to a creative and communal expression.

Encouraging Creative Expressions of Faith:

Through interactive campaigns, the Church can provide a canvas for the youth to artistically express their faith. Whether it's a visual representation of a favourite Scripture, a musical interpretation of a worship song, or a dance that embodies the joy of belief, these challenges unleash a wave of creative expressions that breathe life into the digital space. By fostering a culture of creativity, the Church empowers the youth to explore and communicate their spirituality in ways that resonate with their individuality.

Fostering a Sense of Community Participation:

The essence of interactive campaigns lies not just in the individual expressions but in the collective tapestry they create.

Hashtag campaigns, for instance, become threads that weave together a mosaic of diverse perspectives on faith. Through collaborative projects, the Church nurtures a sense of community participation in which individuals contribute unique pieces to a shared masterpiece.

These campaigns transcend the digital divide, transforming social media from a platform of isolated reflections into a vibrant community square where believers from different corners of the world can converge, share, and celebrate their faith. The digital realm becomes a sacred agora where the collective spirit of the youth resonates in a symphony of diverse expressions.

Creating a Space for Active Spiritual Engagement:

Interactive campaigns go beyond mere visibility; they create a space for active spiritual engagement. Photo challenges might prompt individuals to capture moments of gratitude, hashtag campaigns might encourage sharing personal testimonies, and collaborative projects might unite believers in a digital act of worship. In each instance, the goal is to turn the digital space into a dynamic sanctuary where the youth actively participate in the ongoing dialogue of faith.

The Church, by embracing these interactive initiatives, acknowledges the digital space not merely as a platform for dissemination but as an ecosystem for co-creation. It becomes a curator of experiences, inviting the youth to shape the narrative of their faith actively. In doing so, the Church not only captures the attention of the tech-savvy youth but invites them to be architects of a digital cathedral, where every interactive campaign and challenge contributes to the construction of a vibrant and ever-evolving community of believers.

Embracing Innovative Approaches to Deliver Messages and Create Meaningful Experiences

Embracing Vulnerability as a Strength:

In the landscape of digital communication, the power of authenticity lies in embracing vulnerability as a strength. The Church, through its authentic storytelling, refuses to hide behind a facade of perfection. Instead, it opens the door to the messy, imperfect aspects of faith journeys. This vulnerability becomes a powerful tool for connection, as it communicates that perfection is not a prerequisite for a meaningful relationship with the Divine. By sharing the struggles, doubts, and triumphs authentically, the Church invites others to embrace their own imperfections and find solace in a community that accepts and understands.

The Everyday as Sacred:

Departing from traditional pulpit-centric communication, the Church recognises the sacredness in the everyday lives of believers. Through social media, Christianity is not confined to the sacred spaces of churches but extends into the mundane, messy, and beautiful moments of daily existence. This shift in perspective redefines the boundaries of the sacred, encouraging individuals to see spirituality not only in grand ceremonies but in the ordinary routines of life. The Church's narratives become a testament to the Divine's presence in the ordinary, making faith a relevant and integrated part of every moment.

An Inclusive Invitation:

Authentic storytelling becomes a bridge, breaking down the perceived barriers of an unapproachable institution. The Church's message is not distant; it's an inclusive invitation to engage with faith on a personal level. By showcasing the genuine humanity of believers, the Church communicates that Christianity is for everyone, regardless of their past, struggles, or doubts. The digital narrative becomes a warm welcome, inviting individuals into a community where they can explore their faith, free from judgment and preconceived notions.

Faith as a Dynamic Relationship:

Christianity, as portrayed in the authentic stories shared, is no longer a set of rigid doctrines. It transforms into a dynamic and evolving relationship with the Divine. The narratives illustrate that faith is not a static adherence to rules but a living, breathing connection that adapts to the complexities of contemporary existence. By presenting Christianity as a lived experience, the Church encourages individuals to view their spirituality as an ongoing journey rather than a destination, fostering a sense of curiosity and openness to growth.

A Relatable Community of Seekers:

In the digital sphere, authenticity becomes the cornerstone of the Church's image. It redefines the Church from an institution of perfect saints to a relatable community of real people navigating faith in a broken world. This shift is an acknowledgment that Christianity is not about having all the answers but about the collective journey of seeking, questioning, and growing. The Church positions itself as a companion in the struggles of life, resonating with the inherent humanity of every individual. This authenticity becomes a magnetic force, drawing in those who seek genuine connections and a safe space to explore their spiritual identity.

Capturing the Essence of Humanity:

The vulnerability displayed in authentic storytelling resonates profoundly with Generation Z and Generation Alpha. In a world inundated with carefully curated content, these younger generations crave authenticity and relatable role models. The Church's willingness to showcase the imperfections of its members communicates a genuine humanity that is both refreshing and relatable. It becomes a space where young individuals see not flawless figures but fellow travellers on a spiritual journey, navigating the complexities of faith in a way that aligns with their own experiences and struggles.

A Transformative Opportunity for Connection:

In conclusion, humanising the message of Christianity through authentic storytelling is not just a strategic approach; it's a transformative opportunity for connection in the digital age. By unveiling imperfect yet sincere journeys, breaking down perceived barriers, and presenting Christianity as a lived experience, the Church becomes a beacon of authenticity. In a world hungry for genuine connections, the vulnerability showcased in these narratives not only captures attention but opens doors for meaningful engagement. It resonates with the evolving spiritual quests of the younger generations, inviting them to be active participants in a narrative that embraces the messiness and beauty of the human experience.

Envisioning a Global Sanctuary:

As technology evolves, the concept of a sanctuary expands beyond physical walls. Imagine a virtual sanctuary where believers, scattered across continents, can gather in a shared digital space to worship and partake in sermons. Virtual reality, with its immersive capabilities, allows individuals to step into this ethereal sanctuary, fostering a sense of togetherness that transcends geographical boundaries.

In this digital cathedral, believers can experience the collective energy of a global congregation. Virtual reality transforms the act of worship into a shared journey, where the barriers of distance dissolve, and the collective spirit of the faithful converges in a virtual realm. It becomes a sacred space that unites believers in a profound and immersive communion, redefining the very essence of what it means to gather in worship.

Augmented Reality: Breathing Life into Biblical Narratives

Unlocking Three-Dimensional Storytelling:

Generation Z is characterized by the fact that this generation has grown up in a world where digital technology is ubiquitous and plays a central role in various aspects of their lives. Unlike previous generations, Gen Z has experienced an unprecedented level of connectivity and access to information from an early age. As Generation Alpha continues to come of age, there is a noticeable shift in their preferences and engagement with technology, and augmented reality (AR) and Virtual Reality (VR) are technologies that hold particular appeal to this generation.

Augmented reality emerges as a revolutionary tool, unlocking three-dimensional storytelling capabilities for ancient biblical narratives. The traditional approach of reading these stories from the pages of a book is transcended as AR applications infuse them with a vibrant, dynamic presence. The characters, settings, and events come to life in a way that transcends the limitations of static text, providing a rich and immersive encounter with the sacred texts.

Interactive Displays and Engaging Exploration:

The power of augmented reality lies in its ability to transform the act of learning about biblical stories into an interactive and engaging exploration. AR applications create displays where characters step out of the pages, inviting users to interact with the narratives in a hands-on manner. This interactive element goes beyond passive reading; it encourages users to actively engage with the stories, fostering a deeper connection and understanding of the rich biblical tapestry.

A Visual and Auditory Extravaganza:

Augmented reality turns a simple Bible reading into a visual and auditory extravaganza. The immersive experience goes beyond static visuals, incorporating dynamic elements that stimulate both sight and sound. Users can witness scenes unfolding before their eyes, accompanied by realistic sound effects that bring an added layer of authenticity to the storytelling. This multisensory approach transforms the exploration of biblical narratives into a captivating journey that resonates deeply with the tech-savvy younger generations.

Bridging Ancient Wisdom and Contemporary Engagement:

For the younger generations, raised in a world saturated with dynamic digital experiences, augmented reality becomes a powerful bridge between ancient wisdom and contemporary engagement. It provides a medium through which the age-old stories of the Bible seamlessly integrate with the preferences and expectations of a generation accustomed to interactive and visually stimulating content. AR applications facilitate a seamless fusion of tradition and innovation, making the exploration of Scripture not only relevant but also exciting for the youth.

Immersive Panoramas and Historical Landscapes:

AR applications have the capability to transform biblical exploration into immersive panoramas where historical landscapes materialise before the observer. Users can virtually step into the settings of biblical events, experiencing the vastness of Noah's Ark or witnessing the grandeur of the parting of the Red Sea. This immersive quality transports individuals beyond the constraints of physical space and time, allowing them to witness the biblical narratives in a manner that goes beyond the imagination.

Making Exploration Exciting and Memorable:

The educational experience facilitated by AR applications goes beyond imparting information; it makes the exploration of Scripture exciting and deeply memorable. The combination of visual richness, interactivity, and immersive storytelling turns the process of learning about biblical narratives into an adventure. This approach aligns with the preferences of the younger generations who thrive on dynamic and captivating experiences, making the exploration of Scripture not just a scholarly pursuit but a thrilling journey of discovery.

In conclusion, augmented reality breathes life into biblical narratives by leveraging technology to create a multi-sensory, interactive, and engaging exploration of sacred texts. It transforms the way individuals, especially the younger generations, connect with and understand ancient wisdom, turning the exploration of Scripture into a contemporary and exciting journey.

The Intersection of Tradition and Innovation

Amplifying the Sacred Experience:

Embracing VR and AR worship experiences positions the Church at the intersection of tradition and innovation. Rather than perceiving technology as a threat to the sacred, the Church recognises it as a powerful tool for amplifying the sacred experience. These immersive technologies are not designed to replace the physical Church but to complement and enhance the worship journey beyond the limitations of physical presence.

Extending the Reach Beyond Physical Limitations:

Virtual reality and augmented reality extend the reach of the Church beyond the confines of physical locations. The Church acknowledges that the spiritual journey is not bound by the walls of a specific building; it can seamlessly transition into the digital realm. VR and AR serve as conduits that transcend geographical barriers, offering believers the opportunity to engage with their faith in a manner that transcends both time and space. The Church becomes a dynamic entity capable of reaching individuals wherever they are, fostering a sense of connection and unity among believers.

Pioneering Redefinition of Worship Dynamics:

By delving into VR and AR, the Church assumes the role of a pioneer in redefining the dynamics of worship. It understands that worship is a multifaceted experience that can embrace innovation without compromising tradition. Instead of resisting change, the Church becomes an advocate for leveraging technology to create more meaningful and immersive worship encounters. This pioneering spirit opens new avenues for spiritual exploration, encouraging believers to encounter the Divine in ways that resonate with the complexities of the modern world.

Recognising the Spiritual Journey's Digital Extension:

The Church's exploration of VR and AR is rooted in the recognition that the spiritual journey is not confined to a specific physical space. Virtual reality and augmented reality serve as extensions of the spiritual path into the digital realm. Believers are invited to navigate this intersection of tradition and innovation, where ancient practices and futuristic technologies converge to create a tapestry of worship that transcends conventional boundaries. The Church becomes a guide in this exploration, facilitating a seamless integration of timeless traditions with contemporary tools.

Conduits for Deeper, Immersive Encounters:

Virtual reality and augmented reality serve as conduits for believers to experience a deeper, more immersive encounter with the Divine. These technologies go beyond the limitations of traditional worship formats, offering a more profound engagement with spiritual practices. Whether it's virtually entering a sacred space or witnessing biblical narratives come to life in three dimensions, VR and AR elevate the worship experience to new heights. The Church becomes a curator of these immersive encounters, providing believers with tools to connect with their faith on a profound and personal level.

Inviting Believers to Navigate Ancient and Futuristic Realms:

In the intersection of tradition and innovation, the Church extends an invitation for believers to navigate both ancient and futuristic realms of worship. VR and AR become pathways where age-old traditions are seamlessly interwoven with cutting-edge technologies. Believers are encouraged to embrace this harmonious blend, recognising that innovation does not dilute the essence of tradition but amplifies it in ways that resonate with contemporary sensibilities.

In conclusion, the intersection of tradition and innovation, facilitated by the exploration of VR and AR in worship, positions the Church as a dynamic force that adapts to the evolving needs of its congregation. By leveraging technology to enhance rather than replace sacred experiences, the Church navigates a path where tradition and innovation coalesce to create a worship environment that is both rooted in history and responsive to the demands of the digital age.

A Vision for the Future:

The vision of virtual reality and augmented reality worship experiences is not merely speculative; it is a glimpse into the evolving landscape of spirituality. It envisions a future where believers can seamlessly integrate technology into their worship, where the sacred and the digital coexist in a symbiotic dance. As the Church explores these frontiers, it invites the faithful to embark on a journey that transcends the physical and delves into the limitless possibilities of the digital spiritual experience.

Gamification of Spiritual Growth

Bridging Ancient Wisdom and Contemporary Trends:

In navigating the ever-evolving cultural landscape, the Church stands in a unique position to bridge the gap between ancient wisdom and contemporary trends. Recognising the prevalence of gaming culture among the youth, a profound opportunity emerges—the gamification of spiritual growth. This transformative approach acknowledges the shifts in cultural dynamics and seeks to meet the younger generations on familiar ground, inviting them to explore and deepen their faith through the language of games and interactive experiences.

Acknowledging the Prevalence of Gaming Culture:

The acknowledgement of the prevalence of gaming culture among the youth is a key starting point. The Church understands that digital gaming has become an integral part of the social fabric, shaping how young individuals engage with entertainment, connect with others, and seek personal challenges. Rather than viewing this as a distraction, the Church sees it as a cultural language through which meaningful conversations about spirituality can take place.

A Profound Opportunity for Engagement:

The gamification of spiritual growth represents a profound opportunity for engagement. It recognises that the traditional methods of imparting spiritual teachings may not resonate as effectively with a generation deeply immersed in the interactive and competitive nature of gaming. By embracing gamification, the Church opens a door for the younger generations to actively participate in their own spiritual development, turning what might have been perceived as a solemn and distant journey into an accessible, engaging, and enjoyable experience.

Transforming Solemnity into an Engaging Journey:

Infusing interactive apps, games, and challenges with the teachings of the Bible transforms the often-perceived solemnity of spiritual development into an engaging and enjoyable journey. Instead of approaching spiritual growth as a serious and somber endeavour, gamification introduces an element of play, competition, and achievement. This shift in perspective allows the youth to view their spiritual journey not as a chore but as an exciting quest filled with challenges, rewards, and opportunities for personal growth.

Interactive Apps as Spiritual Tools:

Interactive apps become more than mere tools; they become vehicles for spiritual exploration. These apps leverage the interactive nature of gaming to deliver biblical teachings in ways that captivate the attention of the younger generations. Whether through quiz-style challenges, narrative-driven games, or collaborative missions, these apps offer a dynamic platform for engaging with the core tenets of faith. Each interaction becomes a step in the journey of spiritual growth, encouraging a consistent and personalised exploration of one's beliefs.

Games as Parables of Faith:

In the gamification of spiritual growth, games become modern-day parables of faith. They present scenarios, challenges, and decision points that mirror the complexities of real-life situations. By navigating these virtual landscapes, players can apply biblical principles, make ethical choices, and experience the consequences of their actions within the context of the game. This experiential learning approach transforms abstract theological concepts into tangible lessons that resonate with the lived experiences of the youth.

Fostering Community and Collaboration:

Gamification fosters a sense of community and collaboration among the younger generations. Multiplayer games and collaborative challenges create spaces where individuals can share their spiritual journeys, discuss biblical teachings, and support each other in their quest for growth. The competitive elements become avenues for friendly competition, encouraging healthy dialogue and camaraderie among participants. The Church, by embracing gamification, not only facilitates individual spiritual growth but also nurtures a vibrant and interconnected community.

In conclusion, the gamification of spiritual growth is a strategic and innovative approach that leverages the language of gaming to make the journey of faith accessible, engaging, and enjoyable for the younger generations. By transforming spiritual development into a dynamic and interactive experience, the Church adapts to the cultural dynamics of the digital age, fostering a pathway for the youth to explore and deepen their connection to their faith in ways that align with their contemporary preferences and cultural influences.

Tapping into the Language of Play:

Games have an inherent ability to captivate attention, stimulate creativity, and encourage perseverance. Recognising this, the Church can tap into the language of play to create spiritual experiences that resonate with the youth. Gamification offers an innovative approach, turning spiritual development into a dynamic adventure where biblical principles are not just learned but lived.

Through interactive apps and games, the Church can invite the younger generation to embark on quests that mirror the challenges and triumphs of biblical narratives. These digital journeys become more than educational tools; they become portals where players actively engage with the foundational tenets of their faith. The language of play becomes a conduit for imparting wisdom, fostering a deeper understanding of Scripture through experiential learning.

Encouraging Meaningful Rituals:

Gamification introduces an element of ritualistic engagement with spiritual practices. Prayer, often seen as a traditional and personal act, can be transformed into a communal and interactive experience. Through gamified challenges, believers can participate in collective prayer initiatives, fostering a sense of unity and shared purpose. The act of prayer becomes not just a solitary endeavour but a collaborative effort, reinforcing the communal nature of faith.

Scripture memorisation, a cornerstone of spiritual growth, can be infused with the excitement of competition. Gamified challenges can prompt individuals to memorise verses, with rewards and recognition for achievements. This not only enhances the retention of Scripture but also creates a sense of accomplishment, turning the process of memorisation into a joyful and fulfilling endeavour.

Fostering a Sense of Community and Connection:

In the world of gamification, community and connection are not byproducts but integral components. The Church, through gamified spiritual growth initiatives, can foster a sense of community among believers. Interactive apps and challenges become virtual meeting grounds where individuals can share experiences, offer support, and celebrate milestones in their spiritual journeys.

Multiplayer games designed around biblical themes can create virtual spaces where believers collaborate, learn, and grow together. The gamified experience becomes a unifying force, breaking down barriers and fostering connections among individuals who might otherwise never cross paths. In this virtual realm, the Church becomes a facilitator of community building, using gamification as a conduit for forging meaningful relationships.

Instilling Values through Gameplay:

Gamification allows the Church to instill values not through sermons but through gameplay. Interactive apps can simulate real-life scenarios where players must make decisions aligned with biblical principles. The consequences of these decisions within the game become a reflection of the values embedded in Scripture. Through this experiential learning, the teachings of the Bible are not just heard but internalised, as players navigate ethical dilemmas and moral choices.

In conclusion, the gamification of spiritual growth is not a departure from tradition but an evolution in how the Church engages with the youth. By integrating play, competition, and community into the fabric of spiritual development, the Church creates a space where the journey of faith is not perceived as burdensome but as an exhilarating quest. In doing so, the Church not only speaks the language of the younger generations but also invites them to actively participate in the timeless and transformative narrative of spiritual growth.

In the grand tapestry of religious evolution, "Embracing Technology and Innovation" emerges not merely as a call for adaptation but as a profound acknowledgment of the seismic shift occurring in the way the Church connects with and ministers to Generation Z and Generation Alpha. It transcends the notion of keeping pace with societal changes; it is a recognition of the transformative power inherent in these technological tools—a power capable of reshaping the very essence of spiritual engagement.

A Recognition of Transformative Power:

At its core, embracing technology and innovation in the context of religious practice is an affirmation that these tools are not just neutral vessels for communication; they are dynamic catalysts for transformation. The recognition goes beyond a surface-level acknowledgment of contemporary trends; it delves into the understanding that technology has the potential to reshape the very fabric of religious experiences.

This transformation is not merely about adopting new tools but understanding that these tools have the capacity to revolutionise the way individuals perceive, interact with, and internalise their faith. It's a recognition that the digital realm is not a distraction from the sacred but a space where the sacred can manifest in ways previously unimagined.

Connecting with the Hearts and Minds:

By exploring the role of technology, the Church embarks on a journey to connect with the hearts and minds of the youth. It recognises that the language of communication has evolved, and the narrative of faith must adapt accordingly. Technology becomes a bridge, a medium through which the timeless truths of the faith are conveyed in ways that resonate with the contemporary sensibilities of younger generations.

Leveraging social media is not a superficial attempt at relevance; it's an acknowledgment that the digital landscape is where conversations are unfolding, where ideas are shared, and where relationships are formed. Through social media, the Church has the opportunity to be present in the spaces where the youth naturally gravitate, engaging in meaningful dialogue and fostering connections that transcend the physical boundaries of traditional congregations.

Fostering a Thriving and Inclusive Community:

Embracing innovative approaches is not a departure from tradition; it is an evolution of community building. The Church recognises that the concept of community is no longer confined to physical gatherings; it extends into the digital spaces where individuals seek connection, support, and shared purpose. Through innovative approaches, the Church becomes a curator of experiences, creating environments where the youth can actively participate in the shaping of their faith.

This evolution is not exclusionary; it is deeply inclusive. It acknowledges that diversity exists not only in physical spaces but also in the myriad ways individuals engage with their spirituality. The Church becomes a mosaic, rich in different expressions of faith, where the collective journey is celebrated, and each unique voice contributes to the harmonious tapestry of the community.

For Generations to Come:

The concluding thought is a poignant reminder that this embrace of technology and innovation is not a fleeting trend but a legacy for generations to come. It is an investment in the continuity of the Church's mission, ensuring that the seeds planted today will grow into thriving spiritual landscapes for future generations.

The Church, by embracing these transformative tools, becomes a living testament to the adaptability of faith. It demonstrates that the essence of spirituality remains timeless, even as the methods of expression evolve. The narrative woven through technology and innovation becomes a chapter in the ongoing story of the Church, a story that spans generations and speaks to the enduring and transformative nature of faith in a rapidly changing world.

Chapter 7: Investing in Education and Discipleship

Introduction:

This chapter will look at the critical importance of investing in education and discipleship programmes within religious groups, with a special emphasis on youth. We will look at biblical passages that emphasise the importance of prioritising educational and spiritual growth, developing comprehensive discipleship programmes, and providing young people with the tools and information they need to handle the current world's issues.

Investing in education and discipleship is a cornerstone of religious groups' holistic development of youngsters. This deliberate commitment to young people's varied development includes not only the teaching of knowledge but also the cultivation of their spiritual well-being. Religious communities lay the groundwork for a strong foundation that supports youth on their faith journey by emphasising both educational and spiritual components.

The integration of education and discipleship is an effective technique for developing well-rounded people. Educational pursuits, both secular and religious, provide adolescents with the cognitive tools they need to negotiate the world's complexities. Discipleship programmes that guide people in applying their knowledge within the framework of their faith supplement and expand this academic basis. The interaction of these two pillars ensures holistic development of the youth's mind, spirit, and character.

Comprehensive discipleship programmes, which provide a disciplined framework for spiritual growth, are critical in this process. These programmes are meant to fulfil the varying needs of young people while taking into account the various stages of their spiritual growth. Religious communities foster not only doctrinal comprehension but also the growth of virtues and ethical principles, by incorporating age-appropriate study groups, mentorship efforts, spiritual retreats, and community service projects.

The scriptural allusions, such as Matthew 28:19-20, emphasise the divine obligation to invest in education and discipleship. This commandment is a call to action, a recognition that faith is a dynamic force that motivates individuals to learn, grow, and share their views with others, rather than a passive possession. The responsibility to nurture and guide the youth stems from the recognition that they are the torchbearers of the faith, tasked with the mission of carrying forward the teachings and values passed down through generations.

Investing in education and discipleship also means investing in resilience. In a world of perpetual change and challenges, today's youngsters require a stable foundation to weather life's storms. Education prepares people to adapt and thrive in a variety of circumstances, whereas discipleship strengthens their spiritual resilience by developing a deep-seated faith that can withstand life's ups and downs.

As religious groups consider the value of these investments, they are motivated by a sense of responsibility to empower the youth. This empowerment entails more than just knowledge transfer; it entails the development of critical thinking, moral judgement, and a genuine commitment to carrying out faith beliefs. Religious communities thus contribute not only to the personal development of youngsters but also to the constructive transformation of the communities and societies in which they live.

Finally, the confluence of education and discipleship is a powerful formula for the complete development of young people within religious communities. These communities fulfil a sacred responsibility by prioritising their educational and spiritual progress, executing extensive discipleship programmes, and equipping them with appropriate skills and knowledge. They nurture and guide the youth, empowering them to become faithful and resilient beacons of light in the world around them, not merely knowledgeable persons.

Biblical Groundwork:

1. Proverbs 22:6 (WEB) "Train up a child in the way he should go, and when he is old he will not depart from it." This verse emphasises the long-term importance of early training and education. It is a guiding concept for investing in youth, highlighting the transformative function of education and discipleship in creating lifelong faith.

Proverbs 22:6 (WEB) emphasises the tremendous importance of early instruction and education in defining the trajectory of an individual's life, with its timeless wisdom. "Train up a child in the way he should go, and when he is old he will not depart from it." This verse serves as a guidepost, illustrating the long-term impact that intentional upbringing and education may have on a person's character, beliefs, and values.

This biblical precept, at its core, alludes to the importance of formative events during childhood. It implies that the impressions formed during this pivotal period, particularly in matters of faith and moral development, have a long-lasting impact that transcends the passage of time. This verse becomes a rallying cry for the adoption of educational and discipleship efforts that begin early and give a solid basis for a lifelong journey of faith in the context of investing in the youth within religious communities.

"Train[ing] up a child" suggests a deliberate and intentional approach to education and discipleship. It entails not just the transmission of knowledge but also the development of a value system that is consistent with the teachings of the faith. Religious educational programmes, particularly those for young people, play an important role in establishing the ideals of love, compassion, and moral integrity from a young age. These programmes serve as a fertile field for the planting of seeds of faith, with the hope that they will grow into deeply rooted convictions as the child ages.

Furthermore, the verse emphasises the ever-changing character of education and discipleship. It is not just about providing information; it is also about personalising guidance to the specific path that each child should take. Recognising the multiplicity of individual abilities, weaknesses, and inclinations, religious groups are compelled to develop educational and discipleship programmes that address the unique requirements of each young person. This tailored method attempts to cultivate a religion that is not only inherited but also internalised, guiding the individual through life's trials and decisions.

The verse follows with the guarantee that "when he is old he will not depart from it," emphasising the impact's enduring character. Investing in adolescents has a long-term impact on their lives, offering a moral compass and spiritual anchor that remains firm even in the face of worldly temptations and challenges. This tenacity attests to the transforming power of early education and discipleship, demonstrating that principles taught in young people continue to impact character and decisions long into adulthood.

This biblical precept takes on new meaning in the context of religious communities. It inspires a commitment to establishing environments that promote the holistic development of youth by merging educational and discipleship efforts that are consistent with faith teachings. By embracing this approach, religious institutions not only fulfil a sacred obligation but also contribute to the development of persons whose lives reflect the long-lasting influence of early faith teaching.

2. Deuteronomy 6:6-7 (WEB):
"These words, which I command you today, shall be on your heart; and you shall teach them diligently to your children, and shall talk of them when you sit in your house, and when you walk by the way, and when you lie down, and when you rise up."
This chapter emphasises the complete incorporation of spiritual teachings into daily life. It encourages a continuous and immersive approach to education and discipleship, recognising that these values should pervade all parts of a person's life.

Deuteronomy 6:6-7 (WEB) paints a striking picture of education and discipleship, emphasising the incorporation of spiritual teachings into the fabric of daily life. "These words, which I command you today, shall be on your heart; and you shall teach them diligently to your children, and shall talk of them when you sit in your house, and when you walk by the

way, and when you lie down, and when you rise up."
This passage advocates for a continuous, immersive, and all-encompassing engagement with spiritual principles, rather than a structured approach to learning.

The instruction to keep these words "on your heart" denotes a thorough internalisation of the teachings. It involves more than mechanical memorisation; it implies a profound grasp of and personal connection with the spiritual ideas and values revealed in sacred books. This instruction becomes a guiding concept for religious organisations committed to the holistic development of youth, emphasising not just the transfer of information but the nurturing of a sincere commitment to the tenets of faith.

The instruction to teach young people diligently emphasises the need of passing on this spiritual treasure to the next generation. It encourages religious communities to be deliberate and proactive in their educational and discipleship endeavours, ensuring that wisdom and teachings are not lost but are passed forth with diligence and care. This commitment entails developing educational settings that promote active learning, as well as fostering an environment in which inquiries are encouraged and curiosity is fostered.

The next phrases, "when you sit in your house, and when you walk by the way, and when you lie down, and when you rise up," give a clear image of this educational and discipleship journey's ongoing nature. It promotes a way of living in which spiritual discussions are effortlessly integrated into the fabric of daily activity. This comprehensive integration recognises that faith should pervade every instant and every space in an individual's life, rather than being confined to specific periods or places.

In practise, this chapter encourages religious groups to develop educational and discipleship programmes that go beyond the confines of official venues. It promotes family discussions on spiritual matters, creating a climate in which parents, as primary educators, actively engage their young people in meaningful conversations about faith. It envisions a society in which spiritual discussion is not limited to the bounds of a place of worship, but extends into the everyday and remarkable moments of life.

Furthermore, the verse encourages people to be aware of the ongoing nature of their spiritual path. It implies that faith is not compartmentalised, reserved for special situations, but rather a constant companion in every step of life's journey. This viewpoint promotes living religion, in which the ideas taught are applied in real-life situations, shaping attitudes, decisions, and relationships.

Reflecting on Deuteronomy 6:6-7, religious groups are reminded of their profound obligation to establish an atmosphere in which faith teachings are not just studied but honestly carried out. They contribute to the formation of individuals whose lives are testaments to the enduring impact of spiritual wisdom woven into the very fabric of their life, by embracing a continuous and immersed approach to education and discipleship.

3. 2 Timothy 3:16-17 (WEB) says, "Every Scripture is God-breathed and profitable for teaching, for reproof, for correction, and for instruction in righteousness, that each person who belongs to God may be complete, thoroughly equipped for every good work."

Emphasising the transformational power of Scripture, this text highlights the role of education and discipleship in developing individuals to be ready for a life of service and good acts. It emphasises the all-encompassing character of spiritual development through God's Word.

The deep proclamation in 2 Timothy 3:16-17 (WEB) that "every Scripture is God-breathed" serves as a foundational truth for the transformational power of divine wisdom. This chapter not only emphasises Scripture's hallowed and authoritative nature, but it also lays out its practical consequences for education, discipleship, and the holistic development of persons within religious communities.

The statement that Scripture is "profitable for teaching, for reproof, for correction, and for instruction in righteousness" lays the context for comprehending the Word of God's varied role. It evolves into a dynamic educational instrument that goes beyond simply transmitting knowledge. It is a source of instruction, providing counsel on how to handle life's complexity according to divine principles. Furthermore, it provides a framework for correction and reproof, establishing the feeling of accountability and moral judgement required for personal growth and spiritual maturity.

The chapter emphasises that the ultimate purpose of Scripture-based education and discipleship is to equip persons for righteousness. It posits a transforming process in which humans are not only informed but actively sculpted and moulded into righteous creatures. This training in righteousness entails more than just a theoretical grasp; it entails the actual application of divine principles in daily life, cultivating a character that is consistent with the values revealed in the Scriptures.

Furthermore, the passage states that the overarching goal is for people to be "complete, thoroughly equipped for every good work." This completeness refers to a holistic development that includes not only intellectual understanding but also moral integrity, emotional maturity, and a deep spiritual connection. It envisions persons who, by their engagement with Scripture, are thoroughly prepared to engage in acts of kindness, service, and charity, favourably contributing to the well-being of others and the wider community.

This chapter becomes a guiding concept for the construction of educational and discipleship programmes in the context of religious communities. It advocates for an approach that sees Scripture as a living and transformational resource capable of moulding people holistically. Religious education, then, becomes more than a set of teachings; it becomes an immersing experience in which the heart, mind, and soul are all involved in the process of spiritual formation.

The holistic aspect of this educational and discipleship process is critical in developing individuals who not only know the Scriptures but also embody the virtues and ideals they contain. It calls on religious communities to foster situations in which people are encouraged not only to study the Word of God but also to internalise its teachings, allowing them to permeate every area of their lives.

People who interact with the transformative power of Scripture become living witnesses to the great impact of divine wisdom. They are not only equipped for personal righteousness but also for acts of service and goodness in the world. In summary, 2 Timothy 3:16-17 emphasises the broad scope of spiritual development through Scripture, asking believers to go on a path that transforms their entire being for a life of purpose, service, and devotion.

1. Holistic Development

The biblical parallels emphasise a profound notion of education and discipleship that goes beyond mere knowledge transfer. Instead, they call for a more holistic approach that includes the development of a person's character, values, and faith. The goal is to develop a well-rounded individual who embodies the qualities of love, compassion, and moral integrity, rather than just intellectual growth. This comprehensive growth includes emotional and spiritual aspects, resulting in persons who are resilient, empathic, and strongly linked to their faith. The emphasis is on building an atmosphere within religious communities that fosters the mind, heart, and soul, ensuring that young people emerge not only knowledgeable but also virtuous and firm in their beliefs.

2. Long-Term Impact:

The biblical wisdom provided in 2 Timothy 3:14-15 implies that the impact of education and discipleship is not ephemeral but lasts a lifetime. Early engagement in spiritual education is considered vital, providing the foundation for a long-term relationship with God. The incorporation of spiritual ideas into daily life guarantees that faith is an ever-present guide, influencing decisions, actions, and attitudes at all stages of life. This long-term view encourages religious organisations to prioritise and engage in youth education and discipleship, recognising that seeds planted early can bear fruit throughout their faith journey.

3. The Bible as the Foundation:

The verses of 2 Timothy 3:14-15 emphasise that any meaningful educational programme within religious communities must be based on God's Word. Scripture is the eternal and authoritative guide that provides the concepts, teachings, and tales that create our understanding of faith. This fundamental role of Scripture assures that the education delivered is not arbitrary but rather in accordance with divine wisdom. It encourages religious groups to organise their teachings around sacred texts, highlighting the need of biblical literacy and a real connection with God's Word as fundamental components of spiritual growth.

4. Continuous Engagement

The call to carefully educate in various life situations emphasises the concept of ongoing interaction with spiritual principles. The verses exhort believers to keep a constant dialogue with God, incorporating spiritual lessons into all aspects of their lives. This constant engagement extends beyond the bounds of formal learning environments, stressing the point that faith is not a separate component of one's identity, but rather an intrinsic part of one's existence. Spiritual ideas are not taught and learned in isolated moments in time but are woven into the fabric of daily life. This topic encourages religious organisations to establish circumstances that allow for continuous reflection, conversation, and application of spiritual insight, fostering a relationship with God that pervades every moment and situation in an individual's life.

Strategies for Implementation:

1. Curriculum in Depth:

Religious groups can build educational programmes that effortlessly blend academic disciplines and spiritual teachings to establish a holistic curriculum. This strategy ensures that the students obtain a well-rounded education that tackles not only intellectual development but also spiritual growth. Religious communities provide a comprehensive learning experience that enables students to discover the interconnectedness of knowledge and their faith, by weaving faith into diverse disciplines such as physics, literature, and history. This comprehensive curriculum promotes an environment in which students can investigate the connections between their academic interests and the tenets of their religious beliefs.

2. Programmes for Mentoring and Discipleship:

Creating mentorship and discipleship programmes entails matching experienced members of the religious community with young people. This fosters significant connections that extend beyond formal schooling, providing personalised assistance on the spiritual journey. Mentorship programmes provide a safe space for youngsters to ask questions, discuss spiritual issues, and receive practical counsel on how to apply religious teachings in their daily lives. These programmes not only allow knowledge transfer, but they also contribute to the creation of deep, supporting relationships within the community, promoting a sense of belonging and faith continuity.

3. Participation in the Community:

Encouraging community participation in education and discipleship activities is critical for fostering a shared commitment to the spiritual development of youth. This can mean involving parents, elders, and other community members in educational activities, attending events, and taking part in mentorship programmes. The religious community's broader involvement promotes the idea that education is a collaborative effort, emphasising shared ideals and a unified commitment to fostering the next generation in their faith.

4. Integration of Technology:
Utilising technology is critical for properly engaging the tech-savvy youth. Online platforms, digital resources, and interactive tools can help to improve educational and discipleship programmes. Virtual spaces can help to stimulate debates, offer access to a variety of learning materials, and provide chances for remote mentoring. Religious communities that embrace technology ensure that the message of faith stays current and accessible in the digital era, reaching youth where they are and promoting an environment of continual learning.

5. Applications in Practise:
It is critical to create programmes that assist the practical application of spiritual ideas in order to translate theoretical knowledge into real experiences. This could include organising service projects, mission trips, or other hands-on activities that encourage young people to actively participate in acts of compassion, empathy, and community service. Practical application not only reinforces religious teachings but also helps students to embrace these ideas in their daily lives, building a sense of duty and purpose within the religious community and the larger society.

6. Regular Evaluation
Implementing evaluation systems ensures that education and discipleship programmes stay successful and relevant. Regular assessments enable religious groups to analyse the

impact of their programmes, identify areas for improvement, and adapt their tactics in response to the changing needs of the youth and community. This continuing evaluation process fosters adaptability and response, ensuring that education and discipleship activities remain aligned with the aims of holistic development and lasting effect for the religious community's youth.

Religious communities can design and sustain education and discipleship programmes that have a tremendous impact on the spiritual growth and development of youth, by diving into biblical ideas and gaining inspiration from these fundamental writings. The commitment to investing in the next generation indicates a greater appreciation for the transformational potential of education and discipleship as important components of a vigorous and enduring religion.

1. Prioritising youth educational and spiritual development

Numerous occasions in the Bible emphasise the importance of education and the pursuit of knowledge.
"The fear of Yahweh is the beginning of knowledge," Proverbs 1:7 (WEB) declares, "but the foolish despise wisdom and instruction."

Prioritising youth intellectual and spiritual growth is a timeless need that has its roots not only in modern society but also in ancient wisdom, as evidenced by several passages in the Bible. The sacred literature, particularly Proverbs 1:7, emphasises the profound relationship between the fear of the Lord and the beginning of understanding. This verse acts as a guiding concept, establishing spiritual education as the foundation for the construction of worldly wisdom and insight.

The search of scholastic and spiritual enrichment reveals that these two domains are inextricably linked. The biblical world-view emphasises that true knowledge begins with reverence for the Divine, implying that understanding God's teachings creates the framework for gaining significant insights and discernment in the world. As a result, committing to spiritual study becomes more than just a religious obligation but also a route to holistic enlightenment.

Furthermore, the emphasis on adolescent educational and spiritual growth reflects a broader vision of education that goes beyond purely academic activities. It includes the development of moral ideals, ethical behaviour, and a sense of purpose, as well as the development of persons who are not only intellectually adept but also morally upright and spiritually grounded.

This biblical perspective resonates with the challenges and possibilities that young people confront today. As society gets more complex, the importance of a solid educational foundation that encompasses spiritual and moral components becomes even more apparent. When integrated with spiritual concepts, education provides students with the tools to negotiate the difficulties of the modern world with a moral compass and a resilient spirit.

Prioritising youth educational and spiritual development is a multidimensional endeavour that entails teaching an appreciation for spiritual principles while cultivating a passion for knowledge. It is a call to combine the pursuit of wisdom with an uncompromising dedication to moral ideals, forming individuals who not only thrive in their chosen disciplines but also positively contribute to society's well-being. As we draw inspiration from biblical passages, we are reminded that the journey of education is a transformative process that nurtures the mind, spirit, and character of the youth, empowering them to lead purposeful and impactful lives of spiritual education as the foundation for acquiring worldly wisdom and understanding.

Religious groups must prioritise young spiritual and educational development by providing chances for learning and growth. Offering lessons, workshops, and seminars on Scripture, theology, and moral values is one example. Mentoring programmes and personal instruction from spiritual leaders are very important in supporting young people's intellectual and spiritual development.

Religious communities play a critical role in creating the moral and intellectual environment of the next generation. Recognising this critical role, these communities must actively prioritise the educational and spiritual development of the youth through a range of purposeful programmes.

The introduction of educational programmes within religious institutions is one important option for supporting this development. These communities provide a structured framework for young people to dive deeper into the rich tapestry of their faith by offering lessons, workshops, and seminars on Scripture, theology, and moral values. These educational opportunities not only help them better grasp religious beliefs, but they also foster critical thinking and serious contemplation on how these ideas might be applied to modern issues.

Mentoring programmes are another important component in the overall development of young people in religious communities. Personal supervision from experienced spiritual leaders fosters a supportive environment in which young people can not only learn about their faith but also gain practical insights and advice from those who have travelled a similar route. This mentorship develops a sense of belonging, community, and support, providing a crucial resource for navigating life's complexity.

Furthermore, the incorporation of technology and creative teaching methods inside religious communities can improve the educational experience. To make educational programmes more accessible and interesting for the youth, online platforms, interactive learning tools, and multimedia materials can be used. In a continuously changing world, embracing modern educational methodologies ensures that religious teachings remain current and relatable.

Fostering an atmosphere of open debate is critical in parallel with formal schooling. Providing opportunities for young people to raise questions, express doubts, and engage in meaningful debates helps to foster a dynamic and growing understanding of faith. This promotes a durable and authentic faith that can endure the stresses of the modern world by encouraging a sense of ownership over one's spiritual journey.

Spiritual growth extends beyond the intellectual sphere to include character development and virtue cultivation. Religious communities can help by organising community service programmes, promoting ethical behaviour, and boosting social justice commitment. These initiatives convert spiritual ideas into concrete deeds, encouraging young people to live out their faith in ways that benefit both themselves and the larger community.

In essence, educating and spiritually developing youth within religious communities necessitates a diverse approach. These communities can inspire a generation of individuals who are not only well-versed in their religious traditions but also equipped to navigate the complexities of the modern world with wisdom, compassion, and a strong moral compass. They can accomplish this by providing diverse learning opportunities, fostering mentorship relationships, embracing technological advancements, and promoting a holistic understanding of faith.

2. Putting Thorough Discipleship Programmes in Place

Discipleship entails helping people on their faith journeys and giving them the resources and assistance to help them grow closer to God. Jesus urges His disciples in Matthew 28:19-20 (WEB) to "Go and make disciples of all nations...teaching them to observe all things that I commanded you." This mandate emphasises the importance of complete discipleship programmes in spreading and reinforcing faith teachings.

Religious organisations should develop discipleship programmes that address the requirements of various age groups within the young population. Age-appropriate Bible study groups, mentorship programmes, spiritual retreats, and community service initiatives can all be part of this. Young people can strengthen their connection to their faith and the community through these programmes, while also receiving assistance on how to implement biblical teachings in their daily lives.

As expressed in Matthew 28:19-20, discipleship is a powerful call to action for believers to not only accept their faith but also actively share it with others. This biblical mandate emphasises not only the necessity of personal spiritual progress but also the responsibility to pass on knowledge and wisdom to others. In response, religious communities should design discipleship programmes that are comprehensive, dynamic, and suited to the varying requirements of the youth community's various age groups.

Recognising the distinct stages of spiritual development that individuals go through during their youth is an important component of good discipleship. Religious organisations can create age-appropriate Bible study groups that address the unique issues and questions that different age groups encounter. These clubs build a sense of camaraderie and a shared spiritual journey by providing a supportive atmosphere for young people to explore and improve their understanding of the Scriptures.

Mentorship programmes are important in discipleship because they provide a more personalised and relational approach to spiritual assistance. Creating mentorship relationships between experienced believers and young people gives a forum for exchanging insights, resolving personal problems, and negotiating the complexity of faith in the modern world. Through these interactions, young people not only get spiritual direction but also experience lived instances of faith, prompting them to mimic and internalise Christ's teachings.

Within discipleship programmes, spiritual retreats can be transforming experiences. These retreats provide a reprieve from daily activities, allowing room for meditation, prayer, and greater connection with God. Retreats enable young people to disengage from distractions and focus on their spiritual journey, establishing a genuine engagement with their faith.

Community service projects are another important aspect of discipleship programmes. Engaging in acts of service based on Jesus' teachings of compassion and love demonstrates faith in action. Young disciples not only contribute constructively to society by participating in community service, but they also internalise the ideals of selflessness and humility, transforming their faith into meaningful and concrete influence.

In addition, technology can be used to supplement conventional discipleship approaches. Virtual platforms, internet resources, and interactive apps can help young people access spiritual information at any time and from any location. Incorporating technology into discipleship programmes guarantees that the Christian message remains relevant and accessible in the digital era.

Finally, creating effective discipleship programmes for youth requires a careful and holistic strategy that takes into account the unique needs of different age groups. Religious communities can foster a nurturing environment in which young people not only deepen their relationship with God but also learn to live out their faith authentically in the world, by incorporating age-appropriate study groups, mentorship, spiritual retreats, community service, and leveraging technology.

3. Providing Adolescents with the Skills and Knowledge

To effectively manage the problems of the modern world, it is critical to provide adolescents with appropriate skills and information anchored in religion. In 2 Timothy 2:15 (WEB), the Apostle Paul encourages his young disciple, saying, "Give diligence to present yourself approved by God, a workman who doesn't need to be ashamed, properly handling the Word of Truth." This verse emphasises the importance of both spiritual depth and practical wisdom in the journey of faith.

Religious communities must invest in youth education and practical counsel that addresses modern issues from a faith-based viewpoint. This can involve discussions about ethical decision-making, relationships, media literacy, and social justice. By providing adolescents with a strong moral compass, critical thinking abilities, and a thorough understanding of their faith, they will be able to effectively navigate the complexity of the modern world.

The powerful impact of discipleship programmes goes far beyond religious ceremonies; it pervades the entire fabric of people's lives, turning them into beacons of faith and compassion. As believers respond to the call of Matthew 28:19-20, a dynamic tapestry of spiritual growth, information sharing, and transforming encounters unfolds within the outlines of these comprehensive discipleship projects.

Recognising the various stages of spiritual development that characterise adolescence, religious societies become designers of specialised discipleship techniques. Age-appropriate Bible study groups develop as safe havens for young minds to wrestle with the complexities of Scripture, discovering not just answers but also a supportive community that shares in the collective journey of comprehending and applying their faith's teachings. Camaraderie thrives in these gatherings, forming relationships that strengthen individuals in their spiritual search.

Mentorship programmes, which are an essential component of effective discipleship, enable a personal and relational approach to spiritual teaching. Seasoned believers become live testaments to the enduring power of faith as a result of these mentorship connections. They negotiate the maze of obstacles that modern life presents as seasoned guides, providing essential insights and practical examples of how to implement Christ's teachings. These connections' reciprocity creates a dynamic interchange of wisdom and inspiration.

Spiritual retreats within discipleship programmes are extremely transforming. These retreats serve as sanctuaries for meditation, prayer, and communication with God, providing refuge from the tumult of daily life. Young people immerse themselves in a meaningful encounter with their faith here, amidst the calm of nature or the tranquillity of hallowed sites, emerging renewed and spiritually invigorated.

Community service projects are a visible reflection of discipleship in action. These efforts, founded on Jesus' teachings of compassion and love, move young disciples into the arena of selfless service. By performing acts of kindness and constructively contributing to society, they internalise virtues of humility and empathy, bridging the gap between their religion and the practical needs of the world around them.

Technology effortlessly interacts with conventional discipleship methods in the digital age, providing a diverse platform for continual learning. Virtual environments, internet resources, and interactive apps transcend physical barriers, allowing young people to access spiritual content whenever and wherever they want. This integration guarantees that the faith message remains relevant and resonant, bridging the gap between ancient knowledge and modern concerns.

Finally, effective youth discipleship programmes take a careful and holistic approach that reflects the unique needs of different age groups. Religious communities foster a caring environment by combining age-appropriate study groups, mentorship, spiritual retreats, community service, and technology. Young people not only improve their relationship with God in this atmosphere, but they also learn to truly act out their religion, becoming catalysts for positive change in the world.

Conclusion:

Investing in education and discipleship is critical for the holistic development of religious youth. We establish a strong foundation for their religious journey by prioritising their educational and spiritual progress, executing extensive discipleship programmes, and providing them with necessary skills and knowledge. As we consider the biblical allusions that emphasise the need of investing in education and discipleship, we are reminded of our obligation to nurture and guide the youth, enabling them to become faithful and resilient individuals in the world around them.

Prioritising Youth Educational and Spiritual Development:

Prioritising the educational and spiritual development of youth is critical from the standpoint of the Christian Church, as they are not only the Church's future but also valuable members of the Body of Christ in the present. The Bible contains concepts and counsel that emphasise the significance of nurturing and equipping the next generation. Consider the following biblical references and principles:

1. Proverbs 22:6 — Holistic and Intentional Education:
Proverbs 22:6 serves as a guiding principle for intentional and holistic education, emphasising the obligation to train up young people in the Lord's ways. This verse emphasises the importance of deliberate and purposeful education, not merely in academic issues but more importantly in religious matters. According to this chapter, prioritising the intellectual and spiritual development of adolescents entails transmitting biblical principles that shape their sense of morality, ethics, and the character of God. It goes beyond the classroom to include a holistic approach that nurtures their minds, hearts, and characters. The emphasis is on developing a strong foundation of religion early in life, which will serve as a guiding factor throughout their paths.

2. Deuteronomy 6:6-7 — Intentional and Consistent Teaching:
Deuteronomy 6:6-7 lays out a plan for regular and focused teaching, emphasising the importance of incorporating God's rules into all aspects of daily life. Prioritising youth intellectual and spiritual development, according to this chapter, entails building an atmosphere in which faith concepts are not compartmentalised but are seamlessly integrated into daily activities. It encourages parents, elders, and educators to have continual talks about God's Word, allowing it to become a natural part of family life and

community connections. The comprehensive method indicated here anticipates a constant immersion in spiritual teachings, promoting an environment in which adolescents can consistently learn, question, and apply these concepts throughout their lives.

3. Psalm 78:4 — Transmitting God's Faithfulness:

Psalm 78:4 emphasises the need of passing on stories and testimonials of God's faithfulness to future generations. This verse emphasises the significance of telling the stories of God's work, especially His laudable works, might, and miracles. Prioritising youth spiritual growth, as indicated by this verse, entails making sure that the rich history of God's interactions with His people is not hidden but publicly shared. It necessitates a dedication to retelling and praising God's faithfulness throughout history as well as within the context of one's faith community. This purposeful storytelling promotes a sense of identification, connection, and continuity within the faith, laying the groundwork for the youth's personal religious journey.

In essence, these Scriptures guide the Christian perspective on the importance of young educational and spiritual growth. They advocate for purposeful and holistic education, regular integration of faith into daily life, and narrative to pass along God's faithfulness. Together, these principles contribute to a complete approach that tries to influence the character, values, and spiritual foundation of the faith community's younger generation.

Consider the following practical ways for prioritising youth educational and spiritual development:

1. Age-Appropriate Education:

Tailoring teaching techniques, resources, and programmes to the individual needs and developmental stages of youth is more than a pedagogical strategy; it is the foundation of effective and impactful education within a faith community. Recognising the youths' different ages, interests, and cognitive capacities is critical for developing a dynamic and inclusive educational atmosphere that truly promotes their spiritual growth. The following points expand on the significance and practicalities of personalising education for youth:

A. Understanding Distinctive Qualities:
Recognising that different age groups have distinctive characteristics and developmental needs is the first step in properly personalising instruction. Adolescents, for example, can be struggling with identity formation and complex moral reasoning, whereas younger young people might benefit more from hands-on activities and visual aids. Understanding these distinct features enables educators and leaders to provide information and activities that are appropriate for each group's developmental stage.

B. Using Creative and Interactive Methods
Creativity and engagement are essential components of age-appropriate learning. The use of multimedia presentations, hands-on activities, and group discussions not only accommodates to the diverse learning styles of young people, but it also makes the educational experience more interesting and memorable. Visual aids, technology integration, and interactive exercises help to bring biblical teachings to

life, allowing young people to connect with and internalise the lessons in meaningful ways.

C. How to Recognise Individual Learning Styles

Each adolescent has a distinct learning style that is impacted by characteristics such as cognitive preferences, personality, and prior experiences. Tailoring education entails recognising and respecting these unique learning styles. Some people excel at visual learning, while others prefer aural or kinaesthetic methods. Educators may build a more inclusive and successful learning environment by identifying and adapting these variances, ensuring that each kid can grasp and apply the teachings in a way that meets their own abilities.

D. Encouraging a Dynamic and Inclusive Environment

A developmentally appropriate educational method provides a dynamic and inclusive environment in which every youth feels seen, appreciated, and inspired to engage actively. Leaders can provide a secure space for open talks and religious inquiries by respecting the diversity among the young community. This inclusivity fosters a sense of belonging, encouraging young people to express themselves and engage with the content in ways that reflect their many viewpoints and backgrounds.

E. Inspiring Youth Participation

Tailoring education for youth entails deliberate attempts to encourage their participation. Incorporating features that correspond with their interests, whether cultural, technological, or artistic, aids in capturing and maintaining their attention. This motivation is critical for instilling in young people a positive attitude towards learning about faith, as well as inspiring a lifetime curiosity and exploration of their spiritual path.

Finally, adapting teaching techniques, resources, and programmes to the individual requirements and developmental phases of youth is a purposeful and intentional strategy that improves the effectiveness of education within a faith community. It recognises youth diversity, encourages creativity and interactivity, and respects individual learning styles, ultimately creating an environment in which youth are inspired to actively participate and explore their faith in ways that align with their unique stages of development.

2. Youth Bible Studies

It is important to create an intimate and supportive space for exploring and increasing their grasp of God's Word via frequent small-group Bible studies designed for youth. These studies should target current difficulties and obstacles in their lives. Encourage open dialogue, inquiries, and the application of biblical ideas to their everyday lives. This approach not only improves their understanding of Scripture but also allows for a more personalised and interactive investigation of faith, developing a sense of community and a shared spiritual journey among the youth.

Organising regular small-group Bible studies for youth reflects a deliberate and effective method to nurture their spiritual development within a faith community. This method acknowledges the distinct demands and dynamics of the youth demographic and seeks to create a space that goes beyond standard education. Here's a more in-depth look at the relevance and essential components of these customised small-group Bible studies:

A. Support and Intimacy:

Small group settings naturally encourage intimacy and support. A forum where youth can express their views, concerns, and questions in a more personal environment is vital for those navigating the challenges of adolescence and young adulthood. Because these groups are small, true connections can grow, resulting in a supportive environment in which people feel heard, understood, and supported in their faith journeys.

B. Exploring the Word of God in Context:

Tailoring Bible studies for youth entails tackling contemporary themes and challenges in their lives. Connecting Scripture's timeless principles with real-life problems and questions that today's youth encounter helps to bridge the gap between ancient teachings and modern experiences. This contextual investigation deepens their knowledge of God's Word by highlighting its relevance to their current situation, establishing a stronger relationship to the biblical story.

C. Questions and Open Discussions:

Encouraging open discussions and inviting inquiries provides a dynamic learning environment. In their search for knowledge and purpose, youth may have a variety of opinions and questions about faith and life. Small-group Bible studies create a secure environment for these discussions, allowing individuals to express themselves, share personal experiences, and seek clarification on biblical principles. This openness not only improves the learning experience, but it also helps to build critical thinking skills and a solid faith foundation.

D. Applying Biblical Principles:
One of the primary purposes of these specialised courses is to make it easier for young people to apply biblical concepts in their daily lives. Discussing how Scripture's teachings relate to their experiences, challenges, and decisions allows individuals to integrate faith into their daily lives. This practical application promotes a complete knowledge of Christianity, by emphasising that God's Word's lessons are relevant and transforming in their journey through adolescence and young adulthood.

E. Personalised and Interactive Exploration:
A more personalised and engaging examination of faith is possible in a small group environment. Each person can actively participate in the material by contributing to debates and offering thoughts. This participatory style encourages youth to take responsibility for their spiritual progress by instilling a sense of ownership in their religion journey. It also allows for peer-to-peer learning as participants learn from one another's viewpoints and experiences, further reinforcing the group's feeling of community.

F. Improving Community Spirit:
These small-group Bible studies help to build a close-knit community among the youth. A shared examination of God's Word, mutual support, and

collective participation in conversations all contribute to a sense of belonging. The group transforms into a spiritual family, with members walking alongside one another, sharing the joys and hardships of their faith journeys. This shared experience develops long-lasting bonds and promotes the notion that individuals are not alone in their quest for a greater grasp of God's Word.

Finally, organising specialised small-group Bible studies for youth is a deliberate and purposeful way to develop a rich and supportive atmosphere for their spiritual growth. These studies contribute considerably to the holistic development of youth within a faith community through intimacy, contextual exploration, open conversations, practical application, participatory exploration, and a sense of community.

3. Relationships with Mentors:

Matching young people with older Christian mentors is an effective technique for giving personalised direction and support in their religious journey. These mentorship relationships provide a forum for discussing personal issues, sharing hardships, and learning from the experiences of others. Regular one-on-one or small group encounters foster a trusting environment, allowing for deeper spiritual growth. Mentors act as role models, providing knowledge, support, and a sense of belonging, while assisting youth in navigating the obstacles of adolescence and developing a strong foundation in their religion.

Pairing young people with experienced Christian mentors is a planned and effective technique that recognises the importance of personal supervision and support in a religious community's youth faith journey. Beyond traditional educational techniques, this mentorship model aims to create a more personalised and connected foundation for spiritual growth. (For a more in-depth look at the significance and the important components of mentoring relationships for young people, see Chapter 5: Empowering Youth Leadership.)

Finally, matching young people with older Christian mentors is a holistic and relational method that addresses the unique needs and obstacles that youth face on their religious journey. Mentorship becomes a transformative force, nurturing the spiritual growth and development of the next generation within the faith community, through personalised guidance, answering individual questions, regular meetings, creating a supportive environment, building trust, role modelling wisdom, and navigating the challenges of adolescence.

4. Projects of Service and Outreach:

Engaging youth in service and outreach projects allows them to put their beliefs into action in a hands-on way. These projects allow them to put their skills and talents to work for the Kingdom of God, establishing a feeling of purpose and communal responsibility. Encourage participation in programmes that have a direct influence on their community, instilling a desire to serve others and promoting a comprehensive perspective of Christian discipleship. Youth who actively participate in service not only contribute positively to society, but they also create a stronger connection between their faith and real-world applications.

Engaging young people in service and outreach projects is a dynamic and effective technique that goes beyond theoretical understanding, actively involving young people in the actual manifestation of their religion. This hands-on approach allows them to apply biblical principles to real-world problems, developing a comprehensive grasp of Christian discipleship. Here's a more in-depth look at the importance and major factors of incorporating youth in service and outreach projects:

A. Practical Application of Faith:

Service and outreach programmes give young people a real way to put their faith into action. Engaging in hands-on projects allows youth to actually display love, compassion, and service to others rather than simply learning about Christian ideals in a classroom setting. This experiential learning approach is helpful in cementing the link between their religious beliefs and their practical implementation in the world.

B. Using Your Skills and Talents:

These projects allow young people to find and use their unique abilities and talents for the Kingdom of God. Service projects allow young people to serve in ways that correspond with their capabilities, whether through event planning, creative arts, or technical skills. This not only helps students recognise their abilities, but it also gives them a feeling of purpose and fulfilment in using their talents for the greater good.

C. Developing a Sense of Purpose:

Participating in service projects gives adolescents a sense of purpose and meaning. Understanding that their actions can have a good impact on others and contribute to the community's well-being instills a strong sense of fulfilment. This sense of purpose becomes a driving force in their lives, inspiring people to continue looking for ways to make a positive difference in the lives of others.

D. Community Service and Connection:
Service and outreach projects inspire youth to adopt a feeling of communal responsibility. They develop a heightened awareness of the problems around them by actively participating in programmes that directly influence their local community. This increased awareness develops a sense of belonging to the larger community, reinforcing the concept that their faith requires them to be actively involved in addressing social concerns and contributing to the well-being of others.

E. Promoting a Holistic View of Discipleship:
Youth obtain a complete view of Christian discipleship through involvement in service projects. Discipleship is more than just intellectual pursuits or spiritual practises; it also includes practical, loving action in the world. This holistic viewpoint promotes the notion that living one's faith entails a balance of knowledge, spiritual growth, and active service to others.

F. Contributing to Society in a Positive Way:
Youth can positively contribute to society by actively participating in service programmes. Their acts have a direct impact on the well-being of individuals and communities, whether through community clean-up efforts, food drives, or outreach programmes. This positive contribution promotes civic duty and

strengthens the notion that faith is inextricably tied to social justice and societal well-being.

G. Bridging the Gap Between Faith and Action:
Service initiatives allow students to see the direct connection between their beliefs and real-world applications. Their religious principles and teachings come to life when they actively engage in acts of service and outreach. This experiential learning method allows them to have a better knowledge of the practical ramifications of their faith, fostering a more real and lived expression of Christian principles.

To summarise, including youth in service and outreach programmes not only allows them to actively apply their faith but also instils a sense of purpose, community duty, and a comprehensive understanding of Christian discipleship. Through these programmes, young people make a meaningful contribution to society, gain practical skills, and strengthen the bond between faith and action, building a lifelong commitment to service and compassionate living.

5. Integrate Technology
In the digital age, leveraging technology is critical for supplementing educational and spiritual development. Make available internet tools, devotionals, podcasts, and interactive apps that enhance biblical comprehension and spiritual growth. Technology integration ensures that educational materials remain relevant, engaging, and accessible to today's tech-savvy students. Using digital tools to enable continuous learning allows students to explore and strengthen their faith outside of typical classroom settings.

Using technology to enhance educational and spiritual growth is a critical strategy, especially in a digital age where connectivity and accessibility play critical roles in the lives of the young people. Integrating diverse digital tools ensures that educational materials remain relevant, engaging, and accessible to a technologically savvy age. Here's a more in-depth look at the significance and major components of using technology for youth education and spiritual growth:

A. Online Resource Access:

Technology has enabled a plethora of online tools to supplement traditional learning techniques. By giving youth access to curated websites, publications, and online libraries, they can learn about biblical studies, theology, and spiritual practises. This accessibility allows individuals to explore further into certain topics of interest, supporting a self-directed and exploratory learning method.

B. Podcasts and Devotionals:

Digital platforms provide a vast library of devotionals and podcasts that adapt to a wide range of learning styles. Youth can engage in informative debates, biblical teachings, and inspirational stories through written or audio content. Individuals can acquire spiritual insight through listening, reflection, and discussion in this dynamic and participatory format, which fits diverse learning styles.

C. Interactive Applications:

Interactive apps for spiritual development provide a hands-on and engaging experience. These apps could contain daily devotionals, interactive Bible studies, prayer guides, and discussion forums. These apps provide an immersive learning environment by including gamification aspects or interactive features, making spiritual development more pleasurable and participative for tech-savvy youngsters.

D. Attention and Engagement:
Technology keeps educational materials relevant and engaging for today's youth. Using multimedia features such as movies, graphics, and animations can improve the presentation of biblical teachings and make them more approachable to the audience. This method connects with a generation that is accustomed to visual and interactive content, boosting their receptivity and participation in the learning process.

E. Ongoing Education:
Digital tools support continual learning by allowing access to content at any time and from any location. Youth can engage with educational and spiritual materials outside of typical classroom settings, whether through e-books, online courses, or virtual discussions. This adaptability accommodates their hectic schedules while also encouraging a lifelong quest for knowledge and spiritual improvement.

F. Beyond Boundaries Exploration:
Technology removes geographical constraints, allowing young people to learn about religious communities and cultural situations from around the world. Virtual connections and online platforms allow them to converse with people from around the globe, extending their understanding of spirituality and

promoting a more open and interconnected world-view.

G. Teaching Methods Innovation:
The incorporation of technology promotes innovation in teaching approaches. Virtual reality (VR), augmented reality (AR), and other developing technologies can create immersive learning experiences that bring biblical narratives to life. These novel ways capture the attention of young people, making their educational experience more memorable and meaningful.

H. Digital Platforms for Community Building
By providing forums for virtual gatherings, talks, and joint projects, digital tools aid in community formation. Online forums, social media groups, and video conferencing allow adolescents to connect with others who share their interests, share insights, and develop a supportive digital community to supplement their in-person connections within the religious community.

I. Learning Preferences Adaptation:
Technology enables customisation and adaption to individual learning preferences. Whether a person prefers visual content, interactive exercises, or written materials, digital platforms can accommodate a variety of learning styles. This adaptability ensures that educational and spiritual resources are tailored to each youth's specific needs and preferences.

Finally, leveraging technology for educational and spiritual development is a strategic and necessary approach in today's context. Religious communities can meet the evolving needs of tech-savvy youth by providing access to online resources, devotionals, podcasts, and interactive apps, and by embracing innovative teaching methods, fostering a dynamic and constantly evolving journey of faith and knowledge.

6. Promoting Genuine Worship:
Allowing youth to actively participate in worship services fosters a sense of belonging and ownership in the faith community. Participating in the worship team, leading prayers, sharing testimonies, or participating in creative arts fosters an environment in which their voices and contributions are valued and celebrated. Encourage authentic worship that is appropriate for their cultural and generational context, promoting a diverse and inclusive worship experience. By actively involving youth in worship, you not only nurture their spiritual growth, but you also contribute to the vibrancy and authenticity of the worship life of the entire faith community.

Providing opportunities for youth to actively participate in worship services is a transformative strategy that not only nurtures their spiritual growth but also significantly contributes to the vibrancy and authenticity of the worship life of the entire faith community. Here's a more in-depth look at the significance and key components of involving youth in worship:

A. Promoting a Feeling of Belonging:
Engaging youth in worship services actively promotes a sense of belonging within the faith community. They feel a stronger connection to the community and a sense of ownership in the shared spiritual journey

when they actively contribute to the worship experience, whether through music, prayers, or other creative expressions.

B. Appreciating and Honouring Contributions:
Involving youth in worship or other aspects of the service sends a strong message that their voices and contributions are valued and celebrated. This affirmation is critical for their spiritual development and confidence, as it encourages them to actively participate and share their unique gifts and talents within the faith community.

C. Worship Experience that is Diverse and Inclusive:
Actively engaging youth in worship allows them to express authentic worship that is relevant to their cultural and generational context. This diversity contributes to a more inclusive worship experience by reflecting the demographic richness of the faith community. Embracing various worship styles and creative expressions ensures that the worship environment resonates with a diverse range of participants.

D. Promoting Leadership Positions:
Allowing youth to lead prayers, share testimonies, or participate in creative arts encourages the development of leadership skills. These experiences not only help them grow personally but also prepare them to take on more active roles in the faith community. It develops leadership skills that extend beyond the worship setting and into other aspects of their lives.

E. Promoting Genuine Worship:

Youths' active participation in worship fosters authentic worship experiences. Their genuine faith, enthusiasm, and passion contribute to a dynamic and spiritually vibrant environment. Authenticity in worship connects with all members of the faith community, fostering a deeper connection to the Divine and improving the overall worship environment.

F. Developing Creative Expressions:

Involving youth in creative arts during worship services fosters a culture of creativity. This could include music, visual arts, drama, or other innovative forms of worship. Giving these creative expressions a platform allows youth to engage with their faith in ways that resonate with their generation, making worship more meaningful and relevant to their experiences.

G. Developing a Leadership Pipeline:

Involving youth in worship actively creates a pipeline for future leaders in the faith community. They gain valuable experience and skills as they take on roles in worship services, which they can then transfer to other leadership positions. This intentional cultivation of leadership potential ensures a smooth transition of responsibilities within the community over time.

H. Contributing to Vibrancy and Authenticity:

The active involvement of youth infuses energy, enthusiasm, and authenticity into worship services. Their fresh perspectives, passion, and innovative ideas contribute to the overall vibrancy of the faith community. The intergenerational collaboration in worship reflects the diversity of the community and strengthens the authenticity of the worship experience.

In conclusion, actively involving youth in worship services is a holistic approach that goes beyond mere participation; it fosters a sense of belonging, celebrates their contributions, promotes diversity, encourages leadership development, cultivates creative expressions, builds a leadership pipeline, and contributes to the vibrancy and authenticity of the entire faith community's worship life. This intentional inclusion ensures that worship becomes a dynamic and inclusive expression of the collective faith journey.

Remember to create a safe and welcoming environment where youth can ask questions, express doubts, and grow their understanding of God. Empower them to become leaders, disciples, and active participants in the Church community. Seek guidance from experienced youth pastors, educators and parents who can provide wisdom and support in effectively nurturing the younger generation.

By prioritising the educational and spiritual development of youth, Christian churches invest in the future of the Church while empowering young individuals to live out their faith, impact their communities, and become lifelong disciples of Christ.

Creating a safe and welcoming environment for youth within the Christian Church is essential for fostering a thriving community where young individuals can freely explore their faith, ask questions, and express doubts. This environment should empower them to become leaders, disciples, and active participants in the broader Church community. Here's an expanded exploration of the key elements involved in establishing such an environment:

Creating a Safe and Welcoming Environment for the Youth:

1. Open Dialogue:
A nurturing environment for youth encourages open dialogue and welcomes questions. It's crucial to create a space where young individuals feel comfortable expressing their doubts and seeking answers. This approach fosters a culture of curiosity and continuous exploration of faith, allowing youth to grow in their understanding of God and Christianity.

2. Empowering Youth Leadership:
Empowerment is a fundamental aspect of creating a welcoming environment. Provide opportunities for youth to take on leadership roles within the Church community. This may include involvement in planning events, leading worship, participating in decision-making processes, or engaging in outreach initiatives. By entrusting them with responsibilities, youth develop a sense of ownership in the community and gain valuable leadership experience.

3. Discipleship and Mentorship Programs:
Implement discipleship and mentorship programs that pair youth with experienced leaders, pastors, or mature members of the congregation. These programs create meaningful relationships where young individuals can receive guidance, support, and wisdom from those who have walked the path of faith for a longer time. Mentorship provides a personalised approach to spiritual growth and helps youth navigate the complexities of their faith journey.

4. Safe and Inclusive Community:

Establishing a safe and inclusive community is paramount. Youth should feel accepted and valued for who they are. This involves fostering an environment free from judgment, where diversity is celebrated, and each individual feels seen and heard. An inclusive community promotes a sense of belonging, encouraging youth to actively engage in Church life.

5. Guidance from Experienced Leaders:

Seek guidance from experienced youth pastors, educators, and parents who can provide wisdom and support in effectively nurturing the younger generation. Drawing on the experience of those who have successfully worked with youth can offer insights into best practices, potential challenges, and effective strategies for creating a positive and impactful environment.

6. Educational Programs:

Prioritise educational programs that cater to the specific needs and interests of youth. These programs should go beyond traditional approaches, incorporating interactive and technology-enhanced methods to capture and maintain their attention. The goal is to make educational experiences enjoyable, relevant, and conducive to spiritual growth.

7. Cultivating Lifelong Discipleship:

The overarching aim of creating a welcoming environment for youth is to cultivate lifelong discipleship. By investing in their spiritual and educational development, Christian churches contribute to the long-term commitment of young individuals to their faith. The Church becomes a place where youth not only learn about Christianity but also actively live out their faith, impact their communities, and continue their journey as disciples of Christ throughout their lives.

In conclusion, the establishment of a safe and welcoming environment for youth in the Christian Church involves encouraging questions, empowering youth leadership, implementing discipleship programs, fostering inclusivity, seeking guidance from experienced leaders, prioritising relevant educational programs, and ultimately cultivating a culture of lifelong discipleship. This holistic approach ensures that the Church becomes a nurturing and transformative space for young individuals to grow spiritually, engage actively, and carry their faith into the future.

Implementing Comprehensive Discipleship Programmes that Meet the Needs of Different Age Groups:

Here are some steps you may consider:

1. Assess the Needs: Start by assessing the specific discipleship needs of different age groups within your Church community. Consider conducting surveys or interviews to gather information on spiritual growth, challenges, and learning preferences.

Assessing the needs of different age groups within a Church community is a critical first step in developing effective discipleship programs. This process involves understanding the unique characteristics, challenges, and learning preferences of individuals at various stages of life. Here's an expanded exploration of this essential step:

A. Understanding Spiritual Growth:

Begin the assessment by gaining a deep understanding of the spiritual growth trajectories within the Church community. Recognise that individuals at different ages may be experiencing distinct phases of their faith journeys. Consider the foundational aspects of faith for young people, the identity formation for teenagers, and the depth of theological exploration for adults.

B. Conducting Surveys and Interviews:
Utilise surveys and interviews as valuable tools for gathering insights. Develop targeted questionnaires that explore spiritual practices, areas of spiritual growth, and perceived challenges. Interviews can provide qualitative data, allowing individuals to express their thoughts, experiences, and desires for discipleship in a more nuanced manner. Ensure that the survey questions are age-appropriate and sensitive to the diverse needs of the congregation.

C. Identifying Learning Preferences:
Assess the learning preferences of different age groups to tailor discipleship programs accordingly. Some individuals may thrive in interactive group discussions, while others may prefer personal study. Understanding how various age groups engage with educational materials helps in crafting discipleship initiatives that resonate with their preferred learning styles.

D. Analysing Challenges and Concerns:
Explore the challenges and concerns faced by different age groups in their faith journeys. This could include obstacles such as doubt, time constraints, or

a lack of resources. Identifying these challenges allows for the development of discipleship programs that address specific needs, providing support and guidance where it is most needed.

E. Considering Developmental Stages:
Recognise the developmental stages of individuals within each age group. Young people, teenagers, young adults, and older adults have unique needs based on their cognitive, emotional, and social development. Tailoring discipleship programs to align with these stages ensures that the content and approach are developmentally appropriate and resonate with the life experiences of each group.

F. Incorporating Technology:
Assess the role of technology in the lives of different age groups. Consider whether certain age brackets are more inclined to use digital platforms for learning and engagement. This insight allows for the integration of technology into discipleship programs, ensuring accessibility and relevance for all members of the Church community.

G. Analysing Existing Programs:
Evaluate the effectiveness of existing discipleship programs within the Church. Assess what has worked well and where improvements are needed. Analysing the strengths and weaknesses of current initiatives provides a foundation for refining and enhancing discipleship efforts to better meet the needs of the community.

H. Ensuring Inclusivity:

Pay attention to inclusivity by considering the needs of diverse demographics within the Church community. This includes individuals with varying cultural backgrounds, learning abilities, and life experiences. An inclusive assessment ensures that discipleship programs are designed to meet the needs of the entire congregation, fostering a sense of unity and belonging.

I. Considering Family Dynamics:
Recognise the role of family dynamics in discipleship. Assess how different age groups within families can engage in discipleship together. Understanding family structures and dynamics helps in developing programs that cater to the holistic spiritual growth of families, recognising that discipleship is not only an individual but also a communal journey.

J. Creating a Discipleship Task Force:
Form a discipleship task force or committee that includes representatives from different age groups. This diverse group can provide valuable insights and perspectives, ensuring that the assessment is comprehensive and reflective of the entire Church community.

In conclusion, assessing the needs of different age groups within a Church community is a multifaceted process that involves understanding spiritual growth, conducting surveys and interviews, identifying learning preferences, analysing challenges, considering developmental stages, incorporating technology, evaluating existing programs, ensuring inclusivity, and recognising family dynamics. This comprehensive approach lays the groundwork for developing discipleship programs that are tailored to the specific needs and dynamics of the congregation, fostering a more impactful and inclusive spiritual journey for all members.

2. Formulate Objectives: Based on the needs assessment, outline clear objectives for each age group. These objectives should align with biblical principles and the overall mission of the Church. Examples could include fostering spiritual formation, equipping believers for ministry, nurturing a Christ-centred world-view, and developing strong faith foundations.

Formulating clear objectives for each age group is a crucial step in the development of effective discipleship programs within a Church community. These objectives serve as guiding principles that align with biblical teachings and contribute to the overarching mission of the Church. Here's an in-depth exploration of the process of formulating such objectives:

A. Fostering Spiritual Formation:
Objective: Cultivate a deep and personal relationship with God among individuals at every stage of life. Rationale: Spiritual formation is the core of discipleship. By focusing on fostering spiritual growth, the Church aims to guide individuals in developing a meaningful and transformative connection with God. This objective involves encouraging practices such as prayer, meditation, and studying Scripture, fostering a continuous journey of spiritual development.

B. Equipping Believers for Ministry:

Objective: Equip believers with the knowledge, skills, and spiritual maturity necessary for active ministry.
Rationale: Discipleship is not only about personal growth but also about preparing individuals to serve others. This objective aims to empower members of the Church community to identify and utilise their unique gifts for the betterment of the Church and the broader community. It involves providing practical training, mentorship, and opportunities for hands-on ministry experiences.

C. Nurturing a Christ-entered World-view:
Objective: Instill a Christ-centred world-view that influences how individuals perceive and engage with the world.
Rationale: Discipleship extends beyond the walls of the Church. This objective seeks to shape the perspectives and values of individuals in alignment with the teachings of Christ. It involves exploring how faith informs ethical decision-making, social engagement, and relationships, fostering a world-view rooted in love, justice, and compassion.

D. Developing Strong Faith Foundations:
Objective: Establish and strengthen the foundational beliefs and doctrines of the Christian faith among individuals of all ages.
Rationale: A solid understanding of foundational Christian beliefs is essential for a resilient and enduring faith. This objective involves systematic teaching of core doctrines, biblical principles, and theological concepts. It aims to equip believers with a robust foundation that can withstand challenges, doubts, and external influences.

E. Encouraging Discipleship in Daily Life:
Objective: Encourage the integration of discipleship principles into everyday life, fostering a continuous and practical application of faith.
Rationale: Discipleship is not confined to specific Church activities but should permeate every aspect of life. This objective focuses on helping individuals live out their faith authentically in their families, workplaces, and communities. It involves providing guidance on applying biblical principles to real-life situations and nurturing a lifestyle of discipleship.

F. Building Intergenerational Connections:
Objective: Facilitate meaningful connections and mentorship opportunities between different age groups within the Church.
Rationale: Intergenerational relationships are essential for a holistic discipleship experience. This objective aims to create a sense of community where wisdom is shared across generations. It involves fostering mentorship programs, joint activities, and collaborative learning experiences that bridge the gap between older and younger members of the Church.

G. Promoting a Culture of Inclusivity:
Objective: Ensure that discipleship programs are inclusive and accessible to individuals with diverse backgrounds, abilities, and life experiences.
Rationale: Discipleship should be inclusive, recognising the diversity within the Church community. This objective focuses on creating discipleship materials, activities, and environments that accommodate the unique needs of all members.

It involves promoting an atmosphere where every individual feels welcomed and valued in their journey of faith.

H. Measuring Spiritual Growth:
Objective: Develop mechanisms to measure and track the spiritual growth of individuals over time.
Rationale: To assess the effectiveness of discipleship programs, it is essential to have measurable outcomes. This objective involves creating evaluation tools, progress metrics, and feedback mechanisms that enable the Church to understand the impact of discipleship initiatives on the spiritual development of individuals.

I. Promoting Personal Responsibility in Discipleship:
Objective: Encourage individuals to take personal responsibility for their discipleship journey, actively seeking growth and engagement.
Rationale: Discipleship is a partnership between the individual and the Church. This objective empowers individuals to proactively pursue their spiritual growth, engage in self-directed study, and seek out opportunities for mentorship and community involvement.

J. Aligning Objectives with Church Mission:
Objective: Ensure that the formulated discipleship objectives align harmoniously with the overall mission and vision of the Church.

Rationale: The discipleship objectives should seamlessly integrate with the broader goals of the Church. This involves aligning the discipleship mission with the core values, vision, and purpose of the Church community to create a cohesive and unified approach to spiritual development.

In conclusion, formulating objectives for each age group within a Church community involves a thoughtful process that aligns with biblical principles and the overarching mission of the Church. These objectives are not static but evolve over time as the needs and dynamics of the congregation change. By establishing clear and meaningful objectives, the Church can create discipleship programs that are intentional, impactful, and conducive to the spiritual growth of every individual within the community.

3. Curriculum Development: Develop curriculum materials that align with the objectives and incorporate biblical teachings. Utilise various resources, including the Bible, study guides, devotionals, books, and multimedia tools. Ensure age-appropriate content with engaging and relevant teaching approaches.

Curriculum development is a crucial aspect of designing effective discipleship programs within a Church community. Developing a well-structured curriculum ensures that educational materials align with the established objectives, incorporating biblical teachings and fostering an environment conducive to spiritual growth. Here's an in-depth exploration of the curriculum development process:

A. Aligning with Objectives:
Objective: Ensure that the curriculum directly supports the outlined discipleship objectives for each age group.
Process: Begin by carefully reviewing the formulated objectives. Identify key themes, topics, and learning

outcomes that should be addressed in the curriculum. Every element of the curriculum, from lesson plans to supplementary materials, should align with the overarching discipleship goals.

B. Incorporating Biblical Teachings:
Objective: Integrate foundational biblical teachings, principles, and narratives into the curriculum.
Process: Design curriculum materials that prioritise the Word of God. This involves selecting relevant passages from the Bible, creating study guides that explore key theological concepts, and incorporating biblical narratives that resonate with the developmental stages of each age group. Ensure that the curriculum emphasises the centrality of Scripture in shaping the understanding of faith.

C. Utilising Various Resources:
Objective: Utilise a diverse range of resources, including the Bible, study guides, devotionals, books, and multimedia tools.
Process: Curate a collection of resources that cater to different learning styles and preferences. Incorporate traditional materials like printed study guides and devotional books for in-depth reading. Integrate multimedia tools such as videos, podcasts, and interactive apps to appeal to the tech-savvy youth. Ensure that these resources are not only informative but also engaging and accessible.

D. Ensuring Age-Appropriate Content:
Objective: Tailor the content of the curriculum to the specific needs and developmental stages of each age group.

Process: Recognise the unique characteristics, interests, and challenges faced by different age groups. Design age-appropriate content that speaks to their experiences and encourages active participation. For example, consider using storytelling and visual aids for the youngest people, while providing more in-depth theological discussions for teenagers and adults.

E. Creating Engaging Teaching Approaches:
Objective: Foster engagement through teaching approaches that are creative, interactive, and relevant.
Process: Design lessons that go beyond traditional lecture formats. Incorporate interactive activities, group discussions, case studies, and real-life applications of biblical principles. Integrate multimedia elements such as videos, graphics, and music to enhance the learning experience. By creating dynamic and participatory sessions, the curriculum can capture the attention and interest of learners.

F. Adapting to Learning Styles:
Objective: Acknowledge and accommodate diverse learning styles within the Church community.
Process: Recognise that individuals have different preferences when it comes to learning. Some may thrive in visual environments, while others prefer textual or auditory learning. Ensure that the curriculum includes a mix of learning modalities, allowing participants to engage with the material in ways that resonate with their preferred styles. This inclusivity enhances the accessibility and effectiveness of the curriculum.

G. Encouraging Critical Thinking:
Objective: Promote critical thinking and application of biblical principles in real-life situations.
Process: Design lessons that encourage participants to question, analyse, and apply the teachings of the Bible. Incorporate case studies, role-playing, and scenario-based discussions that prompt participants to think critically about how their faith informs their decisions, actions, and relationships.

H. Providing Flexibility:
Objective: Create a curriculum that allows for flexibility and adaptation to the evolving needs of the Church community.
Process: Recognise that the Church community is dynamic, and individuals may be at different stages of their faith journey. Design a curriculum that can be adjusted based on feedback, emerging needs, or specific contextual factors. This flexibility ensures that the curriculum remains relevant and responsive to the changing dynamics of the Church community.

I. Integrating Evaluation Components:
Objective: Include evaluation components to assess the effectiveness of the curriculum and the achievement of learning objectives.
Process: Incorporate assessment tools such as quizzes, reflective assignments, and group projects to gauge participants' understanding and application of the material. Regularly evaluate the effectiveness of the curriculum through feedback mechanisms, allowing for continuous improvement based on the insights gained from participants and facilitators.

J. Promoting Lifelong Learning:
Objective: Cultivate a culture of lifelong learning and spiritual growth within the Church community.
Process: Design the curriculum with the overarching goal of instilling a passion for continuous learning. Emphasise the importance of ongoing personal study, reflection, and engagement with spiritual practices beyond the structured discipleship programs. Encourage participants to view discipleship as a lifelong journey rather than a finite educational experience.

In conclusion, curriculum development for discipleship programs involves a thoughtful and intentional process that aligns with objectives, incorporates biblical teachings, utilises diverse resources, ensures age-appropriate content, employs engaging teaching approaches, adapts to learning styles, encourages critical thinking, provides flexibility, integrates evaluation components, and promotes lifelong learning. By following these principles, churches can create discipleship curricula that are not only educational but also transformative, fostering spiritual growth and maturity within the Church community.

4. Age-Specific Programmes: Tailor discipleship programs to specific age groups, such as children, youth, young adults, adults, and seniors. Consider factors like learning styles, cognitive abilities, and life stages to design age-appropriate activities, lessons, and discussions.

Designing age-specific discipleship programmes is essential for addressing the unique needs, developmental stages, and learning styles of individuals across different age groups within a Church community. Here's a detailed expansion on the importance and strategies for implementing age-specific programmes:

Strategies for Implementing Age-Specific Programmes:

A. Young People (Ages 0-12):

Importance: Young people have a natural curiosity and receptivity to spiritual teachings. Early exposure to foundational biblical stories, values, and principles lays the groundwork for their faith journey.

Strategies:
- Utilise engaging storytelling, visual aids, and interactive activities to introduce biblical narratives.
- Foster a nurturing environment that emphasises God's love, kindness, and basic moral values.
- Incorporate age-appropriate worship songs, crafts, and games to make learning enjoyable.
- Encourage parental involvement to reinforce spiritual teachings at home.

B. Youth (Ages 13-18):

Importance: Adolescence is a critical period for identity formation and decision-making. Tailored discipleship programs help address questions, doubts, and challenges specific to this age group.

Strategies:
- Organise youth Bible studies that discuss relevant topics and explore how faith applies to their daily lives.

- Facilitate open discussions on issues like peer pressure, identity, and relationships from a biblical perspective.
- Foster mentorship relationships with older, mature Christians who can provide guidance and support.
- Engage them in service projects, encouraging a hands-on application of their faith.

C. Young Adults (Ages 19-30):

Importance: Young adults navigate the transition to independence, career, and relationships. Discipleship programs should address the challenges and opportunities of this life stage.

Strategies:
- Provide in-depth Bible studies that explore theological concepts and encourage critical thinking.
- Address topics like vocation, relationships, and societal engagement from a Christian world-view.
- Facilitate small group discussions for mutual support and accountability.
- Encourage involvement in mentorship.

D. Adults (Ages 31-60):

Importance: Adults often face the pressures of career, family, and societal responsibilities. Discipleship programs can support them in integrating faith into their various roles.

Strategies:
- Offer Bible studies that apply Scripture to the challenges of marriage, parenting, and work.

- Provide opportunities for spiritual retreats and reflection amidst busy schedules.
- Facilitate group discussions on topics like stewardship, ethical decision-making, and community engagement.
- Encourage involvement in ministry and leadership roles within the Church.

E. Seniors (Ages 61 and above):

Importance: Seniors bring a wealth of life experience and wisdom. Discipleship programs can focus on reflection, legacy, and continued spiritual growth.

Strategies:
- Offer Bible studies that delve into deeper theological discussions and the application of lifelong lessons.
- Provide opportunities for seniors to share their testimonies and insights with younger generations.
- Organise fellowship events that foster a sense of community and belonging.
- Encourage engagement in mentorship roles, allowing seniors to pass on their wisdom to younger members.

F. Intergenerational Activities:

Importance: Creating opportunities for different age groups to interact fosters a sense of unity, mutual understanding, and mentorship within the Church community.

Strategies:
- Organise intergenerational worship services, where various age groups actively participate.

- Facilitate mentorship programs that connect individuals from different life stages.
- Plan community service projects that involve participants of all ages working together.
- Incorporate events like family retreats or Church-wide gatherings to strengthen bonds across generations.

In conclusion, tailoring discipleship programs to specific age groups is a strategic approach that recognises the diverse needs, challenges, and strengths within a Church community. By understanding the unique characteristics of each age group, churches can design programs that effectively nurture spiritual growth, address relevant life issues, and create a supportive community for individuals at every stage of their faith journey.

5. Small Groups and Mentoring: Encourage the formation of small groups based on age or life stages. These groups can provide opportunities for fellowship, accountability, prayer, and deeper discussions. Enlist mentors or discipleship leaders who can walk alongside individuals within each group, offering guidance and support.

The establishment of small groups and mentoring relationships within a Church community is a powerful strategy for fostering a sense of connection, accountability, and spiritual growth. Here's a detailed expansion on the importance and implementation of small groups and mentoring in discipleship:

1. Importance of Small Groups

Fellowship and Community Building:

- Small groups create an intimate setting where individuals can form meaningful connections, build friendships, and share life experiences.
- Fellowship within these groups fosters a sense of belonging and encourages a supportive community.

Accountability and Discipleship:
- Small groups provide a platform for mutual accountability, where members can challenge and encourage one another in their faith journeys.
- The sharing of struggles, victories, and prayer requests contributes to a culture of discipleship within the group.

Deeper Discussions and Understanding:
- In smaller settings, individuals feel more comfortable expressing their thoughts and asking questions, leading to more profound discussions on matters of faith.
- Small groups allow for in-depth exploration of Scripture, theology, and personal application of biblical principles.

Prayer and Spiritual Support:
- Members of small groups can pray for one another, offering spiritual support in times of need or celebration.
- Prayer becomes a central component, strengthening the spiritual bond within the group.

2. Implementing Small Groups:
Formation Based on Age or Life Stages:

- Consider organising small groups based on age groups or life stages to ensure that members share similar experiences and can relate to one another.
- Life-stage-oriented groups allow individuals to connect with others who are facing similar challenges and transitions.

Facilitation of Discussions:
- Designate group leaders or facilitators who can guide discussions, ensuring that the conversation remains focused on spiritual growth and mutual support.
- Provide resources, discussion topics, or study guides to facilitate meaningful conversations during group meetings.

Regular Meeting Schedule:
- Establish a consistent meeting schedule to foster regularity and commitment among group members.
- Consistent meeting times allow individuals to plan and prioritise their participation, strengthening the group's cohesion.

Incorporate Social Activities:
- Integrate social activities or gatherings within the small group, creating opportunities for members to build friendships beyond the formal discussion setting.
- Social events contribute to a sense of community and enhance the overall experience of being part of a small group.

3. Importance of Mentoring Relationships:
Guidance and Support:

- Mentoring relationships involve a more experienced individual providing guidance, wisdom, and support to someone at an earlier stage of their faith journey.
- Mentors offer insights based on their own experiences, helping mentees navigate challenges and make informed decisions.

Role Modelling and Encouragement:
- Mentors serve as role models, demonstrating a mature and authentic faith through their actions and attitudes.
- Regular encouragement and affirmation from mentors contribute to the mentees' spiritual growth and confidence in their journey.

Personalised Discipleship:
- Mentorship allows for personalised discipleship, addressing the specific needs, questions, and struggles of the individual.
- One-on-one interactions create a space for deeper exploration of faith and a more tailored approach to spiritual development.

Building a Trusted Relationship:
- Trust is a foundational element of mentoring relationships. Creating a safe and confidential space allows mentees to open up about their concerns and seek guidance without fear of judgment.

4. Implementing Mentoring Relationships

Identify Potential Mentors:
- Identify individuals within the Church community who exhibit a mature and steadfast faith, a willingness to

invest in others, and a capacity for empathy and understanding.

- Invite them to consider serving as mentors, emphasising the impact they can have on the spiritual journeys of others.

Matchmaking Process:

- Facilitate a matchmaking process to pair mentors with mentees based on compatibility, shared interests, or specific areas of spiritual focus.
- Ensure that both mentors and mentees have the opportunity to express their preferences and expectations.

Establish Clear Goals:

- Define clear goals and expectations for the mentoring relationship. This may include specific topics to be covered, frequency of meetings, and desired outcomes.
- Clearly communicated goals provide a framework for the mentorship journey and help both parties stay focused.

Regular Check-Ins:

- Encourage regular check-ins between mentors and mentees to discuss progress, address challenges, and celebrate milestones.
- Consistent communication fosters a sense of continuity and ensures that the mentoring relationship remains purposeful and effective.

Provide Training and Resources:

- Offer training sessions or resources for mentors to enhance their mentoring skills and provide guidance on effective discipleship.
- Equip mentors with tools, study materials, or discussion guides that can aid in facilitating meaningful conversations.

In conclusion, the establishment of small groups and mentoring relationships plays a vital role in creating a dynamic and supportive discipleship culture within a Church.

5. Worship and Service Opportunities: Integrate discipleship with worship and service opportunities. Encourage active participation in Church gatherings, outreach programs, mission trips, and community service. This helps individuals apply their faith practically, fostering a holistic discipleship experience.

Integrating discipleship with worship and service opportunities is a holistic approach that encourages individuals to not only deepen their understanding of faith but also apply it in practical ways. Here's an in-depth expansion on the importance and implementation of combining discipleship with worship and service:

A. Importance of Integrating Discipleship with Worship

Authentic Expression of Faith:
- Worship is a natural response to the recognition of God's goodness, grace, and majesty.
- Integrating discipleship with worship allows individuals to authentically express their growing faith and gratitude.

- Actively participating in worship services becomes an opportunity for individuals to connect with God on a personal level.

Spiritual Growth Through Music and Prayer:
- Worship often involves music and prayer, which can be powerful tools for spiritual growth. Engaging in worship helps individuals internalise biblical truths through lyrics and connect with God in prayerful reflection.
- Worship becomes a medium through which individuals can experience spiritual transformation and a deepening of their relationship with God.

Community Building:
- Worship is a communal activity that unites believers in a shared experience of reverence and adoration. Integrating discipleship with worship strengthens the sense of community within the Church.
- Sharing in worship fosters a collective identity, reminding individuals that they are part of a larger body of believers on a shared faith journey.

B. Implementation of Integrating Discipleship with Worship

Encourage Active Participation:
- Promote active participation in various elements of the worship service, including singing, prayer, Scripture reading, and reflection.
- Provide opportunities for individuals to use their talents and gifts in contributing to the worship experience, such as joining the worship team, leading prayers, or participating in drama or creative arts.

Thematic Worship Services:
- Design worship services with specific themes that align with the discipleship objectives of the Church. This could involve thematic sermon series, special events, or seasonal emphases that reinforce discipleship principles.
- Thematic worship services help individuals make connections between biblical teachings and their practical application in everyday life.

Incorporate Discipleship Elements:
- Integrate discipleship elements into the worship service, such as moments of reflection, testimonies, or discussions related to the sermon topic.
- Provide study guides or discussion questions that connect the worship theme to discipleship principles, encouraging further exploration and application during small group discussions.

C. Importance of Integrating Discipleship with Service Opportunities

Practical Application of Faith:
- Service opportunities provide a tangible way for individuals to apply their faith in real-world situations. Engaging in acts of service aligns with the teachings of Jesus, who emphasised love and compassion through actions.
- Connecting discipleship with service encourages individuals to live out their faith authentically.

Community Impact:

- Service opportunities, such as outreach programs, mission trips, and community service initiatives, allow individuals to positively impact their local community and beyond.
- Discipleship that includes service emphasises the role of believers as agents of change and love in the world.

Spiritual Growth Through Service:
- Serving others is a transformative experience that contributes to spiritual growth. It fosters qualities such as humility, empathy, and selflessness, which are integral to a mature faith.
- Integrating discipleship with service creates a holistic discipleship experience, where faith is not confined to theoretical knowledge, but is actively lived out in service to others.

D. Implementation of Integrating Discipleship with Service Opportunities

Promote Outreach and Mission Trips:
- Encourage participation in outreach programs, mission trips, and initiatives that address the needs of the local community or global missions.
- Provide information and organise events that raise awareness about service opportunities, allowing individuals to discover areas where they can contribute their time and skills.

Community Service Initiatives:
- Organise community service initiatives within the local neighbourhood. This could involve volunteering at shelters, organising food drives, or participating in environmental cleanup projects.

- Discipleship becomes a practical expression of love for the community through meaningful service projects.

Reflective Debrief Sessions:
- After participating in service opportunities, facilitate reflective debrief sessions where individuals can share their experiences, insights, and the impact of their service on their faith journey.
- Incorporate discussions on how the principles of discipleship were applied during service, fostering a deeper understanding of the connection between faith and action.

Empowerment Through Service Roles:
- Provide opportunities for individuals to take on leadership roles in service initiatives. This empowers them to use their skills and passions to make a meaningful contribution to the community.
- Leadership roles in service activities enhance discipleship by encouraging individuals to take ownership of their faith in practical ways.

In conclusion, integrating discipleship with worship and service opportunities creates a well-rounded and transformative experience for individuals within a Church community. It encourages them not to exist within the body of the Church as a passive participant but to become a fully integrated active part of the Body of Christ.

7. Regular Evaluations and Adjustments:
Continuously evaluate the effectiveness of the discipleship programs through feedback, assessments, and discussions with participants and leaders. Make adjustments as

necessary to better meet the evolving needs of different age groups.

Regular evaluations and adjustments are crucial components of maintaining effective discipleship programs within a Church community. (For a detailed expansion on the importance and implementation of regular evaluations and adjustments in discipleship, see Chapter 5: Empowering Youth Leadership.)

Equipping Youth with Relevant Skills and Knowledge to Navigate the Challenges of the Modern World:

In equipping youth with relevant skills and knowledge to navigate the challenges of the modern world from a Christian Church perspective, here are some steps to consider, along with potential biblical references:

1. Biblical Foundation:

Ground the discipleship program on a biblical foundation, emphasising the importance of seeking wisdom and guidance from God's Word. Encourage youth to study and apply Scriptures relevant to their daily lives, such as Proverbs 3:5-6 and Psalm 119:105.
Establishing a robust biblical foundation is paramount in shaping a discipleship program that nurtures the spiritual growth and resilience of youth. By emphasising the centrality of God's Word, participants can be guided by timeless truths that provide a solid framework for navigating life's challenges. Here's an expansion on grounding the discipleship program on a biblical foundation:

A. Profound Wisdom from Proverbs 3:5-6:

- The cornerstone of the discipleship program rests on Proverbs 3:5-6 (WEB), which implores believers to "Trust in Yahweh with all your heart, and don't lean on your own understanding. In all your ways acknowledge him, and he will make your paths straight." This verse encapsulates the essence of surrendering to God's wisdom and acknowledging His sovereignty in every aspect of life.

- Through reflective study and discussion, youth can delve into the profound wisdom embedded in this passage. They can explore the implications of trusting God wholeheartedly, recognising the limitations of human understanding, and the promise of God's guidance when we submit our ways to Him.

B. Guidance through Psalm 119:105:
- Psalm 119:105 (WEB) serves as a guiding light in the discipleship journey, stating, "Your word is a lamp to my feet, and a light for my path." This imagery underscores the illuminating power of God's Word, providing clarity and direction in the often challenging and uncertain paths of life.

- Encourage participants to engage in a systematic study of Psalm 119, exploring the richness of God's precepts and their relevance to contemporary challenges. Discuss how the Scriptures, like a lamp, not only reveal the immediate steps to take, but also illuminate the broader path of righteousness.

C. Application to Daily Lives:
- The discipleship program should actively promote the practical application of biblical principles in the day-

to-day lives of the youth. This involves not only studying the Scriptures but also discerning how these teachings relate to their personal experiences, relationships, and decision-making processes.

- Facilitate small group discussions, workshops, and activities that encourage participants to share real-life scenarios and explore how Proverbs 3:5-6 and Psalm 119:105 can be applied in navigating challenges at school, in relationships, and in personal growth.

D. Interactive Learning Methods:

- Foster an interactive and engaging learning environment within the discipleship program. Utilise creative methods such as role-playing, case studies, and group projects to make the biblical teachings come alive. This not only enhances comprehension but also encourages active participation and personal reflection.

- Incorporate multimedia resources, contemporary examples, and testimonies that illustrate the transformative impact of relying on God's wisdom, as outlined in the selected verses. This dynamic approach helps bridge the gap between ancient wisdom and the complexities of the modern world.

E. Encouraging a Lifelong Habit of Study:

- Instill in the youth a passion for lifelong learning and exploration of God's Word. Equip them with tools for independent Bible study and encourage the formation of study groups. This empowers them to continue seeking wisdom beyond the structured program, fostering a habit of continual spiritual growth.

- Remind participants that Proverbs 3:5-6 and Psalm 119:105 are not merely verses to be memorised but guideposts for an ongoing relationship with God. Encourage them to view the Scriptures as a living source of wisdom that evolves with them through different stages of life.

By grounding the discipleship program on the timeless wisdom encapsulated in Proverbs 3:5-6 and Psalm 119:105, the Church can lay a foundation that empowers youth to navigate the complexities of the modern world with a steadfast reliance on God's Word. This approach not only imparts knowledge but fosters a transformative journey of faith and spiritual maturity.

2. Understanding Culture and Challenges:

Engage youth in discussions where they openly express their concerns and challenges related to the modern world. Address topics such as technology, peer pressure, identity, relationships, morality, and ethical dilemmas. Consider 1 Peter 5:8-9 to highlight the need for awareness and vigilance in navigating worldly challenges.

Recognising the multifaceted nature of the modern world, it is crucial to engage youth in open discussions that provide a platform for them to express their concerns and challenges. By addressing a spectrum of topics including technology, peer pressure, identity, relationships, morality, and ethical dilemmas, the Church can foster an environment that acknowledges the complexity of the issues young individuals face. Drawing inspiration from 1 Peter 5:8-9, these discussions can underscore the importance of awareness and vigilance in navigating the challenges of the world.

A. Open Dialogues on Modern Challenges:
Establish a safe and open space for youth to express their thoughts and concerns. Create forums, discussion groups, or retreats specifically designed to delve into the challenges posed by the modern world. Encourage participants to share their experiences and perspectives on topics such as the pervasive influence of technology, the pressures of peer interactions, the quest for identity, and the complexities of relationships.

B. Exploration of Technology's Impact:
Dive into discussions regarding the impact of technology on the lives of youth. Address issues such as social media, online interactions, and the potential challenges of constant connectivity. Explore how biblical principles can guide responsible and mindful use of technology, emphasising the importance of maintaining a balance between virtual and real-world experiences.

C. Peer Pressure and Identity Formation:
Discuss the realities of peer pressure and the quest for identity. Through open conversations, help youth navigate the challenges of conforming to societal expectations while staying true to their Christian values. Reference biblical examples of individuals who remained steadfast in their faith despite external pressures, encouraging youth to draw strength from their identity in Christ.

D. Navigating Relationships:

Explore the dynamics of relationships, both romantic and platonic, within the context of Christian values. Discuss the challenges of maintaining healthy relationships, setting boundaries, and making decisions that align with biblical principles. Reference passages that emphasise love, respect, and mutual support in relationships, fostering a deeper understanding of God's design for human connections.

E. Morality and Ethical Dilemmas:

Delve into discussions surrounding morality and ethical decision-making. Address contemporary ethical dilemmas and equip youth with a biblical framework for making ethical choices in challenging situations. Reference Scriptures that provide moral guidance, emphasising the importance of maintaining integrity and righteousness in all aspects of life.

F. 1 Peter 5:8-9: Awareness and Vigilance:

Integrate 1 Peter 5:8-9 (WEB) into the discussions to highlight the biblical perspective on the need for awareness and vigilance. The passage states, "Be sober and self-controlled. Be watchful. Your adversary, the devil, walks around like a roaring lion, seeking whom he may devour. Withstand him steadfast in your faith, knowing that your brothers who are in the world are undergoing the same sufferings."

Use this Scripture as a foundation to emphasise the importance of being alert to the challenges posed by the world. Discuss practical ways to resist negative influences, stand firm in faith, and support one another in the face of shared struggles. This biblical perspective serves as a reminder that the challenges faced by the youth are not unique, and with vigilance and faith, the youth can overcome.

G. Practical Strategies and Solutions:
Conclude the discussions with practical strategies and solutions rooted in biblical teachings. Empower youth with tools for discernment, resilience, and faith-based decision-making. Encourage the formation of accountability partnerships within the community, fostering an environment where individuals can support each other in living out their faith amidst the challenges of the modern world.

By actively engaging youth in open discussions and considering the insights provided by 1 Peter 5:8-9, the Church can create a space that not only addresses the specific challenges of the modern era but also equips young individuals with the wisdom and strength derived from biblical principles. This approach fosters a holistic understanding of their faith that is relevant and applicable to the complexities of their lives.

3. Teach Critical Thinking:
Equip youth with critical thinking skills, encouraging them to evaluate ideas and influences in light of biblical values. Emphasise discernment and the ability to make morally informed decisions. Reference Romans 12:2 in emphasising the importance of not conforming to the patterns of the world but being transformed by the renewing of the mind.

Teaching critical thinking skills is an essential component of equipping youth to navigate the complexities of the modern world with a strong foundation in Christian values. By encouraging them to evaluate ideas, influences, and choices through the lens of biblical principles, the Church can empower young individuals to develop discernment and make morally informed decisions. Drawing inspiration from Romans 12:2, the emphasis is on the transformative power of renewing the mind and avoiding conformity to worldly patterns.

A. Introduction to Critical Thinking:

Begin by introducing the concept of critical thinking and its relevance in the context of faith. Explain that critical thinking involves the ability to analyse, evaluate, and discern information, ideas, and influences. Emphasise that this skill is instrumental in navigating the complexities of the modern world while maintaining a steadfast commitment to biblical values.

B. Biblical Foundation—Romans 12:2:

Anchor the teaching of critical thinking in Romans 12:2 (WEB), which states, "Don't be conformed to this world, but be transformed by the renewing of your mind, so that you may prove what is the good, well-pleasing, and perfect will of God." Use this Scripture as a foundation to convey the transformative power of renewing the mind according to God's Word, enabling youth to discern God's will amidst worldly influences.

C. Discernment in Decision-Making:

Guide youth through practical exercises that involve discernment in decision-making. Encourage them to evaluate choices, media messages, and cultural norms in light of biblical values. Provide scenarios that challenge them to think critically about the consequences of different actions and how those align with their Christian beliefs.

D. Analysing Cultural Influences:

Explore contemporary cultural influences that may impact the world-view of young individuals. This could include discussions on popular media, societal norms, and prevailing ideologies. Equip youth with the skills to critically analyse these influences, questioning whether they align with or diverge from biblical teachings.

E. Ethical Considerations:

Introduce ethical considerations in critical thinking by discussing real-world scenarios where ethical dilemmas arise. Challenge youth to assess these dilemmas through the ethical framework provided by Christian values. Explore the concept of moral reasoning and ethical decision-making, emphasising the importance of integrity in personal and professional spheres.

F. Engage in Scripture Study:

Encourage a deep engagement with Scripture as a means of developing critical thinking skills. Guide youth in studying passages that address moral, ethical, and philosophical questions. Discuss how biblical principles can be applied to various situations and how a thorough understanding of Scripture enhances their ability to think critically about contemporary issues.

G. Questioning Assumptions:

Foster an environment that encourages questioning assumptions and societal norms. Challenge youth to identify underlying assumptions in various contexts and evaluate whether those assumptions align with a biblical world-view. This exercise promotes a mindset of thoughtful inquiry and prevents unquestioning acceptance of cultural trends.

H. Practical Application and Role-Playing:

Facilitate role-playing exercises that simulate real-life situations. These scenarios can include peer pressure, moral dilemmas, or conflicting value systems. Encourage youth to apply critical thinking skills in these scenarios, demonstrating how they can navigate challenges while staying true to their Christian convictions.

I. Community Dialogues:

Organise community dialogues or panel discussions where youth can engage with individuals who have navigated complex issues with a strong foundation in Christian principles. This exposure to diverse perspectives and experiences enhances their ability to think critically and consider different viewpoints while maintaining a commitment to biblical values.

J. Encouraging Intellectual Humility:

Emphasise the importance of intellectual humility in the pursuit of truth. Teach youth that critical thinking involves acknowledging the limitations of one's own understanding and being open to continuous learning. This attitude fosters a humble approach to knowledge, recognising that God's wisdom surpasses human comprehension.

Incorporating these elements into the teaching of critical thinking aligns with the biblical directive in Romans 12:2, guiding youth to transform their minds according to God's will. By fostering critical thinking skills, the Church empowers young individuals to engage with the world thoughtfully, discerningly, and faithfully, contributing to their personal growth and the broader mission of the Christian community.

4. Apologetics:

Train youth in apologetics, helping them understand and defend their faith in an increasingly secular world. Teach them to provide rational reasons for their beliefs while respecting others. Utilise passages like 1 Peter 3:15 to emphasise the importance of being prepared to give a reason for their hope.

In the face of an increasingly secular world, equipping youth with the tools of apologetics becomes imperative for fostering a robust and informed faith. Apologetics involves not only understanding one's own beliefs but also being able to articulate and defend them rationally, all while maintaining a respectful dialogue with those who hold different perspectives. Drawing inspiration from passages like 1 Peter 3:15, which encourages believers to be prepared to give a reason for their hope, the training in apologetics becomes a crucial aspect of navigating the challenges of a secular culture.

A. Introduction to Apologetics:

Begin by introducing the concept of apologetics to the youth. Explain that it is the reasoned defense of the

Christian faith, encompassing the ability to articulate beliefs, respond to challenges, and engage in respectful conversations with those who may hold differing world-views.

B. Biblical Foundation — 1 Peter 3:15:

Ground the training in 1 Peter 3:15 (AMP), which states, "But in your hearts set Christ apart [as holy— acknowledging Him, giving Him first place in your lives] as Lord. Always be ready to give a [logical] defense to anyone who asks you to account for the hope *and* confident assurance [elicited by faith] that is within you, yet [do it] with gentleness and respect." Emphasise the dual importance of being prepared to defend one's faith and doing so with a spirit of gentleness and respect.

C. Understanding Core Christian Beliefs:

Ensure that youth have a good understanding of key Christian values. This involves a comprehensive grasp of the Bible, the nature of God, the person of Jesus Christ, and the essential beliefs of the Christian world-view. This basic knowledge sets the basis for effective engagement in apologetics.

D. Addressing Common Challenges:

Identify frequent difficulties and objections raised against Christianity in the secular world. These could include issues regarding the existence of God, the veracity of the Bible, the problem of evil, and moral objections. Equip youth with reasoned responses to these difficulties, focusing on both biblical principles and logical reasoning.

E. Logical Reasoning and Critical Thinking:

Integrate components of logical reasoning and critical thinking into the instruction. Teach youth how to develop effective arguments and evaluate the validity of diverse claims. This skill set boosts their ability to engage in meaningful discussion and successfully express the rational basis for their religion.

F. Mock Debates and Role-Playing:

Facilitate role-playing exercises and mock discussions to give students hands-on experience defending their religion. This interactive approach allows youth to practise apologetic ideas in simulated talks, allowing them to improve their communication skills and successfully respond to diverse viewpoints.

G. Cultural Importance:

Link apologetics to current cultural issues. Investigate the ways in which Christian beliefs intersect with and provide insights into subjects such as science, morality, philosophy, and social justice.
Demonstrating the applicability of the Christian world-view to current issues strengthens the youth's ability to engage in critical dialogue with the secular world.

H. Respectful Participation:

Stress the significance of courteous apologetics engagement. Encourage young people to approach discussions with humility, understanding that they may not have all of the answers. Encourage respect for other people's beliefs while boldly expressing the rational basis for their own.

I. Creating Bridges, Not Walls:

Teach adolescents how to use faith talks to build bridges rather than walls. Highlight the shared human experience and the search for truth. Encourage them to identify common ground with others, creating a climate conducive to dialogue and mutual understanding.

J. Lifelong Learning and Humility:
Instill a culture of lifelong learning and intellectual humility. Apologetics is a dynamic field in which there is always more to learn and comprehend. Encourage young people to embrace the journey of lifelong learning, acknowledging that intellectual humility is a virtue that goes hand in hand with the quest of truth.

By including these aspects into apologetics training, the Church equips young people to face the difficulties of an increasingly secular world with confidence and conviction. This method not only deepens their personal faith but also places them in a position to connect meaningfully with others, encouraging a spirit of conversation and understanding in the midst of varied faiths.

5. Prayer and Spiritual Disciplines:

Instill in young people the need of seeking God's guidance via prayer and participating in spiritual disciplines such as Bible reading, fasting, worship, and fellowship. Encourage regular prayer for guidance and strength in dealing with difficulties. Refer to James 1:5, which assures believers that they can ask God for wisdom and that He will gladly grant it to them.

The importance of prayer and spiritual exercises in developing a resilient and grounded faith cannot be emphasized enough, especially for young people navigating the challenges of the modern world. Teaching young people to seek God's wisdom via prayer and to engage in spiritual disciplines such as Bible reading, fasting, worship, and fellowship is critical for developing a deep relationship with God. The necessity of constant prayer for guidance and strength is based on James 1:5, which assures believers that God abundantly offers wisdom to those who seek it.

A. An Overview of Spiritual Disciplines:

Begin by explaining to youth the concept of spiritual disciplines and how these practises are intentional strategies of establishing a stronger relationship with God. Show how these disciplines have played a role in the spiritual journeys of believers throughout history.

B. Biblical Basis—James 1:5:

Foundation the teaching on James 1:5, which says, "But if any of you lacks wisdom, let him ask of God, who gives to all liberally and without reproach, and it will be given to him." This Scripture serves as a foundational promise that encourages believers, including youth, to seek God's wisdom through prayer.

C. Prayer as a Mode of Communication with God:

Emphasise that prayer is a dynamic communication with a loving and responsive God, not just a routine. Teach youth that they can express their ideas, concerns, and appreciation to God through prayer, while also asking His guidance and wisdom in all aspects of their lives.

D. Bible Study and Meditation:
Emphasise the significance of regular Bible reading and meditation. Encourage young people to acquire the habit of reading and meditating on Scripture, emphasising that the Bible is a source of insight, guidance, and spiritual nourishment. Encourage them to read several books and passages that address their individual problems and concerns.

E. Fasting as a Spiritual Practise:
Introduce fasting as a discipline to enhance their reliance on God. Explain that fasting is the temporary cessation of some activities or foods in order to focus on prayer and spiritual meditation. Discuss how fasting can help to develop self-control, spiritual sensitivity, and a greater experience of God's presence.

F. Worship as a Way of Life:
Teach youth that worship is more than just a Church service. Encourage them to live a worshipful lifestyle, exhibiting reverence and awe for God in their daily activities. In order to create a stronger connection with God and a perspective that transcends worldly concerns, emphasise the transformational potential of worship.

G. Friendship and Community:
Emphasise the significance of community and fellowship as essential components of spiritual growth. Encourage young people to participate

actively in Church activities, small groups, and events that build a sense of belonging and mutual support. Describe how sharing spiritual journeys with others enriches their faith experience.

H. Guided Prayer for Strength and Guidance:
Explain how to structure prayers for direction and strength. Encourage young people to be explicit in their petitions, seeking God's wisdom for academic decisions, job options, relationships, and personal development. Give examples of Bible prayers that demonstrate a deep desire for God's guidance.

I. Personal Accounts:
Include personal experiences from those who have experienced the transformational effect of prayer and spiritual exercises. Real-life examples can inspire and demonstrate the influence of these practises in overcoming problems and making life-changing decisions with God's help.

J. Consistency and Adaptability:
Teach youth that spiritual disciplines may be adjusted to their own preferences and schedules. Stress the significance of consistency above perfection. Encourage them to try out different disciplines to see what resonates with their personal spiritual journey.

K. Reflection and Evaluation:
Assist youth in analysing and reflecting on their spiritual exercises on a regular basis. Encourage people to evaluate the influence of prayer and other practises on their life, noting areas of progress and areas that may require correction. This reflecting

process adds to a dynamic and ever-changing spiritual experience.

By instilling the importance of prayer and spiritual practises, the Church provides youth with transforming skills for overcoming the problems of modern life. This comprehensive method fosters a resilient faith that seeks God's counsel, finds strength in His presence, and engages in a lifelong spiritual journey.

6. Mentoring and Role Models:

Match young people with adult Christians who can act as mentors and role models. These connections can provide direction, support, and accountability. Highlight Scriptures such as Titus 2:3-5 that emphasise the importance of elder generations guiding younger generations in the faith.

Connecting young people with adult Christians who can act as mentors and role models is a transforming and important part of spiritual development. These interactions go beyond basic instruction; they provide advice, support, and accountability, developing young people's character and faith. Highlighting texts like Titus 2:3-5 emphasises the biblical underpinning for intergenerational mentorship and the importance of elder generations passing on wisdom and faith to the younger generations.

A. An Overview of Mentoring and Role Models:

Begin by discussing mentoring and the importance of having role models in one's religion journey. Explain that these interactions are not just about learning but also about seeing the lived-out faith of mature Christians directly.

B. Biblical Basis—Titus 2:3-5:

Titus 2:3-5 (WEB) states "that older women likewise be reverent in behavior, not slanderers nor enslaved to much wine, teachers of that which is good, that they may train the young wives to love their husbands, to love their children, to be sober minded, chaste, workers at home, kind, being in subjection to their own husbands, that God's word may not be blasphemed."

C. Selecting Potential Mentors:

Assist youth in locating prospective mentors within the Church community or larger Christian groups. Encourage them to seek out others whose faith, character, and life experiences are consistent with their values and goals. This procedure necessitates careful consideration and prayerful discernment.

D. Create Genuine Relationships:

Stress the significance of true relationships between mentors and mentees. These bonds extend beyond formal meetings and include shared experiences, open communication, and a common commitment to growth. Encourage both parties to spend time getting to know each other personally.

E. Faith and Life Decision Guidance:

Make it clear that mentoring connections extend beyond spiritual topics to include other parts of life. Mentors can help you navigate difficult life decisions, job choices, relationships, and personal development. Mentors provide unique perspectives and insights by drawing on their own experiences.

F. Assistance with Spiritual Disciplines:

Emphasise the importance of mentors in supporting and encouraging spiritual practises such as prayer, Bible study, and worship. Mentors can share their personal practises, offer advice on overcoming obstacles, and hold youth accountable to help them stay consistent in their spiritual journey.

G. Challenge Encouragement:

Recognise that difficulties are an unavoidable part of life. During tough times, mentors can provide a listening ear, empathetic support, and godly wisdom. This relational support system helps young people enduring hardships to develop resilience and faith.

H. Accountability and Development:

Emphasise the significance of accountability in mentoring relationships. Setting objectives, sharing progress, and holding one other accountable for spiritual and personal growth are all part of this. Accountability develops a sense of duty and commitment to the mutual religious journey.

I. Exemplifying Christ-like Behaviour:

Remind mentors of the importance of modelling Christ-like behaviour through their actions and attitudes. Mentors are living models of the religion they proclaim, and their actions have a significant impact on the spiritual formation of the young they mentor. Encourage mentors to demonstrate values like love, patience, and humility.

J. Rejoicing in Milestones and Achievements:

Recognise and celebrate milestones and accomplishments within the mentoring relationship. Recognise and affirm the mentorship-induced growth, accomplishments, and good changes. These occasions highlight the importance of the connection and encourage both mentors and mentees to continue investing in their spiritual journey.

K. Increasing the Impact:
As mentees grow in their faith, encourage them to consider becoming mentors themselves. This multiplicity of impact produces a circle of growth within the community, where individuals consistently participate in the spiritual development of others, as indicated in Titus 2.

The Church develops a culture of intergenerational support and growth by combining these factors into the practise of mentoring and emphasising the scriptural foundation provided by Titus 2:3-5. These mentorship relationships become essential to youth spiritual development, laying the groundwork for a lifelong journey of religion.

7. Training:
Provide training in real life skills such as financial stewardship, time management, communication skills, healthy relationships, and leadership development. While not expressly biblical, these abilities are consistent with biblical ideals of good living and resource management.

Practical life-skills training is a helpful and comprehensive strategy to prepare adolescents for success in different facets of their lives. The Church can enable young people to handle the problems of the modern world by addressing issues such as financial stewardship, time management, communication skills, healthy relationships, and leadership development. Although these abilities are not specifically biblical, they are consistent with overall biblical themes of wise living, resource stewardship, and responsible leadership.

A. Financial Management:

Financial stewardship education emphasises biblical principles of prudent financial management and responsible stewardship. Teach young people the importance of budgeting, saving, and charity giving. Discuss the value of contentment, giving, and avoiding financial traps, matching these lessons with biblical teachings on appreciation, confidence in God, and appropriate resource management.

B. Time Administration:

Time management abilities are essential for living a balanced and purposeful life. Assist young people in developing appropriate time-management methods, emphasising the biblical notion of redeeming time (Ephesians 5:16). Encourage them to prioritise their activities according to their values, ambitions, and pursuit of God's purposes in their lives.

C. Communication Abilities:

Effective communication is the foundation of healthy relationships and prosperous endeavours. Training in verbal and nonverbal communication, active listening, and conflict resolution is available. While not expressly biblical, these qualities are consistent with the ideals of compassion, patience, and the significance of edifying speech mentioned in several texts, including Ephesians 4:29.

D. Good Relationships:
Healthy connections are the foundation of a happy life. Provide advice on developing and sustaining healthy relationships, including friendships, family ties, and romantic relationships. While not technically biblical, these teachings correlate with the ideals of love, forgiveness, and mutual respect emphasised in texts such as Colossians 3:12-14.

E. Development of Leadership:
Leadership development focuses on developing skills that enable youth to lead with integrity and positively affect others. Develop their decision-making, problem-solving, and collaborative skills. Connect these abilities to biblical values of servant leadership, humility, and the call to use one's power for the greater good (Matthew 20:26-28).

F. Solving Problems and Making Decisions:
Instill problem-solving and decision-making abilities in youth, emphasising the necessity of seeking God's guidance in all decisions. Connect these abilities to biblical themes such as seeking knowledge (Proverbs 2:6) and trusting in the Lord's guidance (Proverbs 3:5-6).

G. Setting and Planning Goals:
Provide training on goal setting and achievement in order to promote a sense of purpose and direction. Encourage young people to match their ambitions with their values and to seek God's guidance in their

aims. This is consistent with biblical ideas such as seeking God's will (James 4:13-15) and entrusting one's plans to the Lord (Proverbs 16:3).

H. Resilience and Adaptability:
Instill in young people the value of adaptation and resilience in the face of life's obstacles. While not expressly biblical, these abilities are consistent with the biblical ideas of endurance, persistence, and confidence in God's faithfulness during adversity (James 1:2-4).

I. Dispute Resolution:
Provide conflict resolution training that emphasises biblical themes of reconciliation and forgiveness (Matthew 18:15-17). Give youth the skills they need to negotiate disagreements with humility, seek repair, and sustain good relationships.

J. Cultural Awareness:
Develop cultural competency abilities in youth so that they can engage with varied perspectives and navigate a globalised environment. While not expressly biblical, this corresponds with the biblical call to love one's neighbour (Matthew 22:39) and the Great Commission (Matthew 28:19).

K. Volunteering and Service:
Foster a spirit of service and volunteerism by linking these efforts to biblical principles of love for others and the call to serve one another (Galatians 5:13; Mark 10:45). Teach young people the joy and fulfilment that comes from contributing to their communities.

Incorporating practical life-skills training into the Church's youth programme shows a commitment to holistic development. While these abilities are not expressly biblical, linking them with overall biblical concepts increases their applicability and creates a well-rounded understanding of responsible living, stewardship, and leadership in the context of one's religion.

Remember that biblical references should be utilised in context and carefully evaluated to guarantee proper application. Consultation with Church leaders and study of pertinent texts will aid in the appropriate incorporation of biblical truth within the programme.

Chapter 8: Nurturing Relationships and Community

In the ever-evolving landscape of the Christian Church, the eighth chapter of our theological exploration delves into a pivotal aspect of faith and communal living—Nurturing Relationships and Community. As we navigate the complexities of a rapidly changing world, our focus turns to the generations that stand on the precipice of shaping the future: Generation Z and Generation Alpha. This chapter seeks to illuminate the profound significance of fostering meaningful connections and building robust communities within the context of the Christian faith.

Fostering a Sense of Belonging and Community Among the Youth:

The foundational stones of a thriving Christian community are laid in the hearts and minds of its youth. Within the pages of this chapter, we explore strategies to cultivate a sense of belonging among the younger members of our congregations. As we acknowledge the unique challenges and opportunities that Generations Z and Alpha bring to the table, we seek to understand how the Church can become a sanctuary where the youth not only find solace but actively engage in the shared journey of faith.

Promoting Healthy Relationships and Friendships Within the Church:

Amidst the noise and clamour of a digitally connected yet emotionally distant world, the Christian Church stands as a beacon of hope for fostering genuine relationships and friendships. This section of our exploration delves into the principles that underpin healthy connections, examining how the Church can be a nurturing environment where individuals, irrespective of age, find companionship and support. From addressing the challenges posed by social media to promoting face-to-face interactions, we delve into the transformative power of authentic relationships within the Body of Christ.

Creating Opportunities for Intergenerational Bonding and Support:

In a society that often compartmentalises generations, the Christian Church holds a unique potential to bridge generational gaps and foster intergenerational unity. This subsection explores practical ways in which the Church can facilitate meaningful connections between the wisdom of older generations and the fresh perspectives of the youth. As we envision a Church where mentorship, guidance, and support flow seamlessly between the seasoned veterans of faith and those just embarking on their spiritual journeys, we uncover the beauty of a multigenerational community bound together by a shared commitment to Christ.

As we embark on this chapter, let us embrace the call to build a Church where relationships are not only nurtured but celebrated—a community that transcends generational divides and reflects the boundless love of our Creator. In exploring these themes, we invite you to join us in envisioning a Church where the tapestry of faith is woven with threads of genuine connection, forging a path forward for Generations Z and Alpha within the timeless embrace of Christian community.

Fostering a Sense of Belonging and Community Among the Youth:

In this section, we will look at the importance of Fostering a Sense of Belonging and Community Among the Youth, and creating a sense of community in religious settings, with a particular emphasis on youth. We will look at biblical allusions that emphasise the importance of belonging, healthy relationships and friendships, and chances for intergenerational bonding and support.

1. Creating a Sense of Belonging and Community Among Young People:

The Bible emphasises the necessity of belonging to a community on numerous occasions. According to 1 Corinthians 12:27 (WEB), "Now you are the body of Christ, and members individually." This verse emphasises the idea of the Church as a cohesive community, with each member having a distinct and valuable function. Fostering a sense of belonging and community among youth becomes critical in this situation.

Religious communities should prioritise fostering circumstances in which youth feel welcome, accepted, and respected. Organising youth-centred events, small groups, and activities that encourage participation, collaboration, and shared experiences can be part of this. Furthermore, offering outlets for adolescents to communicate their opinions, concerns, and ideas creates a sense of community ownership and empowerment.

Developing a Sense of Belonging and Community in Young People

A. Understanding the Biblical Call:

1 Corinthians 12:27 articulates the biblical mandate for community. This metaphor emphasises the Church's adherents' connectivity and interdependence. It not only emphasises each member's uniqueness but also their essential role in the broader spiritual body. As fundamental members of this body, the youth are active contributors to the vibrancy and progress of the community rather than passive participants.

B. Creating Friendly Environments:

Belonging begins with the creation of situations that are not just physically welcome but also emotionally and spiritually uplifting. Youth should go to places where they feel accepted, valued, and understood. As Christian communities, we must be diligent in breaking down obstacles that prevent youth from feeling valued members. This entails creating an environment in which variety is appreciated and differences are accepted as distinct contributions to the community's collective identity.

C. Youth-Centred Activities and Events:

Organising events and activities specifically tailored for youth is vital for reinforcing a sense of belonging. These events could range from dramatic worship meetings designed specifically for the younger generation to engaging Bible studies that address their specific questions and concerns. Providing outlets for artistic expression, such as painting, music, or drama, allows youth to connect with their faith on a personal level while also cultivating a sense of community through shared experiences.

D. Intimacy and Connection in Small Groups:

Small groups provide an intimate environment in which deeper ties can form. Youth can engage in meaningful conversations, share their spiritual experiences, and encourage one another by creating smaller, more intimate places within the broader group. Small groups provide a setting for true relationships to emerge, fostering a sense of belonging that extends beyond the surface.

E. Strengthening Youth Voices:

Recognising and amplifying the views of the community's young is critical for establishing a sense of belonging. Inviting them to share their testimony and encouraging them to lead in various capacities allows the youth to take ownership of their Church community. This empowerment not only increases their sense of belonging, but it also fosters leadership qualities that will benefit the community in the long run.

F. Developing Spiritual Mentorship:

Pairing youth with spiritual mentors in the community creates a link between generations. This mentorship gives the youth direction, encouragement, and a sense of belonging. Older community members can offer their wisdom and experiences, weaving a rich tapestry of intergenerational relationships that add to a sense of belonging and community.

To summarise, developing a sense of belonging and community among youth is a biblical commandment as well as a practical necessity. By welcoming youth as active and vital members of the Body of Christ, religious groups may foster spiritual growth and cultivate a profound sense of belonging that will last through the various seasons of life.

2. Fostering Healthy Church Relationships and Friendships:

The Bible contains guidance on how to cultivate healthy relationships and friendships. Proverbs 13:20 (WEB) says, "One who walks with wise men grows wise, but a companion of fools suffers harm." This Scripture emphasises the need of surrounding oneself with positive influences and cultivating relationships that correspond with God's standards.

It is critical to establish good relationships and friendships among youth within religious communities. This entails cultivating mutual respect, empathy, and love for one another. Youth may grow together, encourage one another, and build meaningful connections based on shared values by organising group activities, service projects, and frequent reunions.

Healthy Relationships and Friendships in the Church:

A. The Biblical Basis for Healthy Relationships:
Proverbs 13:20 is a guideline for developing healthy relationships within the Church. This verse emphasises the transformational power of association, asking believers to surround themselves with people whose influence accords with God's knowledge. The Church establishes a firm foundation for interpersonal ties that contribute to spiritual growth by grounding the pursuit of healthy friendships in such biblical principles.

B. Encourage Mutual Respect and Empathy:

Mutual respect and empathy are essential for healthy Church relationships. Encouraging youth to genuinely understand and appreciate one another's differences fosters an environment in which varied viewpoints are valued. This entails cultivating a culture in which people actively listen, attempt to understand, and respond with empathy. By demonstrating these values, the Church community becomes a safe haven for young people to manage the complexity of life together.

C. Love as the Central Principle:
The biblical injunction to love one another (John 13:34-35) is essential for developing healthy relationships within the Church. By fostering a love culture, youth learn to see each other through the prism of Christ's unconditional love. This principle promotes forgiveness, selflessness, and a commitment to building each other up, fostering an environment conducive to healthy friendships.

D. Activities for Groups and Shared Experiences:
Organising group activities is a great strategy to encourage youth bonding. Participating in community service projects, partaking in leisure activities, or uniting together in Church creates long-lasting friendships. These activities allow the youth to not only have fun together but also to witness and participate in each other's personal and spiritual development.

E. Service Projects for a Common Good:
Participating in service initiatives helps to teach the concepts of selflessness and teamwork. The youth

learn the importance of collaboration and build a common sense of purpose by working together to help the community. Service initiatives not only improve interpersonal ties, but they also add to the Church's goal of love and compassion.

F. Regular Connection Gatherings:
Regular and consistent gatherings offer a rhythm for the youth to connect. These could include gatherings of youth groups, study sessions, or fellowship events. The regularity of these gatherings allows relationships to develop over time, offering a supportive framework for life's ups and downs.

G. Guidance Mentorship Programmes:
Creating mentorship programmes within the Church provides a framework for the growth of good relationships. Mentors are older, more experienced members who provide direction, knowledge, and support to the youth. These mentoring ties help to weave a web of healthy connections throughout the Church community.

To summarise, developing good relationships and friendships inside the Church is a multidimensional endeavour that necessitates deliberate efforts based on biblical principles. The Church guarantees that the youth not only grow in faith together but also form lasting friendships that last the test of time by cultivating an environment of love, mutual respect, and shared experiences.

3. Creating Possibilities for Intergenerational Support and Bonding:

The Bible emphasises the value of intergenerational ties and assistance. Titus 2:2-4 states (WEB), "Older men should be temperate, sensible, sober minded, sound in faith, in love, and in perseverance: and that older women likewise be...teachers of that which is good, that they may train the young wives." This text emphasises the need of elder generations teaching wisdom, guidance, and support to the younger generations.

Religious communities should foster intergenerational connection and support, ensuring that young people have access to the wisdom and guidance of older members of the faith community. This can include intergenerational activities, mentorship programmes, and chances for joint ministry. By cultivating these ties, the youth can benefit from the experiences, wisdom, and prayers of more experienced people, while older generations find renewed purpose and inspiration in helping the younger ones.

Intergenerational bonding and support, as emphasised in religious teachings such as Titus 2:2-4, are extremely important in building a cohesive and supportive community. Beyond the spiritual framework, there are several practical ways for religious communities to adopt and expand on this principle.

One useful strategy is to organise intergenerational events that bring people of all ages together. These events can range from workshops and seminars to social gatherings, and they serve as an organic platform for the exchange of knowledge and experiences. Structured mentorship programmes can help to formalise this relationship by matching older, more experienced members with younger members seeking assistance on their faith journeys.

Integrating intergenerational perspectives in shared ministry opportunities, in addition to formal programmes, can be revolutionary. Collaborative projects involving both young and old people not only allow for knowledge transmission but also promote a sense of unity and shared purpose. These shared experiences, whether organising community outreach programmes or participating in religious events together, enhance the links between generations.

Furthermore, emphasising the value of storytelling in the community can be an effective form of intergenerational interaction. Encouragement of the older generation to share their life stories, experiences, and spiritual journeys not only provides vital lessons but also humanises their narratives for the younger generation. This interchange fosters empathy, comprehension, and a strong sense of connection.

Prayer circles with members of various ages might provide a spiritual foundation for intergenerational assistance. This shared practise not only unifies the community in a common goal, but it also provides a forum for individuals to express their issues, seek guidance, and receive the community's collective support.

Expanding possibilities for intergenerational connection and support within religious groups can weave a rich tapestry of shared experiences, wisdom, and spiritual growth. As a result, these communities foster a caring atmosphere in which each generation contributes to the overall flourishing, embodying the concepts of mutual respect, mentorship, and shared religion.

Developing Opportunities for Intergenerational Bonding and Support:

1. Bible Advice on Intergenerational Relationships:

Titus 2:2-4 is a foundational text that emphasises the importance of intergenerational connections within the Church community. It describes a mutually beneficial relationship in which the older generation distributes wisdom and the younger generation gets guidance. This biblical wisdom serves as the foundation for recognising that interwoven generations is a divine design intended to benefit the entire community.

Titus 2:2-4 is a timeless pearl of biblical wisdom that illuminates the importance of intergenerational connections within the tapestry of the Christian community. This foundational chapter encapsulates a divine plan, describing a beautiful interplay between seasoned elders and enthusiastic youth, where wisdom flows easily from generation to generation.

This biblical teaching, at its foundation, emphasises the shared duty that older people bear in creating a spirit of sobriety, dignity, and self-control. Their job extends beyond virtuous behaviour to actively connecting with the younger members of the community. The command for elder men to be "sober-minded" and for older women to be "teachers of that which is good" is a heavenly mandate for them to share not just their virtuous examples but also the profound truths learnt through their life experiences.

In return, the younger generation is expected to be receptive, willing to accept the teachings and advice provided by their elders. This receptivity is not a passive absorption of knowledge but an active pursuit of it, an understanding that the wisdom of the older generation is a wellspring of precious ideas. The divine plan revealed in Titus 2:2-4 presents a vision of a community in which intergenerational communication is not only welcomed but essential to its members' spiritual growth and health.

The braiding of generations seen in this biblical Scripture demonstrates God's planned design for community and spiritual development. It conveys the idea that the religious journey should not be undertaken in isolation, but as a community pilgrimage in which each generation performs a distinct and complementary role. With the weight of experience and proved faith, the older generation becomes mentors and guides, while the younger generation, with its passion and fresh insights, infuses life into the community.

This divine design emphasises that the enrichment received from intergenerational interactions goes beyond the mere transmission of knowledge; it includes the development of a communal spirit in which individuals can find peace, inspiration, and a sense of shared purpose. The faith community becomes a living monument to the beauty and power that emerges from the interwoven threads of generations, producing a tapestry that mirrors the divine order and wisdom inherent in God's creation for His people by embracing and embodying this biblical understanding.

2. Intergenerational Events to Bridge the Generational Divide:

Organising events that intentionally bring together people of different ages gives opportunity for shared experiences. These events could range from intergenerational worship sessions and fellowship dinners to collaborative community service projects. Individuals of different generations can interact, break down prejudices, and appreciate the distinct insights each age group provides to the faith community through these common activities.

Intergenerational events are transformative endeavours within a faith community, meant to bridge the gap between age groups and develop a sense of oneness among its members. These deliberate events go beyond the ordinary, establishing spaces where people of different generations can come together, share, and learn from one another. These events, which range from intergenerational worship services to fellowship meals and joint community service initiatives, act as catalysts for the development of meaningful connections that cross age lines.

The faith community encounters a colourful tapestry of worship styles and expressions in the setting of intergenerational worship sessions. Older generations provide a depth of ancient practises and songs, offering a strong sense of continuity and reverence. Simultaneously, the younger generation injects vitality into the worship experience by providing new viewpoints and inventive approaches to spiritual expression. This blending of genres not only enhances the worship experience but also represents the unity and inclusivity inherent in the religion community's variegated fabric.

Fellowship meals take the form of communal tables where generations gather to share not only food but also tales, experiences, and laughs. Breaking bread together becomes a figurative feast where the wisdom of elders is passed down and the excitement of youth pumps vitality into the gathering. These shared meals serve as crucibles for creating connections, dismantling preconceptions, and cultivating a sense of familial belonging among individuals of all ages.

Collaborative community service programmes boost the effect of intergenerational gatherings. Participating in outreach activities as a group allows people of all ages to combine their abilities and talents for a shared goal. This joint effort not only answers community needs, but it also fosters a sense of shared responsibility and mutual respect. The elder age group finds newfound meaning as mentors and guides through such ventures, while the younger generation acquires vital ideas and abilities from their more experienced counterparts.

These purposeful intergenerational activities create hallowed spaces where the richness of each generation's contribution is acknowledged and appreciated. The faith community turns into a vibrant and inclusive tapestry by accepting difference and actively generating chances for shared experiences, weaving together the combined wisdom, energy, and dedication of individuals across generations. It not only bridges the gap but also creates a harmonious symphony, in which the voices of the young and old combine in a celebration of faith, love, and shared community.

3. Personal and Spiritual Growth Mentorship Programmes:

Intergenerational mentorship programmes provide a structured environment for the exchange of knowledge and support. The pairing of elder mentors with younger mentees enables for the transmission of life experiences, spiritual insights, and practical assistance. These programmes not only help the youth's personal and spiritual growth, but they also give the older generation a feeling of purpose and fulfilment as they invest in the next generation of Christians.

Within a Christian community, mentoring programmes emerge as strong conduits for both personal and spiritual growth, establishing a structured framework that promotes the exchange of vital wisdom and support. The basis of these programmes is the deliberate coupling of experienced adults with eager young brains, resulting in a symbiotic relationship that goes beyond simple coaching and dives into the realms of life experiences, spiritual insights, and practical assistance.

The belief that seniors, equipped with the tapestry of their life journeys, have a responsibility to communicate their amassed wisdom to the younger generation is at the heart of intergenerational mentorship. These programmes create a sacred environment for knowledge transmission that goes beyond the theoretical, diving into the complexities of overcoming life's obstacles with faith and resilience. The mentor becomes a living storehouse of experiences, a guide who shares not just the victories but also the tribulations, providing a roadmap for the mentee to navigate the perilous paths of life.

These mentorship programmes become transformative places for personal and spiritual growth for the next generation. The mentor acts as a guide, offering insights into spiritual disciplines, fostering faith discussions, and providing a listening ear for the doubts and uncertainties that frequently accompany the formative years. Beyond knowledge, the mentee develops a sense of belonging and direction, fostering holistic development that transcends beyond academic or professional arenas.

Simultaneously, the mentor discovers fresh meaning and fulfilment in investing in the next generation of believers. Seeing their mentees grow and develop becomes a source of motivation, confirming the influence of their own path and experiences. The act of guiding others is not only a noble gesture, but it is also a way of leaving a lasting legacy within the religion community.

These mentorship programmes help to strengthen and unite the faith community as a whole. Developing these purposeful relationships between generations fosters a culture of mutual respect and collaboration. The mentorship relationship becomes a microcosm of the greater communal ethos, in which people of various ages collaborate for the shared aim of spiritual progress and collective well-being.

In essence, intergenerational mentorship programmes cross generational lines, bridging the knowledge of the past with the hopes of the future. Both mentors and mentees become vital threads in the rich fabric of the faith community as a result of this intentional exchange, weaving a story of progress, continuity, and shared faith that resonates beyond generations.

4. Opportunities for Joint Ministry:
Intergenerational collaboration throughout diverse religious ministries promotes unity and mutual respect. The blending of age groups in ministry gives a platform for shared service, whether it's through worship teams, community outreach activities, or educational programmes. This common goal reinforces the idea that each generation brings distinct

abilities and views to the religion community, resulting in a healthy and dynamic Church community.

Shared ministry opportunities within a Church community emerge as dynamic arenas, where people of many generations come together to share their unique abilities and perspectives in a collaborative spirit. This deliberate mixing of age groups develops a sense of togetherness, mutual respect, and shared purpose, greatly enriching the fabric of the Christian community.

Participation in worship teams is a good example of intergenerational ministry teamwork. The faith community enjoys a harmonic blend of traditional and contemporary worship forms by integrating people of various ages in musical and liturgical expressions. The older generation's knowledge and experience with long-standing songs blend with the younger members' energy and passion for modern manifestations of worship. This collaboration not only produces a diverse and inclusive worship setting, but it also symbolises the faith community's unity in diversity.

Intergenerational collaboration becomes a powerful force for positive change in the realm of community outreach efforts. Whether it's organising philanthropic events, participating in social justice issues, or lending a helping hand to people in need, the combined actions of various age groups multiply the ministry's influence. The seasoned expertise of older people blends with the vigour and original ideas of the younger generation, resulting in a holistic and compassionate approach to community service. This shared service promotes key religious principles by emphasising love, compassion, and a dedication to making a tangible impact in the lives of others.

Intergenerational collaboration benefits educational programmes within the religious setting as well. The inclusion of people of diverse ages in Sunday school courses, Bible studies, and discipleship programmes promotes a rich learning environment. The older generation's wisdom contributes historical and contextual insights, while the younger members' fresh viewpoints inject vigour into conversations. This collaborative learning journey not only broadens individual comprehension but also fosters a culture of shared exploration and growth.

Finally, shared ministry possibilities emphasise the biblical premise that each generation brings distinctive gifts and perspectives to the body of believers. The intertwining of these various contributions results in a harmonious and vivid fabric of faith. By actively engaging people of all ages in ministry, the faith community becomes a living testament to the belief that unity in variety is not only possible but also necessary for the Body of Christ to flourish. The faith community embraces the spirit of collaboration and mutual respect by embracing shared ministry opportunities, providing a dynamic and inclusive place where people of all ages actively participate in the continuing work of faith, service, and community building.

5. Bible Studies and Discussions for All Ages:

Facilitating intergenerational Bible study and debates allows for the interchange of spiritual ideas across generations. Older members can share their faith-walking experiences, while the youth bring new perspectives and questions. These events provide a rich atmosphere for learning, growth, and the formation of relationships that transcend beyond the Church's walls.

Intergenerational Bible studies and debates are a distinct and valuable aspect of a faith community, giving a dedicated area for the exchange of spiritual insights across varied age groups. These events serve as dynamic forums in which the seasoned knowledge of older members intertwines with the fresh perspectives and inquiries of the youth, resulting in a vivid tapestry of shared learning, growth, and relationship-building that transcends far beyond the Church walls.

The purposeful mingling of experiences is at the heart of these intergenerational Bible studies. Older members, who have seen the ups and downs of life, bring a wealth of direct experience with faith's difficulties and victories. Their stories become living testimonies, demonstrating the enduring character of God's faithfulness as well as the transformative power of a faith-filled life. These stories provide a sense of continuity by connecting the current generation to the rich spiritual tradition that has come before them.

At the same time, the youth add a lively and fresh viewpoint to the conversations. Their contemporary-life-shaped questions encourage deliberate investigation and prompt a re-examination of biblical truths in light of changing societal dynamics. The intergenerational discussion creates a mutual exchange of thoughts in which the wisdom of the past collides with the relevance of the present, resulting in a holistic understanding of Scripture that resonates with the faith community's different experiences.

These gatherings promote an environment in which relationships are nurtured through a shared desire of spiritual understanding, rather than by age. The mentorship that naturally emerges from these exchanges attests to the intergenerational relationships developed. Older members serve as spiritual advisors, offering advice and support, while the youth provide an infectious zeal that energises the group's faith journey. Both generations benefit from the viewpoints and contributions of the other in this symbiotic connection.

Furthermore, the impact of intergenerational Bible studies extends beyond the walls of the Church. The relationships developed during these debates pervade daily life, providing a sense of community that spans generations. Shared experiences of diving into Scripture develop a feeling of community, emphasising the idea that faith is a communal journey in which people of all ages participate in and profit from the shared search for spiritual truth.

Intergenerational Bible studies and debates, in essence, function as transforming places in which timeless truths of Scripture connect with modern realities of life. These gatherings become catalysts for building a resilient and interconnected faith community, one where the richness of spiritual insights and the depth of relationships extend far beyond the pages of the Bible and the walls of the Church, by fostering an inclusive environment that embraces the contributions of all generations.

6. Storytelling and Wisdom Circles:
Creating informal settings for sharing life experiences and lessons learned, such as wisdom circles or storytelling sessions, enables the sharing of life stories and lessons acquired. Older members can share their faith journeys, including struggles, joys, and God's faithfulness. These storytelling sessions allow the youth to gain wisdom, receive

encouragement, and interact on a more personal basis with the elder generation.

Wisdom circles and storytelling sessions arise as private and informal settings within a Church community, providing a sensitive conduit for the sharing of life stories and collective wisdom earned on a religion journey. These circles, which are distinguished by a communal spirit of trust and openness, morph into transforming spaces in which the rich tapestry of individual experiences is woven together, creating a narrative that spans generations.

Older members take front stage as storytellers and mentors in the core of wisdom circles. Their life tales, inscribed with indelible signs of adversity, success, and everlasting faith in God, become priceless repositories of wisdom. They not only discuss the complexities of their personal walks with God, but they also highlight the faithfulness and providence that have impacted their lives as they narrate their experiences. These stories serve as living testaments, demonstrating the ongoing character of God's grace and the transformative power of a faith-filled life.

These storytelling sessions are a treasure trove of inspiration and instruction for the next generation. They discover parallels of their own challenges, aspirations, and questions in the histories of elder members. The informal atmosphere promotes an environment in which the youth can gain practical wisdom, learn how to negotiate life's problems, and draw strength from the shared experiences of those who have gone before them on the path of faith. The storytelling sessions serve as a link between generations, allowing the knowledge of the past to resonate with the hopes of the future.

Furthermore, these workshops provide a venue for younger members to connect on a deeper level with the elder generation. The stories recounted go beyond mere anecdotes to build a sense of shared identity and purpose among the spiritual community. These storytelling circles build a culture of mutual understanding by expressing vulnerability and authenticity, fostering relationships that go beyond the surface and into the heart of shared religion.

Wisdom circles and storytelling sessions, in essence, exemplify the notion of handing down the torch of religion from generation to generation. These informal gatherings allow for the organic transmission of wisdom, rather than lectures, through the art of storytelling. The faith community becomes a living narrative in this holy interchange, where the collective tales of individuals merge to build a tapestry that symbolises the enduring legacy of God's faithfulness. These sessions, with their blend of candour, vulnerability, and shared wisdom, contribute to the faith community's resilience and cohesiveness, establishing a space where the continuum of faith is not just acknowledged but actively embraced and celebrated.

7. Partnerships in Prayer Across Generations:
Encouraging prayer connections amongst people of different generations develops an intergenerational culture. Older members can pray for the hopes and problems of the youth, while the younger generation can offer new passion and energy to the community's prayer life. This prayer exchange forges a spiritual link that transcends age.

Facilitating intergenerational prayer connections within a faith community indicates a significant commitment to fostering a culture of interdependence and shared spiritual support. This deliberate connection between older and younger members transcends mere generational divides, resulting in a dynamic synergy in which prayers become threads in a tapestry of common faith, understanding, and mutual support.

In these prayer partnerships, elder members take on the sacred responsibility of praying for the younger generation's hopes, struggles, and dreams. Their prayers are influenced by a lifetime of navigating the intricacies of faith and life. They draw from a fountain of wisdom as they petition on behalf of the youth, requesting God's direction, protection, and favour for those who are commencing on the road of life, with its numerous possibilities and difficulties.

In contrast, the younger generation offers a unique vitality and zest to the community's common prayer life. Their prayers are imbued with a new perspective, free of the fatigue that comes with the passing of time. Their hopes, desires, and concerns become focal points of intercession, resulting in a passionate conversation in which the established wisdom of the elder generation meets the energetic fervour of the youth. This exchange of prayers fosters not just mutual comprehension but also a spiritual relationship that transcends age barriers.

These prayer partnerships go beyond the formality of intercession to build spiritual links that bind people from different generations together in a shared commitment to support one another. The act of praying for someone else fosters a profound sense of responsibility and care, building a community in which individuals actively participate in their other members' spiritual well-being. The faith community becomes a shelter through this interconnected web of prayers, as the collective voices of different generations rise in unison, seeking God's guidance, grace, and blessings.

Prayer partnerships have long-reaching consequences that go far beyond individual issues. The combined prayers create a unifying force that reinforces the faith community's fabric. As older and younger members work together to seek God's wisdom and intervention, a spirit of unity and solidarity develops. The community becomes a living testimonial to the scriptural idea that there is no Jew or Gentile, slave or free, male or female in Christ; because all are one in Him (Galatians 3:28). This oneness is actively manifested via prayer partnerships, breaking down age barriers and creating a lively, intergenerational spiritual community where the collective heartbeat of prayer echoes with the beautiful rhythm of shared faith.

Establishing opportunities for intergenerational bonding and support is about weaving a tapestry of shared faith, wisdom, and mutual care, not just connecting different age groups. By encouraging these relationships on purpose, religious communities can create a resilient and dynamic environment in which each generation plays an important role in the communal journey of religion.

Conclusion:
Nurturing relationships and creating a feeling of community within religious settings is critical for youth development and well-being. We develop a strong community based on love, kindness, and shared religion by fostering a sense of belonging, supporting healthy relationships and friendships, and providing chances for intergenerational bonding and support. We are reminded of our responsibility to provide

spaces where youth can thrive, receive support, and form lifetime connections within the Church family, as we focus on biblical allusions that emphasise the value of nurturing relationships and community.

The threads of connection in the fabric of faith construct a narrative that transcends beyond individual spirituality to encompass the communal journey of a community. The vitality of religious contexts is inextricably linked to the well-being and development of young people, who serve as torchbearers for the future.

Creating a Sense of Belonging and Community Among Young People:

The "Belong, Believe, Behave" model is a framework that describes the psychological and sociological process of how individuals form connections and allegiances. It suggests that people first seek a sense of belonging, then develop beliefs consistent with that group, and finally, exhibit behaviors that align with those beliefs. For Generations Z and Alpha, we see this as a key part of groups they align themselves with.

1. **Make Church Spaces and Gatherings More Welcoming:**

Make Church spaces and gatherings more welcoming and inclusive, so that all youth feel valued and accepted. Encourage one another's hospitality, kindness, and respect. Refer to Romans 12:13 and Hebrews 13:2, which encourage believers to treat one another with hospitality and love.

It is critical to create welcoming environments within the Church in order to foster a sense of belonging and community among the youth. Here are some suggestions, backed up by biblical references:

A. Open Doors of Hospitality: Stress the significance of hospitality as a Christian virtue. Encourage members to open their homes and hearts to one another, creating welcoming environments for all. The Apostle Paul writes in Romans 12:13 (WEB) of the importance of "contributing to the needs of the saints; [and being] given to hospitality." This verse emphasises the idea that hospitality is a way to meet the needs of others while also building a sense of community.

B. Use Inclusive Language: Make sure the language used in church is inclusive and affirming. Encourage the use of words that uplift and show respect for one another. "Let your speech always be with grace, seasoned with salt, that you may know how you ought to answer each one," Colossians 4:6 (WEB) advises. This verse emphasises the importance of gracious communication, fostering an atmosphere of acceptance.

C. Assign Greeters and Mentors: Identify individuals who will serve as greeters, specifically welcoming new youth members. Assign mentors to help newcomers integrate into the community.
"Don't forget to show hospitality to strangers," says Hebrews 13:2 (WEB), "for in doing so, some have entertained angels without knowing it." This verse emphasises the importance of being open and

welcoming to newcomers, as they may bring unexpected blessings to the community.

D. Celebrate Diversity: Recognise and value the diversity of the youth community. Accept diversity in backgrounds, cultures, and personalities. "There is neither Jew nor Greek, there is neither slave nor free man, there is neither male nor female; for you are all one in Christ Jesus," says Galatians 3:28 (WEB). This verse emphasises Christ's unity, transcends worldly divisions, and promotes an inclusive community.

E. Provide Supportive Programmes: Create programmes that address the diverse needs and interests of youth. Create spaces for open dialogue where people can express their ideas and concerns without fear of being judged. Proverbs 11:14 (American Standard Version [ASV]) states, "Where no wise guidance is, the people falleth;
But in the multitude of counsellors there is safety."
This verse encourages the establishment of supportive networks within the community.

F. Address Bullying and Exclusion: Take a firm stance against any form of bullying or exclusion within the youth community. Encourage a culture of kindness and empathy. Ephesians 4:32 (WEB) advises, "Be kind to one another, tender hearted, forgiving each other, just as God also in Christ forgave you." This verse highlights the importance of kindness and forgiveness, fostering an environment where conflicts are resolved in a spirit of love.

G. Regularly Assess and Improve: Continuously assess the inclusivity of Church spaces and gatherings. Seek feedback from the youth and be willing to make adjustments to better meet their needs. Revelation 3:20 (WEB) says, "Behold, I stand at the door and knock. If anyone hears my voice and opens the door, then I will come in to him, and will dine with him, and he with me." This verse serves as a reminder to be attentive to the voice of the community and to respond to their needs.

By actively implementing these strategies and drawing upon biblical principles, a Christian Church can create welcoming environments that foster a strong sense of belonging and community among the youth.

2. Small Group Connections:

Encourage youth to participate in small groups or youth ministries where they can connect with peers who share their faith and values. These smaller communities foster deeper relationships and provide support, accountability, and encouragement. Reference Acts 2:42-47, where the early believers formed small, devoted communities to support and grow together.

Small group connections play a pivotal role in fostering a sense of belonging and community among the youth within a Christian Church. Here's an expansion on the idea, incorporating the reference to Acts 2:42-47:

A. Encouraging Fellowship: Actively encourage youth to participate in small groups or youth ministries within the Church. These smaller communities serve as a space for meaningful fellowship, where individuals can connect with like-minded peers who share their faith and values. Acts 2:42-47 provides a biblical model for this, depicting how early believers devoted themselves to fellowship, breaking bread together and supporting one another.

B. **Deeper Relationships:** Small groups provide an intimate setting for building deeper relationships. In a smaller community, youth can share their joys, struggles, and doubts in a more personal and supportive environment. Proverbs 27:17 (WEB) captures this idea: "Iron sharpens iron; so a man sharpens his friend's countenance." Small groups become a crucible for growth, where individuals can challenge and uplift each other on their spiritual journeys.

C. **Support and Accountability:** Within the context of a small group, youth can find both support and accountability. Galatians 6:2 (WEB) encourages believers to "Bear one another's burdens, and so fulfill the law of Christ." Small groups become a place where members can lean on each other during challenging times, offering a network of care and accountability to help navigate the ups and downs of life.

D. **Prayer and Encouragement:** Acts 2:42 highlights the early believers' commitment to prayer. Similarly, small groups become a space where youth can share their prayer requests, lifting each other up in prayer and providing encouragement. This collective prayer and encouragement strengthen the bonds within the group, fostering a sense of unity and shared spiritual journey.

E. Biblical Study and Growth: Small groups offer a platform for focused biblical study and spiritual growth. Acts 2:42 mentions the early believers devoting themselves to the Apostles' teaching, a principle that can be applied to small groups engaging in Bible study. In these settings, youth can deepen their understanding of Scripture, ask questions, and grow together in their faith.

F. Shared Mission and Outreach: Acts 2:44-45 describes the early believers selling their possessions to meet the needs of others. In a similar vein, small groups can engage in shared mission and outreach initiatives. This might involve community service, evangelism, or supporting local charities, creating a sense of purpose and unity as the group works together for the greater good.

G. Celebrating Spiritual Milestones: Small groups provide a supportive environment for celebrating spiritual milestones. Whether it's baptism, a commitment to Christ, or overcoming personal challenges, Acts 2:47 highlights the believers praising God and enjoying favour with all the people. In small groups, these celebrations become moments of shared joy and encouragement, reinforcing the sense of community.

H. Open Dialogue and Feedback: Create an atmosphere within small groups where open dialogue and feedback are valued. Acts 2:46 mentions the early believers gathering in homes, breaking bread together with glad and sincere hearts. This setting encourages honesty and transparency, allowing youth to express their thoughts and concerns freely.

By encouraging youth to participate in small groups and drawing inspiration from Acts 2:42-47, a Christian Church can provide a framework for deeper connections, spiritual growth, and a strong sense of community among its youth.

3. Service and Mission Opportunities:

Engage youth in service and mission projects where they can actively participate and make a positive impact in their communities. This shared experience of serving others can strengthen bonds and create a sense of purpose. Reference Galatians 5:13, which encourages believers to serve one another through love.

Service and mission opportunities present powerful avenues for cultivating a sense of belonging and community among the youth within a Christian Church. By actively engaging in projects that contribute to the well-being of others, young individuals not only fulfil the teachings of Galatians 5:13 but also form lasting connections with their peers. Here's an expansion on this idea:

A. Participating in Acts of Love: Galatians 5:13 underscores the significance of serving one another through love. Engage the youth in a variety of service activities that reflect this principle, whether it's volunteering at a local shelter, participating in community clean-up efforts, or assisting the elderly. These acts of love not only benefit those in need but also foster a shared commitment to living out Christian values.

B. Building Empathy and Compassion: Service and mission projects provide opportunities for youth to step outside their comfort zones and experience the challenges faced by others. Through hands-on involvement, they develop empathy and compassion, recognising the shared humanity that binds them to the broader community. This shared understanding becomes a powerful bonding factor within the youth group.

C. Strengthening Teamwork: Working together on service and mission projects requires collaboration and teamwork. Whether it's organising a charity event or participating in a mission trip, youth learn to rely on each other's strengths and support one another. This shared effort fosters a sense of unity and belonging as they collectively strive towards a common goal, echoing the biblical principle of the Body of Christ in 1 Corinthians 12.

D. Creating Lasting Memories: Engaging in service and mission activities creates lasting memories for the youth. Shared experiences, such as building homes for those in need or participating in disaster relief efforts, become foundational elements of their collective identity. These shared memories strengthen the sense of community, providing a reservoir of stories that bind the youth together.

E. Developing a Sense of Purpose: Galatians 5:13 not only encourages service but also implies a sense of purpose through love. By actively participating in projects that make a positive impact, youth find a deeper meaning and purpose in their faith. This shared sense of purpose becomes a unifying force, inspiring them to live out their Christian values in tangible ways.

F. Facilitating Spiritual Growth: Service and mission opportunities provide a unique context for spiritual growth. As youth engage in acts of love and service, they often find that their own faith is strengthened. This shared spiritual journey becomes a source of encouragement and mutual support within the group, fostering a community where members are growing together in their relationship with God.

G. Encouraging a Lifestyle of Service: Galatians 5:13 encourages a lifestyle of serving one another through love. By involving youth in ongoing service initiatives, the Church promotes the idea that service is not just a one-time event but a continuous expression of Christian living. This establishes a culture within the youth community where service becomes a natural and integral part of their lives.

H. Reflecting Christ's Love: Ultimately, service and mission projects provide tangible opportunities for youth to reflect the love of Christ to the world. As they actively embody the teachings of Galatians 5:13, serving others becomes a testimony of their faith. This shared commitment to being Christ's hands and feet in the world strengthens the bonds within the youth community, creating a sense of belonging grounded in a common mission.

By incorporating service and mission opportunities into the youth ministry and referencing Galatians 5:13, a Christian Church can effectively foster a vibrant sense of belonging and community among its youth, grounded in the transformative power of love and service.

4. Mentoring and Discipleship:

Pair youth with mature believers who can serve as mentors and invest in their spiritual growth. Through one-on-one or group discipleship relationships, youth can receive guidance, support, and discipleship. Reference Matthew 28:19-20, where Jesus commands his disciples to make more disciples and teach them to observe all that he commanded.

Mentoring and discipleship form a crucial foundation for fostering spiritual growth and a sense of community among the youth within a Christian Church. By following the model set by Jesus in Matthew 28:19-20, where disciples are commanded to make more disciples and teach them, the Church can establish intentional relationships that contribute to the flourishing of its younger members. Here's an expansion on this concept:

A. Intentional Pairing: Actively match youth with mature believers who can serve as mentors. The pairing process should consider compatibility in personalities, interests, and spiritual journeys. Acts 9:26-27 illustrates the importance of Barnabas mentoring Paul, providing support and encouragement during his early days as a follower of Christ.

B. One-on-One and Group Dynamics: Offer both one-on-one and group discipleship settings. While individual mentoring provides personalised attention, group dynamics allow for a communal learning experience. Jesus himself had a close circle of disciples but also engaged with them collectively, fostering a sense of shared growth and community.

C. Life-on-Life Discipleship: Discipleship extends beyond mere instruction; it involves sharing life experiences. Encourage mentors to invest not only in the spiritual aspects of a young person's life but also in their personal and relational development. This holistic approach mirrors the way Jesus interacted with his disciples, addressing both spiritual and practical aspects of their lives.

D. Guidance in Biblical Understanding: Utilise discipleship relationships to deepen the youth's understanding of the Bible. Following Jesus's command in Matthew 28:20 to teach everything He commanded, mentors can guide young believers through the Scriptures, helping them apply biblical principles to their lives. This process contributes to a shared foundation of faith within the youth community.

E. Creating Safe Spaces: Establish an environment within mentoring relationships where youth feel safe to express their doubts, struggles, and questions. Acts 4:36 introduces Barnabas as the "Son of Encouragement," highlighting the supportive role mentors can play in nurturing the emotional and spiritual well-being of the youth.

F. Encouraging Spiritual Practices: In line with Jesus's command to teach disciples to observe all that he commanded, mentors can guide youth in cultivating spiritual practices such as prayer, worship, and meditation. These practices not only deepen the individual's connection with God but also contribute to a shared spiritual language within the youth community.

G. Accountability and Growth: Incorporate accountability into discipleship relationships. Encourage mentors to help youth set spiritual goals and provide the necessary support for growth. Acts 18:24-26 illustrates how Priscilla and Aquila took Apollos aside and explained the way of God more accurately, demonstrating a supportive approach to accountability and growth.

H. Emphasising Reproducible Discipleship: Jesus's command to make disciples who, in turn, make more disciples emphasises a reproducing pattern. Encourage mentors to instil in the youth a sense of responsibility for their spiritual legacy. This not only creates a culture of discipleship within the youth community but also ensures the continuity of the Church's mission.

I. Celebrating Milestones: Acknowledge and celebrate milestones in the discipleship journey. Whether it's a baptism, a commitment to following Christ, or significant spiritual growth, recognise these moments within the youth community. Acts 8:12 illustrates the joy that follows when people respond to the message of Jesus, emphasising the communal celebration of spiritual milestones.

J. Continued Learning and Training: Equip mentors with ongoing training and resources. This ensures that they are well-prepared to guide the youth effectively. Acts 18:25-26 shows how Apollos was instructed further by Priscilla and Aquila, emphasising the importance of continuous learning and mentor development within the Church.

By incorporating mentoring and discipleship relationships into the youth ministry and drawing inspiration from Matthew 28:19-20, a Christian Church can establish a strong foundation for spiritual growth and a vibrant sense of community among its youth.

5. Regular Gatherings and Worship:
Organise regular youth gatherings, worship services, and events specifically designed to meet the needs and interests of young people. Provide a safe space where youth can worship, learn, pray, and fellowship together. Reference Psalm 122:1, which expresses joy and significance in gathering together for worship.

Regular gatherings and worship services tailored for the youth play a vital role in nurturing a sense of community and spiritual growth within a Christian Church. By creating dedicated spaces and events that cater to the unique needs and interests of young people, the Church can foster a vibrant and inclusive community. Here's an expansion on this concept:

A. Youth-Centric Worship Services: Design worship services with the preferences and cultural relevance of the youth in mind. Incorporate contemporary music, engaging visuals, and interactive elements that resonate with younger generations. This approach aligns with the spirit of Psalm 150, emphasising the joyful and exuberant expression of worship.

B. Relevant Teaching and Messages: Tailor the teaching and messages to address the specific challenges and questions that young people face in their faith journeys. Connect biblical principles with real-life situations, providing practical insights for navigating the complexities of adolescence and young adulthood. This approach aligns with 2 Timothy 3:16, highlighting the relevance of Scripture for teaching, rebuking, correcting, and training in righteousness.

C. Interactive Learning Formats: Foster a dynamic learning environment by incorporating interactive formats such as small group discussions, Q&A sessions, and workshops. This allows youth to actively engage with the content, share their perspectives, and learn from one another. Acts 17:11 commends the Berean Jews for examining the Scriptures daily to see if what Paul said was true, emphasising the importance of active engagement in learning.

D. Diverse Programming: Recognise the diversity of interests within the youth community and offer a range of programs and events. From Bible studies and prayer nights to recreational activities and community service projects, provide a well-rounded menu of opportunities for engagement. This diversity mirrors the multifaceted nature of the Body of Christ, as emphasised in 1 Corinthians 12.

E. Creating a Safe and Inclusive Space: Psalm 122:1 expresses joy and significance in gathering for worship. Ensure that the youth gatherings provide a safe and inclusive space where individuals feel welcomed and accepted. Cultivate an atmosphere where authenticity is valued, and young people can freely express their thoughts, doubts, and joys without fear of judgment.

F. Fellowship Opportunities: Facilitate regular fellowship opportunities for youth to connect with one another. This can include post-service gatherings, social events, and retreats. Acts 2:42 describes the early believers devoting themselves to fellowship, emphasising the importance of shared community and mutual support.

G. Encouraging Personal Worship: Beyond organised gatherings, encourage youth to develop a habit of personal worship. Provide resources and guidance on individual spiritual practices such as prayer, meditation, and personal Bible study. This fosters a sense of continuous connection with God and reinforces the idea that worship is a lifestyle.

H. Mentorship and Discipleship Integration: Integrate mentorship and discipleship opportunities within the context of youth gatherings. Acts 2:46 highlights how the early believers continued to meet together daily, providing a model for regular interaction and discipleship. Mentorship within these settings allows for more organic and relational growth.

I. Celebrating Milestones and Achievements: Acknowledge and celebrate the milestones and achievements of the youth within the Church community. Whether it's academic accomplishments, personal growth, or spiritual milestones, recognising these achievements reinforces a culture of encouragement and shared joy, as encouraged in Romans 12:15.

J. Adapting to Changing Needs: Stay attuned to the evolving needs and interests of the youth community. Regularly seek feedback and be willing to adapt programming to meet the changing dynamics of the group. Acts 15:28 emphasises the importance of adapting decisions to the guidance of the Holy Spirit, illustrating the need for flexibility and responsiveness in ministry.

By incorporating these elements into regular youth gatherings and worship services, a Christian Church can cultivate a vibrant and inclusive community that actively engages and supports its young members in their spiritual journey. This approach aligns with the biblical principles of joyful worship, fellowship, and continuous learning.

6. Encourage Authenticity and Vulnerability:

Discourage a culture of pretence or shallow relationships by promoting authenticity and vulnerability among the youth community. Teach them the importance of sharing their struggles, joys, and faith journeys with one another, fostering deeper connections and empathy. Reference James 5:16, where believers are encouraged to confess their sins to one another and pray for each other.

Encouraging authenticity and vulnerability within the youth community is essential for fostering genuine connections and deepening relationships. By creating an environment where young individuals feel comfortable sharing their true selves, the Church can cultivate a community that supports, empathises, and grows together.

A. Emphasising the Value of Authenticity:
Communicate the significance of authenticity as a cornerstone of meaningful relationships within the youth community. Encourage young individuals to embrace their true selves, sharing not only their victories but also their struggles. Romans 12:9 (WEB) encourages believers to "Let love be without hypocrisy," underscoring the importance of sincerity in relationships.

B. Providing Safe Spaces: Create designated safe spaces within the youth community where individuals can express themselves without fear of judgment. These environments, whether in small group settings or during specific events, allow for open dialogue, the sharing of personal experiences, and the building of trust. Proverbs 11:13 (WEB) emphasises the importance of confidentiality in fostering trust: "One who brings gossip betrays a confidence, but one who is of a trustworthy spirit is one who keeps a secret."

C. Modelling Vulnerability: Leaders and mentors within the Church community should model vulnerability by sharing their own experiences, struggles, and faith journeys. This openness creates a culture where vulnerability is normalised and demonstrates that everyone, regardless of their role, is on a continual journey of growth and discovery. The verse 2 Corinthians 12:9 encourages believers to boast in their weaknesses, recognising that God's power is made perfect in weakness.

D. Teaching the Biblical Foundation: Ground the encouragement for authenticity and vulnerability in biblical principles. Reference passages like Psalm 34:18 (WEB), which states, "Yahweh is near to those who have a broken heart, and saves those who have a crushed spirit." Highlight the biblical examples of individuals who openly shared their struggles, such as David in the Psalms and Paul in his letters, to demonstrate the importance of honesty and vulnerability in the faith journey.

E. Facilitating Small Group Discussions: Small group settings provide an ideal platform for fostering authenticity and vulnerability. Through guided discussions, individuals can share their experiences, ask questions, and seek support from their peers. Galatians 6:2, which encourages bearing one another's burdens, becomes a practical guide for these small group interactions.

F. Encouraging Emotional Intelligence: Equip the youth with emotional intelligence skills that enable them to understand and express their feelings effectively. Proverbs 4:23 (WEB) advises, "Keep your heart with all diligence, for out of it is the wellspring of life." Teaching emotional awareness and communication helps build a foundation for honest and open relationships.

G. Embracing Imperfection: Emphasise the beauty of imperfection and the idea that everyone is a work in progress. Romans 3:23 reminds believers that all have sinned and fallen short of God's glory. By acknowledging shared struggles and imperfections, the youth community can foster a sense of humility and understanding, strengthening their connections.

H. Promoting Empathy and Compassion: Encourage youth to actively listen and empathise with one another's stories. Colossians 3:12 urges believers to clothe themselves with compassion, kindness, humility, gentleness, and patience. This approach fosters a community where individuals feel understood and supported, promoting a culture of empathy.

I. Providing Resources for Growth: Offer resources such as workshops, seminars, or literature that guide individuals in their personal and spiritual growth. Psalm 119:105 emphasises the role of God's Word as a lamp to one's feet and a light to one's path. Providing practical tools and guidance supports the youth in navigating their faith journeys authentically.

J. Celebrating Transformations: Celebrate and affirm individuals who courageously share their stories of transformation and growth. Acts 15:3 (WEB) highlights the joy that comes from sharing stories of God's work: "They, being sent on their way by the assembly, passed through both Phoenicia and Samaria, declaring the conversion of the Gentiles. They caused great joy to all the brothers."

By actively promoting authenticity and vulnerability within the youth community and referencing the biblical principles of confession and prayer in James 5:16, a Christian Church can foster a culture of openness, understanding, and mutual support among its young members. This approach contributes to the development of a thriving and spiritually connected youth community.

Remember to seek guidance from Church leaders, study relevant passages in context, and adapt these steps to suit the specific needs of your youth community. The goal is to create a nurturing and supportive Christian community where youth feel they belong and can grow in their faith together.

Fostering Healthy Church Relationships and Friendships:

In the sacred space of the Church, believers come together not only to worship and grow in their faith but also to foster meaningful connections with one another. The Bible emphasises the importance of relationships and the unity of believers in Christ. As members of the Body of Christ, it is our duty to cultivate and promote healthy relationships and friendships within the Church community.

I. The Foundation of Christian Relationships

1. Love and Unity (John 13:34-35)

Jesus, in His earthly ministry, commanded His followers to love one another as He loved them. This sacrificial love is the cornerstone of healthy relationships within the Church. When we genuinely love one another, we reflect the love of Christ and create an environment where friendships can flourish.

In delving deeper into the profound words of Jesus in John 13:34-35 (WEB), we uncover the essence of the Christian life—a life characterised by an extraordinary love. Christ's command to love one another is not a mere suggestion; it is a fundamental principle that underpins the very fabric of our faith community.

As we reflect on the words, "A new commandment I give to you, that you love one another. Just as I have loved you, you also love one another," we are confronted with the radical nature of this divine directive. Jesus, the embodiment of selfless love, sets the standard for our relationships. His love goes beyond the superficial, transcending boundaries and extending even to the sacrificial offering of His own life on the cross.

This love becomes the cornerstone of our relationships within the Church. It is not a love contingent on personal gain or reciprocation, but a selfless, agape love that seeks the well-being of others above our own. It is a love that forgives, heals, and perseveres through trials, reflecting the enduring love that Christ demonstrated throughout His earthly ministry.

Jesus adds, "By this everyone will know that you are my disciples, if you have love for one another." Here, He unveils the transformative power of such love. Our relationships within the Church become a living testimony to the redemptive and transformative love of Christ. When we authentically love one another, we bear witness to the profound impact of Christ's love on our lives, drawing others into the fold through the magnetic force of genuine Christian community.

In practical terms, this love is not confined to sentimental expressions but extends to our actions and attitudes. It prompts us to actively seek the well-being of our brothers and sisters, to empathise with their struggles, and to celebrate their victories. It inspires a unity that transcends differences, making our diversity a source of strength rather than division.

In cultivating this sacrificial love, we create an environment where friendships can truly flourish. Our interactions become more than casual exchanges; they become opportunities to mirror the love of Christ. As we prioritise this love in our relationships, we contribute to the building of a community that reflects the very heart of God—a community characterised by love, unity, and a compelling testimony that draws others into the transformative embrace of Christ's love.

2. Bearing One Another's Burdens (Galatians 6:2)

In the journey of faith, we are called to support and uplift our fellow believers. Building strong relationships involves being there for one another in times of joy and sorrow. By bearing each other's burdens, we fulfil the law of Christ and strengthen the bonds of fellowship within the Church.

As we explore the wisdom encapsulated in Galatians 6:2 (WEB), we uncover a profound aspect of Christian relationships—the call to bear one another's burdens. In the tapestry of our faith journey, this exhortation becomes a thread that weaves us together, fostering a sense of communal responsibility and shared experiences.

The Apostle Paul, writing to the Galatian believers, implores them with these words: "Bear one another's burdens, and so fulfill the law of Christ." The imagery is powerful, depicting the Christian community as a place where the weight of life's challenges is not borne in isolation but is shared collectively. It is an acknowledgment that our individual journeys are interwoven, and the burdens one carries need not be shouldered alone.

This concept of bearing burdens is not limited to the tangible and physical; it extends to the emotional, spiritual, and relational aspects of our lives. In times of joy, we celebrate together, and in times of sorrow, we come alongside one another with empathy and support. The Christian community becomes a refuge, a safe haven where authenticity is welcomed, and vulnerability is met with compassion.

To bear one another's burdens is to step into the shoes of a fellow believer, to share in their struggles, and to offer a helping hand when the weight becomes too much to bear. It is an embodiment of the selfless love Christ demonstrated on the cross—a love that sacrificially takes on the burdens of others, providing solace and relief.

In this act of bearing burdens, we not only fulfil the law of Christ, which is rooted in love and compassion, but we also strengthen the bonds of fellowship within the Church. The shared experience of navigating life's challenges together creates a deep sense of connection. It transforms the Church from a gathering of individuals into a family—a family that walks together through the highs and lows, knowing that in unity the load is lighter.

This mutual support system is a testament to the transformative power of Christ's teachings. It reflects the essence of community that Christ envisioned for His followers—a community characterised by love, empathy, and a shared commitment to each other's well-being. As we embrace the call to bear one another's burdens, we contribute to the building of a resilient and compassionate Church, united in its dedication to embodying the love of Christ in practical, tangible ways.

II. Communication's Role in Church Relationships

1. Speaking the Truth in Love (Ephesians 4:15)

Healthy partnerships require open and honest communication. The Bible teaches us to communicate the truth in love, creating an environment of openness and understanding. By doing so, we help the Body of Christ develop and build trust among believers.

Communication is the key thread that ties hearts and minds together in the rich tapestry of Christian relationships. "But speaking truth in love," Ephesians 4:15 (WEB) says, "we may grow up in all things into him who is the head, Christ."

In this verse, the juxtaposition of "truth" and "love" serves as the foundation for efficient communication within the Church. It is a call to be honest in expressing our thoughts, feelings, and convictions while also surrounding our words with the warmth of love. This delicate balance is more than a suggestion; it is a road to spiritual development and the unity of Christ's body.

"Speaking truth" denotes a dedication to honesty and openness. It necessitates that we speak clearly, honestly, and with integrity. In the context of Christian relationships, the truth includes not just factual correctness but also a representation of God's truth as revealed in His Word. As Christians, we should communicate in accordance with the principles and teachings of Scripture, ensuring that our words are grounded in God's everlasting truth.

The exhortation to speak the truth, however, is not without context—it is inscribed in the transformational power of love. "In love" represents how truth should be communicated. Love softens the edges of our words, ensuring that even the most difficult messages are presented with empathy and love. It is a love that seeks the other person's spiritual well-being, rather than judgement.

Within the Church, this mix of truth and love develops a climate of trust and understanding. Communication that is honest and loving becomes a fuel for growth and maturity. Believers are encouraged to voice their opinions and concerns honestly, knowing that the conversation will be supported by the basis of love. Individuals are free to be themselves, wrestle with questions, and learn from one another in this environment, which fosters true oneness.

Furthermore, expressing the truth in love mirrors Christ's own communication style during His earthly ministry. His remarks, while strong when required, were always filled with a profound, caring love. As Christ's imitators, we are asked to follow in Christ's footsteps, recognising that our words have the potential to create the spiritual landscape of the Church.

In essence, the challenge to speak the truth in love is a call to create a community in which communication is a conduit for unity and growth, rather than a tool for division. Let us endeavour to be vessels of truth wrapped in the mantle of love, as we navigate the complexities of human interaction within the Church. In this way, we will contribute to the growth of the Body of Christ and the strengthening of the relationships that bind us together in Christian fellowship.

2. Avoiding Slander and Gossip (Proverbs 16:28)

Proverbs warns against gossip and slander, recognising the devastation that careless words can cause. We must be careful in the Church about how we speak about one another. Gossip stifles the growth of true relationships and can cause division. Instead, let us season our words with grace and edify our brothers and sisters.

The wisdom of Proverbs 16:28 (WEB) serves as a sobering reminder of the significant impact our words can have on the fabric of connections in the hallowed sphere of Christian fellowship. "A perverse man stirs up strife. A whisperer separates close friends," the text warns.

Gossip and slander are more than just mistakes in etiquette; they are poisonous factors that can damage the Church's roots of trust and unity. Proverbs recognises the damaging impact of thoughtless words, comparing them to a wedge that separates friends. As stewards of Christ's love, we are obligated to be cautious in how we speak about one another, recognising the potential harm that gossip can cause the body of believers.

In its poisonous nature, gossip frequently masquerades as innocent talk. It lives on rumour, half-truths, and sensationalism. Engaging in gossip hampers the formation of true connections in the setting of the Church. It fosters a climate of distrust, generating schisms in the community's close-knit fabric. Gossip shatters the togetherness that should characterise the Body of Christ, substituting strife for harmony and distrust for camaraderie.

Slander, a close relative to gossip, amplifies the damaging power of words. It entails producing false remarks with the purpose to harm someone's reputation. Slander is especially outrageous in the Church, where authenticity and mutual respect should flourish. It not only ruins relationships, but it also taints the Church's witness in the eyes of those who observe its members.

As Christians, our commitment to avoiding gossip and slander stems from the biblical command to love one another. In Ephesians 4:29 (WEB), the Apostle Paul reinforces this principle: "Let no corrupt speech proceed out of your mouth, but only what is good for building others up as the need may be, that it may give grace to those who hear." Our words should be agents of edification and grace rather than of tearing down.

To counteract the damaging influences of gossip and slander, we must make a conscious decision to season our words with grace. This entails speaking with empathy, kindness, and a genuine desire to raise up rather than tear down. It entails establishing a communication culture in which the truth is communicated in love and issues are addressed immediately and confidentially, in accordance with the biblical principles given in Matthew 18:15-17.

We contribute to the preservation of Church unity by refraining from gossip and slander. Our words become healing tools, and our relationships become more resistant to the destructive effects of negativity. Let our communication reflect the transformative power of Christ's love, ensuring that our words contribute to the formation of a community that displays grace, develops trust, and edifies our Christ-followers.

III. Friendship Development Through Fellowship

1. Fellowship Is Important (Hebrews 10:24-25)

Regular fellowship is essential for developing healthy Church relationships. We may encourage one another, share experiences, and build our bond as believers when we meet together. Fellowship, whether through small groups, prayer sessions, or social gatherings, contributes to the body's cohesiveness.

Hebrews 10:24-25 (WEB) reveals a profound truth about the vitality of Christian fellowship: "Let's consider how to provoke one another to love and good works, not forsaking our own assembling together, as the custom of some is, but exhorting one another, and so much the more as you see the Day approaching."

The author emphasises the importance of regular companionship in the lives of believers in these words. The phrase "assembling together" refers to a shared life, a communal journey of faith in which believers come together to raise, encourage, and strengthen one another.

The encouragement to "consider how to provoke one another to love and good works" emphasises the participatory character of friendship. It encourages Christians to be intentional in their interactions, looking for ways to inspire and motivate one another in the pursuit of love and moral life. Fellowship becomes the loom that knits persons together in a common commitment to spiritual growth and Kingdom impact in the tapestry of Christian relationships.

The phrase "not forsaking our own assembling together" has a sense of urgency to it. It recognises some people's tendency to disengage from Church social life, whether owing to busyness, disillusionment, or other circumstances. The author, on the other hand, exhorts believers to resist this temptation, recognising that the power of fellowship rests in the consistency of shared experiences and mutual support.

Small groups, prayer sessions, worship services, and social gatherings are all examples of Church fellowship. Each of these channels offers believers a unique opportunity to interact on a deeper level. Small groups promote closeness by allowing people to share their joys and sorrows in a more intimate atmosphere. Prayer sessions become a collective statement of reliance on God, strengthening intercessional solidarity. In their lightheartedness, social activities create a space for joy and companionship, breaking down boundaries and developing true friendships.

The oneness of the Body of Christ is a practical reality that is fostered through purposeful fellowship; it is not just an abstract concept. Relationships are formed, strengthened, and sustained at these events. Worship, prayer, and mutual encouragement develop a relationship that transcends individual differences, forming a cohesive front against life's hardships and the forces that want to split the community.

As Christians, we are urged to prioritise fellowship as a key part of our spiritual journey, not just as a religious obligation. We contribute to the body's unity by creating a community where love, support, and encouragement flow freely—a community that stands as a monument to the transformational power of shared lives journeying together towards the glorious Day when we will see our Saviour face to face.

2. Hospitality in Action (Romans 12:13)

Hospitality is a powerful display of acceptance and love. We generate possibilities for deeper connections by opening our homes and hearts to fellow believers. In doing so, we mimic Christ's and His disciples' hospitality, providing a climate in which relationships might grow.

The exhortation to practise hospitality, as expressed in Romans 12:13 (WEB), is a timeless appeal to create sacred places within the Christian community. Paul writes of the importance of "contributing to the needs of the saints; [and being] given to hospitality," emphasising the transformational potential of showing one another warmth, openness, and generosity.

In essence, hospitality extends beyond the physical act of opening our doors. It is a heart posture—a conscious decision to welcome others into our life with love and acceptance. The importance of this practise stems from its ability to pave the path for deeper connections and build an environment in which relationships can truly develop.

Hospitality is, at its essence, a strong expression of love. We extend a visible representation of Christ's love for His people when we open our homes to fellow believers. It echoes Jesus' words in Matthew 25:35: (WEB) "For I was hungry and you gave me food to eat. I was thirsty and you gave me drink. I was a stranger and you took me in." When we practise hospitality, we emulate the very heart of Christ, who welcomed sinners and outcasts into His presence with open arms.

Hospitality is not limited to great gestures; it may also be found in the simple pleasures of a shared meal, a pleasant conversation, or a cup of tea served with real concern. These seemingly insignificant acts become channels for deepening relationships, breaking down barriers, and cultivating a sense of belonging.

The biblical command to be kind is inextricably linked to the practise of providing to the needs of the saints. When we open our homes, we create areas where people can share not only physical resources but also the richness of community. It is a reciprocal relationship in which both the host and the guest contribute to each other's well-being, promoting a sense of oneness within the Body of Christ.

When we think about hospitality, we are reminded of the numerous times in the Gospels in which Jesus demonstrated extraordinary hospitality. Jesus demonstrated that everyone is deserving of love and acceptance by having meals with tax collectors and welcoming young people. As His disciples, we are asked to model this radical hospitality by

establishing situations in which others feel seen, heard, and appreciated.

The practise of hospitality becomes a thread that knits individuals into a community in the tapestry of Church ties. It elevates our gatherings from mere congregations to families, and from strangers to friends. Walls fall down and hearts open in the warmth of a welcoming home, creating an environment in which true relationships can take root and grow.

Finally, practising hospitality is a lovely act of stewardship—a realisation that the spaces we live, both physical and emotional, are God-given resources meant to be shared. As we give hospitality, we contribute to the formation of a Church community characterised by love, acceptance, and genuine connections—a community that reflects Christ's love and serves as a beacon of light in a world hungry for authentic relationships.

Conclusion:

Finally, the Bible provides a solid framework for establishing and maintaining strong Church relationships. We contribute to the unity of the Body of Christ by embodying love, practising efficient communication, and prioritising friendship. By adhering to these biblical principles, we may build a community that reflects the love and grace of our Lord Jesus Christ, attracting people and honouring God through our interactions.

Finally, the hallowed pages of the Bible disclose a rich tapestry of wisdom, educating believers in the art of creating and fostering healthy Church connections. As we traverse the complexities of Christian fellowship, three fundamental concepts emerge: love, efficient communication, and fellowship. When woven together, these offer a strong framework for the unity of the Body of Christ.

First and foremost, love is the foundation of genuine Christian relationships. The Bible is replete with Jesus' instruction to believers to love one another as He has loved them (John 13:34-35). This sacrificial, Christ-like love serves as the foundation for the Christian community. It is a love that goes beyond personal preferences, recognising variety within the Body of Christ and cultivating an environment of grace.

The second pillar is effective communication, as instructed in Ephesians 4:15 (WEB). The biblical command regarding "speaking truth in love" encourages Christians to communicate with transparency, honesty, and empathy. This principle protects against the damaging powers of gossip and slander by building an environment in which trust is fostered, understanding is deepened, and connections are strengthened. Through loving communication, the Body of Christ becomes a sanctuary where words are vessels of healing and encouragement.

Fellowship emerges as the third critical component in the biblical plan for healthy relationships, reflecting the significance emphasised in Hebrews 10:24-25. Regular gatherings, whether in small groups, prayer sessions, or social activities, allow Christians to support one another, share their experiences, and build their bonds as members of the Body. This purposeful fellowship fosters a oneness that goes beyond surface ties, transforming the Church into a family where shared lives travel together towards a common goal.

By embodying love, practising effective communication, and prioritising fellowship, we become architects of a community that reflects the love and grace of our Lord Jesus Christ. It is a community that attracts others into its fold, not through pressure or force, but through the magnetic pull of real Christian love. By putting these principles into practise, we honour God via our relationships, demonstrating to the world the transformative power of Christ's love.

In a world eager for authenticity and connection, this community of love and grace shines brightly. It overcomes the limitations of a physical building to become a living, breathing expression of Christ's Body. Relationships in such a community are sacred collaborations, with each member contributing to the flourishing of the whole.

Healthy relationships within the Church serve as a monument to the reconciling and transformative work of the Gospel in the broad tapestry of God's design. We participate in the ongoing story of God's redemptive love as we heed the wisdom inherent in the Scriptures and apply these principles to our interactions, building a community that reflects the very heart of our Lord and Saviour, Jesus Christ.

Creating Possibilities for Intergenerational Support and Bonding:

The Christian community is a tapestry of ages, experiences, and wisdom woven together. Embracing intergenerational unity within the Church is a scriptural requirement, not a suggestion. The Bible emphasises the importance of different generations joining together, each bringing distinct strengths to form a strong and healthy community of believers.

I. The Biblical Basis for Intergenerational Cooperation

1. Elderly Wisdom (Proverbs 16:31)

The Bible praises age-related wisdom, recognising the benefit of learning from the experiences of the aged. Proverbs 16:31 (WEB) says, "Gray hair is a crown of glory. It is attained by a life of righteousness." By developing relationships between younger and older members, we offer opportunities for spiritual wisdom and insight to be transferred.

The books of Proverbs reveal a timeless truth that has echoed throughout the ages: wisdom obtained from a well-lived life is a treasure deserving of praise and respect. The Bible beautifully expresses this sentiment in Proverbs 16:31 (WEB): "Gray hair is a crown of glory. It is attained by a life of righteousness."

This biblical idea provides the foundation for developing intergenerational unity within the Church. The intentional interplay between generations is a sacred calling that recognises the profound beauty in the diversity of life phases within the Body of Christ.

The picture of "gray hair" in Proverbs 16:31 is symbolic, indicating the accumulation of years defined by a devotion to good life. It is a monument to a life lived in pursuit of God's ways, characterised by faith, tenacity, and a deep knowledge of the complexities of the human experience. As a result, this

430

"crown of glory" is more than just a symbol of ageing; it also represents the spiritual prosperity that comes from living a life based on God's Word.

When the Church purposefully develops ties between younger and older members, it creates a dynamic atmosphere for the exchange of spiritual wealth. The older generation becomes a living repository of God's faithfulness and wisdom, with a plethora of experiences to teach and enrich the faith journeys of those in younger seasons of life.

The interchange of spiritual wisdom and insight is a two-way street, not a one-way street. While the older age provides wisdom and understanding, the younger generation gives vigour, new views, and a revitalised fervour for the Kingdom. It's a lovely dance in which the richness of the past blends with the vibrancy of the present to create a symphony that reverberates throughout the Church community.

In essence, Proverbs 16:31 asks us to regard the elderly as valuable producers to the spiritual landscape of the Church, not only as beneficiaries of care. It fosters a culture in which the wisdom gained from years of walking with God becomes a wellspring from which the entire body can draw, ensuring that the flame of faith is carried down from generation to generation.

As the Church embraces this biblical foundation for intergenerational unity, it weaves a tapestry of shared stories, mutual understanding, and a common goal of holiness. It changes the Body of Christ into a multigenerational family, with each member contributing to the overall spiritual life and growth. The beauty of Proverbs 16:31 unfolds in this rich and diverse community—a glowing crown of glory that symbolises not just the passage of time but the enduring legacy of faith lived out in the righteous pursuit of God.

2. Faith Transmission (Deuteronomy 6:6-7)

Deuteronomy emphasises the significance of passing down the faith from generation to generation. We have a responsibility as the Church to ensure that knowledge of God's love and precepts is passed down through generations. Intergenerational ties facilitate this transmission of faith, assisting in the establishment of a solid foundation of spiritual strength.

The echo of Deuteronomy travels through time, serving as a striking reminder of the sacred obligation assigned to the community of faith—the transmission of faith from one generation to the next. In Deuteronomy 6:6-7 (WEB), the Bible says, "These words, which I command you today, shall be on your heart; and you shall teach them diligently to your children, and shall talk of them when you sit in your house, and when you walk by the way, and when you lie down, and when you rise up."

This passage captures the core of faith transmission—a constant, intentional, and pervasive activity that permeates all aspects of life. God's instructions are to be more than just writings on stone tablets; they are to be engraved on the hearts of His people. Faith is not to be transmitted in formal settings, but rather in the ebb and flow of daily life, from the commonplace moments of sitting in one's house to the rhythmic steps taken on life's journey.

This biblical obligation extends beyond individual houses to the collective responsibility of the faith community as the Church. Within the familial embrace of the Church, knowledge of God's love and instructions is to be passed down through generations. Intergenerational bonds arise as a natural conduit for this sacred transfer of faith—a divine relay race in which the baton of spiritual inheritance is passed from the experienced hands of the elders to the eager hands of the younger generation.

The responsibility to faithfully educate is an active involvement that includes living experiences, authentic testimony, and a display of faith in action. It is a mentoring process that occurs not just in formal venues such as classrooms or Church gatherings, but also in the organic talks that occur when sitting, walking, lying down, and getting up. It's a comprehensive approach that recognises the multifaceted character of life and faith, weaving a seamless narrative of God's love into the fabric of daily living.

As a result, intergenerational unity becomes more than a demographic occurrence; it becomes a conduit for the transmission of enduring spiritual strength. Through their faith journeys, seasoned Christians become living testimonies to God's faithfulness. Their tales, successes, and even problems act as beacons, illuminating the route for those who follow. In turn, the younger generation injects vigour, passion, and a new viewpoint into the continuous story of faith, ensuring that the flame remains bright.

When the Church accepts its mission to carry on the faith, it transforms into a dynamic interplay of shared stories, mutual learning, and a collective devotion to God's unchanging truths. Intergenerational ties stop being optional and become an essential aspect of the Church's identity—a vivid tapestry in which every thread contributes to the overall beauty. In this rich ecosystem of religion, passing on God's love and precepts becomes a joyful celebration of the eternal legacy of faith passed down from generation to generation.

II. Creating Intergenerational Bonding Spaces

1. Worship Experiences in Community (Psalm 145:4)

Worship is a strong unifier, bringing believers of all ages together. Psalm 145:4 (WEB) says, "One generation will commend your works to another, and will declare your mighty acts." When people of different ages come together to worship, there is an exchange of spiritual vigour and insight that benefits the entire congregation.

The scriptural rhythm of Psalm 145:4 (WEB) echoes as a poetic anthem in the symphony of communal worship, highlighting the great relevance of shared worship experiences throughout generations "One generation will commend your works to another, and will declare your mighty acts," the psalmist declares, projecting a vision of worship that transcends age and weaves a harmonious tapestry of faith.

Worship, at its core, is a sacred intersection—a point at which diverse lives, formed by unique experiences and viewpoints, unite at the feet of the Almighty. Psalm 145:4 reveals a heavenly choreography in which one generation takes the torch of praise and worship and passes it on to the next in a seamless dance of spiritual continuity.

The Church's shared worship experiences become a transforming arena where the vitality of youth meets the seasoned depth of the elders. The exuberance of people in the bloom of life mingles with the steady beat of those who have walked the landscapes of faith for decades in this hallowed area. It is more than just a coexistence of ages; it is a vibrant exchange—a spiritual dialogue in which testimonies of God's faithfulness are passed down as beloved relics.

When people of different generations come together to worship, there is a dynamic exchange of spiritual vigour and insight. The youthful excitement fills the worship expression with energy, passion, and contagious enthusiasm. Simultaneously, the seasoned worshippers offer a depth of understanding, a wealth of theological insight, and a wealth of experienced wisdom to the worship experience, elevating it to a sacred crescendo.

The intergenerational interaction in worship is about more than just knowledge transfer; it is about the transmission of live faith. It serves as a visual reminder that the God we worship is the same yesterday, today, and forever. Declarations of God's magnificent actions form a ringing chorus that echoes through the ages—a song of faith that connects hearts across the generational span.

Furthermore, shared worship experiences foster a sense of belonging in the Church. The young discover spiritual mentors, while the elders see the continuation of their spiritual legacy. It transforms into a communal celebration in which each generation adds a distinct hue to the vibrant canvas of worship, resulting in a tableau that represents the diversity and unity found in the Body of Christ.

The Church becomes a sanctuary where echoes of praise and adoration resonate through the generations, by creating spaces for intergenerational connection through shared worship experiences. It is a tribute to the God who transcends time and geography, calling His people to share in the vast story of His redemptive work. The Church reflects the magnificent fact that in Christ we are one—a united body expressing the mighty actions of a God who connects us together across generations—as young and old stand together in worship.

2. Discipleship and Mentoring (Titus 2:3-5)

Paul emphasises the necessity of elder women teaching and encouraging younger women in the faith in his epistle to Titus. This mentoring strategy is applicable to all generations within the Church. We give opportunities for spiritual growth and assistance across the generational range by purposefully cultivating mentorship relationships.

The Apostle Paul lays out a timeless plan for intergenerational connection through mentorship and discipleship in his pastoral epistle to Titus. In Titus 2:3-5, God's plan is stated: "that older women likewise be reverent in behavior, not slanderers nor enslaved to much wine, teachers of that which is good, that they may train the young wives to love their husbands, to love their children, to be sober minded, chaste, workers at home, kind, being in subjection to their own husbands, that God's word may not be blasphemed."

This scriptural instruction does not apply only to gender roles; it is a paradigm that applies to all generations within the Church. It emphasises the importance of purposeful mentorship and discipleship relationships as a conduit for spiritual growth and support across generations.

Titus 2:3-5 provides a picture of seasoned believers investing in the spiritual formation of people in the early stages of their faith journeys. It's a lovely interplay in which the wisdom garnered through years of walking with God is shared with individuals on the verge of their Christian journey. The older generation serves as a source of direction, encouragement, and practical wisdom for the younger generation, guiding them through the many facets of faith and life.

Mentorship, in this biblical context, is a personalised journey rather than a one-size-fits-all prescription. It entails the deliberate transfer of not only information but also the manifestation of Christ-like character and virtue. The mentor becomes a living epistle, a real manifestation of the principles and values of God's Word. This relational investment provides the younger generation with not only knowledge but also the means to handle the intricacies of faith in a practical, everyday context.

Furthermore, mentorship and discipleship connections inside the Church develop a sense of belonging and accountability. The mentee finds a safe place to express questions, share challenges, and seek advice. In exchange, the mentor sees the fruit of their investment as they experience spiritual growth and transformation in the lives of individuals they mentor. It is a symbiotic partnership in which both sides contribute to each other's spiritual progress.

The Church becomes a dynamic ecosystem of spiritual growth by purposefully nurturing mentorship and discipleship ties across generations. It turns from a collection of individuals seeking their faith in solitude to a lively community where the baton of faith is carried from generation to generation. This intentional intergenerational investment not only strengthens the Church but also contributes to the faith community's durability and sustainability.

In the spirit of Titus 2:3-5, the Church becomes a living testimony to the transformative power of intentional relationships—a community where the experienced guide the inexperienced, where the wisdom of age blends with the zeal of youth, and where the timeless truths of God's Word are passed down through the generations, through the beautiful dance of mentorship and discipleship.

III. Serving in the Kingdom Together

1. Cooperative Service and Mission (1 Corinthians 12:12-27)

In 1 Corinthians 12, the Apostle Paul's image of the body clearly depicts the interdependence of believers within the Church. Each generation has its own set of gifts and talents to offer, and when these are combined in service, the Body runs smoothly. Intergenerational mission and service collaboration develops a sense of shared purpose and mutual support.

The metaphorical richness of the body, as represented by the Apostle Paul in 1 Corinthians 12:12-27 (WEB), becomes a powerful paradigm for comprehending the Church's

438

intergenerational dynamics. "For as the body is one, and has many members, and all the members of the body, being many, are one body; so also is Christ," Paul states, revealing a deep truth about the connectivity of believers over generations.

Each generation brings its own gifts, talents, and views to the body's rich fabric. The younger generations contribute passion, energy, and new perspectives, whilst the older generations bring knowledge, experience, and seasoned discernment. When these disparate elements come together in service and mission, the body functions smoothly, with each portion complementing the others and expressing the fullness of Christ's Body powerfully.

The call to united service and mission is an invitation to break down generational barriers and recognise that the Kingdom's mission necessitates the combined engagement of all believers. It is an invitation to envision the Church as a mosaic where the exuberance of youth, the steadiness of midlife, and the richness of age combine in a magnificent symphony of devotion to God and people.

Paul's imagery in 1 Corinthians 12 (WEB) contradicts the concept of generational segregation by emphasising that the body does not consist of isolated parts but operates as an integrated whole. Similarly, the foot does not say to the hand, "I have no need for you," and the eye does not say to the ear, "I have no need for you." Analogously, the younger generation does not exist independently of the older, nor does the older act in isolation from the younger. Each generation in the Kingdom requires the other, and their united efforts form a complete and dynamic representation of Christ's Body.

Intergenerational mission and service collaboration develops a sense of shared purpose and mutual support. The seasoned coach and lead the young, who are fired by their zeal, while the young are energised by the vibrancy of the seasoned. Together, they form a tremendous force for good, engaged in Kingdom activity that transcends age-defined bounds and has a long-term impact on the world.

The invitation to combined service corresponds to the essence of the Great Commission, which is to go and make disciples of all nations (Matthew 28:19-20). It is a summons that crosses generations, harnessing the body's collective energy to fulfil the task of advancing God's Kingdom on earth. The Kingdom becomes tangible as generations work side by side in missions, community service, and outreach, and the Church reflects the beauty of unity in variety.

The Church becomes a microcosm of God's Kingdom by offering areas for intergenerational bonding via combined service and mission. It is a strong witness to the world that the transformative work of the Gospel knows no age restrictions, and when generations come together in service, they bear witness to the limitless possibilities of God's love working through His people.

2. Bearing One Another's Burdens (Colossians 3:13-14 [WEB])

Colossians reminds us of the importance of "bearing with one another, and forgiving each other, if any man has a complaint against any; even as Christ forgave you, so you also do. Above all these things, walk in love, which is the bond of perfection." Intergenerational relationships require patience, understanding, and a commitment to love one another.

The words of Colossians 3:13-14 (WEB) serve as a gentle yet powerful guide in the delicate dance of intergenerational relationships: "bearing with one another, and forgiving each other, if any man has a complaint against any; even as Christ forgave you, so you also do. Above all these things, walk in love, which is the bond of perfection."

The advice on "bearing with one another" is an exhortation to practise tolerance and understanding, acknowledging that each generation brings with it its own set of experiences, viewpoints, and even quirks. It recognises that in the Church's magnificent mosaic, different age groups may confront disparities in communication styles, preferences, and cultural nuances. Nonetheless, the command to bear with each other encourages believers to accept these differences with kindness and forbearance.

Bearing with one another is an active display of love and unity, not passive endurance. It entails being willing to listen, empathise, and extend empathy, even when confronted with generational differences. This deliberate decision to bear with one another demonstrates the transformative power of Christ's love, breaking down boundaries and developing a feeling of common humanity within the Body of Christ.

As the journey progresses, forgiveness becomes an important component in intergenerational relationships. It acknowledges that complaints and misunderstandings may emerge, but the command to forgive parallels the heavenly forgiveness believers have received from the Lord. This is similar to the Lord's Prayer, in which Jesus instructs His disciples to pray, "Forgive us our debts, as we also forgive our debtors" (Matthew 6:12 [WEB]). Forgiveness is more than just a transaction; it is a reflection of our Saviour's undeserved love and kindness.

Paul emphasises that love is the overarching virtue that unites all of these parts in perfect unity. This is not a superficial love, but one that reflects Christ's sacrificial and transformational love. It is a love that seeks the well-being of others, crossing generational divides and forging bonds that go beyond mere tolerance to genuine acceptance and caring.

Intergenerational relationships, when founded on the values of bearing with one another, forgiveness, and love, provide witness to the Gospel's reconciling work. It is alive. "There is neither Jew nor Greek, there is neither slave nor free man, there is neither male nor female; for you are all one in Christ Jesus" (Galatians 3:28 [WEB]). The mutual commitment to bear with one another creates a space in which the generational tapestry becomes a harmonious symphony, with each note adding to the overall beauty.

Finally, the command to bear with one another in love is more than just a practical approach to intergenerational relationships; it is an expression of God's innermost heart. As believers manage the intricacies of intergenerational interactions, they embody Christ's transformative love, forging a bond that attests to the oneness found in Him. The Church becomes a living representation of Christ's love, a beacon of unity that draws people into the arms of the Saviour, via these intentional acts of grace and understanding.

Conclusion:

Finally, supporting intergenerational unity within the Church is a calling strongly anchored in biblical teachings. We build the fabric of our Christian community by learning from one another, creating spaces for bonding, and working together in the Kingdom. By doing so, we reflect the interconnection and unity shown in the Body of Christ, providing a lively and supportive atmosphere that bears witness to our Lord's love throughout generations.

To summarise, the requirement of embracing intergenerational unity within the Church is a divine calling deeply woven into the fabric of biblical teachings. As Christians, we are called to participate in a beautiful dance of learning, bonding, and serving together—actions that enhance the fabric of our Christian community and mirror the connectivity and unity exhibited in Christ's body.

The call to "learn from one another" recognises that each generation has unique insights, experiences, and wisdom. It is an encouragement to approach intergenerational relationships with humility and a readiness to learn from the wealth of knowledge that spans life's various seasons. The Church becomes a learning community through this mutual exchange of wisdom, where the young's energetic inquiry blends with the depth of insight supplied by the seasoned, creating a rich and dynamic mosaic of religion.

The purposeful establishment of venues for intergenerational connection, as evident in shared worship experiences, mentorship relationships, and collaborative service, is a manifestation of the divine design for the Body of Christ. It is a conscious decision to tear down barriers, transcend generational silos, and establish ties that reflect Christ's unity. The vitality of youth meets the seasoned wisdom of age in these settings, producing an environment where the generational tapestry is woven into a harmonic and cohesive whole.

Serving together in the Kingdom, drawing on 1 Corinthians 12's analogy of the body, becomes an expression of our joint mission as believers. It acknowledges that each generation brings distinct gifts and perspectives, and that when these are combined in service, the body functions harmoniously. The call to joint service and mission generates a sense of shared purpose and mutual support, resulting in a Kingdom-focused community in which all generations' collective energies move the Church forward in the fulfilment of its divine mandate.

We imitate the connection and unity exemplified in the Body of Christ by engaging in these practises. The various strands of age, experience, and background are carefully woven together, providing a vibrant and supportive environment that bears witness to our Lord's love across generations. The Church becomes a living testament to the transformative power of the Gospel—a community in which the young are mentored, the elderly are energised, and the Body of Christ functions in harmonious oneness.

By embracing intergenerational unity, we not only fulfil a biblical mandate, but we also build a Church community that reflects God's heart. It is a community in which Christ's love transcends generational borders, and where learning, bonding, and service become the threads that connect us together in a tapestry of faith. In doing so, we contribute to the continuous tale of God's redeeming work, leaving a legacy of unity and love that spans generations and attests to our Lord's enduring power throughout the ages.

Conclusion: Cultivating a Theology for the Future

In the quest to retain and grow Generation Z and Generation Alpha within the embrace of the Church, the journey has unfolded as a sacred narrative—a story of transformation, adaptability, and enduring hope. As we stand at the precipice of a future unknown, the chapters of this theological exploration converge into a resounding call: Cultivating a Theology for the Future.

The journey to keep and grow Generation Z and Generation Alpha in the Church has taken them through many different types of settings. We tried to gather all the useful information from the previous chapters in this last one, putting together ideas that will help build a modern religion for the future.

Understanding the Challenges:
The challenges faced by these younger generations are multifaceted, requiring a nuanced approach that acknowledges the complexities of their experiences. Recognising the evolving cultural and social contexts that shape their world-view is imperative. A theology that is both responsive and empathetic can bridge the gap between tradition and the contemporary reality of Generations Z and Alpha.

Rediscovering the Purpose of the Church:
At the heart of this theological exploration lies a rediscovery of the purpose of the Church. It is a call to return to the core tenets of love, compassion, and service. This renewed understanding propels the Church forward, as a dynamic force capable of meeting the spiritual needs of these generations while remaining anchored in its timeless mission.

Creating a Welcoming Environment:

Hospitality becomes a sacred practice when the Church extends open arms to all, embracing diversity and individuality. A theology that prioritises inclusivity fosters an environment where Generations Z and Alpha feel not only accepted but valued for their unique contributions. A welcoming Church is a thriving Church.

Empowering Youth Leadership:
Empowerment is not a concession but a covenant. A theology for the future mandates a deliberate commitment to empowering the youth as leaders today, recognising their agency and potential to shape the trajectory of the Church. The baton is not merely passed but shared, creating a collaborative and intergenerational leadership model.

Embracing Technology and Innovation:
As the world evolves, so must the Church. A dynamic theology acknowledges the role of technology and innovation in shaping the experiences and expectations of younger generations. Integrating these tools becomes an act of worship, enhancing rather than diluting the sacred connection between God and His people.

Investing in Education and Discipleship:
Education is not a means to an end but a lifelong journey of discipleship. A robust theology invests in the intellectual and spiritual growth of Generations Z and Alpha, recognising the symbiotic relationship between knowledge and faith. In doing so, the Church becomes a fertile ground for the flourishing of wisdom and understanding.

Nurturing Relationships and Community:
Community is the heartbeat of the Church, pulsating with the rhythm of shared lives and shared faith. A theology for the

future priorities the intentional cultivation of relationships, fostering a sense of belonging that transcends generational boundaries. In the embrace of a nurturing community, the seeds of faith take root and flourish.

Cultivating a Theology for the Future:

I. Summarising Key Strategies for Relevance

The tactics discussed in the previous chapters come together to form a whole framework, like a colourful tapestry that weaves together different threads to make a dynamic plan for changing how the Church interacts with today's youth. This complicated mosaic isn't just a list; it's a theory that lives and breathes, a theology that comes from a deep understanding.

Basically, this doctrine is a return to the Church's original purpose, which is like a renaissance. It goes beyond the limits of tradition, giving old ideas new meaning and showing how they apply to today. There is no such thing as an end point; rather it is a living force that calls us to show love, kindness, and justice all the time.

The "Welcoming Environment" that this religion creates is not just a show; it is a way of life that changes people. Love's arms are open there without judging, welcoming all the different ways people live their lives. It's not enough to just open doors; we need to take down walls and make a sacred place where being honest and open is not only accepted but also praised.

As an important part of this plan, youth leadership is not just a nice thing to do; it gives young people a lot of power. It's a recognition that the Church's future is not some faraway time, but now, shaped by the opinions, ideas, and passions of the young. It's an invitation for them to take on leadership roles, not as fill-ins but as change agents who can use their unique skills and views to shape the Church's future.

Accepting technology and new ideas is not a hesitant give-in; it's a brave step into the future. It's an acknowledgment that the Word will always be the same, but the way it's sent must change. By using technology to its fullest, the Church doesn't give up on its beliefs; instead, it makes them stronger by reaching people online, beyond physical distance.

Putting money into education and discipleship isn't just a transaction; it's a path that changes people. It means taking care of your mind and heart, knowing that faith is an adventure that lasts a lifetime. Education turns into a holy goal, and discipleship into a shared journey where mentors and mentees go together to learn and grow.

Most importantly, building real relationships and community isn't just a bunch of people getting together; it's a holy meeting. It means committing to making relationships that go beyond one-time chats. Relationships are not a means to an end in this community; they are an end in themselves. This shows how deeply linked the Body of Christ is.

The combination of these strategies, which are part of a responsive and changing theology, is a call for Generations Z and Alpha to not just watch the story of faith unfold, but to actively shape it. It's an invitation for them to share their doubts, questions, hopes, and goals, and to be involved in writing the story of God's saving love as it changes over time. This makes the Church more than just a place they go; it becomes a real example of how the Gospel is still relevant in their lives.

II. Encouraging Long-Term Mindset and Ongoing Adaptation

As we come to the end of this journey of exploration, it becomes clearer that having a long-term perspective and a strong commitment to ongoing adaptation are not just suggestions; they are essential for keeping the Church alive and relevant in a world that is always changing.

It's not true that the Church is a relic from the past, stuck in memories and time. Instead, it is a living, breathing thing that beats with the heartbeat of God and is called to respond quickly to how society is changing. These insights take us from the safety of tradition into the realm of change, recognising that the Gospel is a fact that will never change, but its presentation and use must adapt to the beats of the modern world.

In the future, a theology won't be a set of strict rules. Instead, it will be a live story that people from the past, present, and future will help write. This story asks everyone to stick to long-lasting principles—those basic truths that don't change over time or in society. These timeless ideas hold the Church firmly in the love and kindness of God, which never changes.

However, it is also important to be flexible when cultural norms change. The winds of change are always blowing, and a religion for the future means being ready to change our sails. To do this, people need to be open to new ideas and ready to listen to and learn from different voices inside and outside the Church. It's an acknowledgment that the ways and words used may change over time, but the Gospel's message of hope, salvation, and love stays the same.

The path of faith is more like a marathon than a short sprint. It takes a long time to complete. During this marathon, endurance turns into a holy virtue, persistence into a spiritual practise, and flexibility into a sign of knowledge. People recognise that the path may be long and full of turns, but the goal stays the same: changing people's minds and making the Kingdom come true on earth as it is in Heaven.

In its dedication to a Long-term Mindset and Ongoing Adaptation, the Church accepts its position as a traveller, not a settler, a temporary participant in God's plan to save the world. As we change, grow, and go on this journey together, the Church becomes a live example of how strong faith is, a flame that never goes out and guides each generation. In this way, the Church doesn't just survive time; it grows, staying true to the eternal truths that guide its path.

III. Inspiring Hope for a Vibrant Future Church

This religious symphony ends with the story's joyful crescendo. This hope comes from the fact that today's young people are so excited and involved. In the hearts and minds of Generations Z and Alpha, the idea of a Church that is living and well in the future is not a far-off, vague dream. It is becoming real. What we do today is like setting seeds that will grow into a rich crop that will feed and inspire the Church for a long time.

Things change over time, and the future Church looks like a living work of art. The vivid brushstrokes of this changing mural are the stories of transformation that touch people's lives, change their hearts, and draw them into the story of Christ's salvation. Each story is like a brushstroke that adds to the beauty and depth of the Church's fabric. It gives it life and makes it pulse with life.

The ties formed in real community are like the fine threads that run through this tapestry. They make it strong, interconnected, and full of the different stories of people who found family and belonging in the Church. The community is more than just a bunch of different people; it's a story of shared experiences, mutual support, and growth as a whole. It's related to the Body of Christ and works like a web.

Another thing is that the journey of faith as a whole becomes the big story that ties the Church together across generations. This journey is not a solo one but a pilgrimage with a group of people. Each step forward makes an indelible mark on the path for those who come after. The story goes beyond each person's lifetime, leaving a sense of continuity and a memory that lasts beyond this present moment.

It's not enough to just look forward to the future Church; we need to actively take part in making it happen, working together with the young minds and hearts that are forming faith out of hope. A group of people are working together on it, and the old and new ideas are coming together. The rich customs of the past are dancing with the new rhythms of the future.

In these last few notes, the melody of hope repeats, not as an idea in the air but as a real thing happening right now. The Church of the future, full of life and vitality, will be a tribute to the good management of today—a legacy of love, strength, and a shared dedication to the eternal story of God's grace. As we listen to this last note of hope, may it not only ring in our ears but also in the actions and choices that move the Church forward, always ready to answer God's call to help make the future full of life, love, and unshakeable faith.

When we start the holy work of creating a religion for the future, may it be based on humility, openness, and a firm belief in the God who is beyond the limits of time. These words encourage us to think about religion with a humble heart, knowing that what we know about God is only a small part of the great secret that unfolds over time. This kind of humility makes us want to look at theological terrain with awe and respect, realising that understanding God's truth is a journey, not a final goal.

Additionally, being open makes it possible for the seeds of a religion for the future to grow and take root. People who are open to this are open to the moving of the Spirit, to the doubts and questions that come up in the hearts of seekers, and to the different ways that people show their faith in the Church. That way of being theologically open doesn't mean giving up on core beliefs; it's a reaction to the constantly changing world in which the Church lives, just like the Gospel itself is alive and active.

A deep belief in the God who is outside of time becomes the most important thing in this theological landscape. This trust grounds us in the eternal love and knowledge of God and gives us the strength to confidently ride the waves of change. This trust isn't passive; it's an active giving up of control to God's story of redemption, which has been told for generations and is still being written on the minds of those who seek Him.

As the Church works to develop this theory for the future, may it be a shining light that helps us understand how complicated life is right now. Let it be a lighthouse of love, where kindness isn't just a feeling but a way of life that permeates every contact in the community. Let it be a lighthouse of grace, where the transformative and unconditional nature of God's grace is not only taught but deeply felt, inviting everyone into the embrace of divine love.

Relevance becomes the Church's holy cloak—an ever-present garment that connects the eternal truths of the Gospel to the minds of young people today. The promise is to speak the language of the present generation without watering down the message, knowing that God's eternal truths can deeply connect with the hearts of people living now.

The holy goal of this work is not just to keep and grow new generations in the Church but also to show how beautiful God's story of redemption is as it unfolds. Each life, story, and journey of faith adds to the work of divine grace in the Church, which becomes a living canvas. The Church has always wanted to be a living example to the power of God's love to change lives. May this theology for the future show that the Church's dedication to this goal lives on through the ages.

Who's This Guy?

The larger-than-life Dez Johnston has poured his soul into youth work in both voluntary and paid positions.

From the first time he set foot in a drop in youth cafe in one of the most deprived areas in Glasgow in 2008, God ignited a fire deep in his being to see young people of all backgrounds thrive and be given the opportunity to personally meet Jesus.

Now the Director of Youth for Alpha in Europe, The Middle East and North Africa that fire continues to drive a passion to see younger generations understood and empowered from their own context.

Dez understands that the newer generations of Gen Z and Gen Alpha function drastically different to the older generations before. Dez has made it his mission to research and understand these generations on a profoundly deep levels that he can build, serve and release them. in the most beneficial way.

Printed in Great Britain
by Amazon

38764032R00255